"What's wrong? Why isn't it working? Where is God in all of this?" are questions all Christian business people have struggled with at multiple points in their careers. Successful management consultant Jeff Ahern, in his new book, *Kingdom Business Success*, gives strong, practical, biblical advice on how we can answer these questions and more. This book is an excellent antidote to the secular/spiritual divide that plagues Christians in the business world today and gives a practical means toward helping us integrate our faith and work in a way that truly glorifies God and serves the common good.

- Hugh Whelchel
Executive Director of the Institute of Faith, Work & Economics (www.tifwe.org) and the author of *How Then Should We Work*.

I have known Jeff Ahern very well for many years, personally and professionally. Several years ago, I began to speak to Jeff about writing and about getting some of the amazing truths of God that he has been operating in written and produced into some material that can affect the Body of Christ. I am so blessed that he has accomplished this. Jeff is one of those rare individuals who possess extreme knowledge and humility and is able to deeply understand and articulate spiritual truths as well as leadership skills that he has developed through his extensive background. I give my sincere endorsement to Jeff and pray God's blessings on his material.

- Dave Yarnes
Executive Vice President of MorningStar Ministries
Fort Mill, South Carolina

Once I picked this book up, I couldn't put it down. Rich with real world case studies, heart probing questions that force life-changing reflection, and sprinkled with the dry wit and side-splitting analogies he's known for, Jeff Ahern ties tried and true principles and practices with Kingdom released revelation in ways that leap from the page and propel new approaches. Run toward this book if you want to start doing business WITH God verses FOR God. Challenge yourself to read it if you want to be introduced to God, or become more intimately acquainted in the "all in" way than you ever thought you could. What's stopping YOU from moving forward faster? As Jeff says, "We are all called to become like Him, and when He speaks, worlds are created." There's only one now, and one next. For every man or woman longing to move from player to finisher; for those seeking to take themselves and their business idea or venture higher, faster, and stronger than ever, this book is your "now", and reading it should be your "next!"

- Sher Valenzuela
Owner, First State Manufacturing Inc.

What hope this author brings to a believing business owner's heart to learn of God's interest in the success of an enterprise when properly aligned with His Kingdom Purpose. I first met Jeff Ahern years ago when I attended a Kingdom Business Association conference for the first time, and our paths have crossed several times since. Admittedly, part of me came alive at that conference when the idea that a business could be a ministry was presented. I had never heard it stated so clearly before, but it immediately resonated with me. I knew that I knew it was true. So now what? Jeff answers these questions: who, what, where, when, why and how to do it – in this book. An owner's manual for how to operate a Kingdom-minded enterprise. A step by step approach complete with valuable insight, and real world examples of why some business ideas fail and others succeed, and what you can do differently. This is an invaluable asset to anyone in business who desires to honor the Lord with the work of their hands, but lacks direction. Jeff Ahern not only gives you direction, but also provides a compass, a moral compass which just makes sense. Thank you Jeff for this wonderful book, your obedience in answering God's call to write it, and the Blessing it has been to me and will be to others as well. Get the book! Read the book! Study and apply the principles outlined in it. Use it like a workbook – purposefully – and allow God to bring His Kingdom into your business life in addition to your personal life.

-    **Chuck Christie**
President, Heritage Wealth Management Group

KINGDOM

BUSINESS

SUCCE$$

BRING THE KINGDOM OF HEAVEN INTO YOUR BUSINESS

JEFF AHERN

Kingdom Business Success : Bring The Kingdom of Heaven Into Your Business

Library of Congress Control Number: 2016912819
CreateSpace Independent Publishing Platform, North Charleston, SC

ISBN-13: 978-1535402811
ISBN-10: 1535402814

Cover design by Zizi Iryaspraha S (www.pagatana.com)

DEDICATION

This book is dedicated to the many business owners I have met who have struggled to succeed, and at one time or another found themselves asking the question, *"What's wrong? Why isn't it working? Where is God in all of this?"*

CONTENTS

Introduction

"The thief comes only to steal and kill and destroy; I came that they may have life, and have it abundantly" (John 10:10).

"I don't know what we're doing wrong. It just doesn't seem to be working. Every time we start to see some success in our business or personal finances, it seems something else happens and we take two steps backwards. We can't seem to get ahead. We're doing everything we know to do. We tithe faithfully. We are involved in ministry at our church. We fast and pray and lead a Bible study. There's no sin in our lives that we know of, yet we continue to struggle to make our company profitable and pay all of our bills. *What's wrong? Why isn't it working? Where is God in all of this?*"

I closed my portfolio and took a long hard look at Paul before attempting to respond to his question. Although this lament was coming from one of my clients, it was not a new problem or question being posed to me, nor one I hadn't asked myself at one time or another. I was tempted to tell Paul that if I had heard this question once, I had heard it a thousand times. But I knew this response would not answer his question nor provide the solace he was looking for from me as his business confidant. Moreover, although I believed I could provide some insight into Paul's business challenges and some specific changes that would help him on the path to solve his problems, if I was going to be honest with myself, I didn't have the answer. But I felt I should know the answer to his question. That was my job as a business consultant, wasn't it?

I couldn't keep avoiding this question and pretend the elephant was not in the room. I had to find the answer, if for no one else but myself. Paul's question was the quintessential question to the struggles I had known in my own life and business ventures. *I* needed to know the answer. Where was the abundant life, the God-type of life Jesus promised those who would follow Him and what did I have to do to start seeing this abundance in my own life and business?

1

Kingdom Business Success

During most of my professional career, I have been involved in providing some type of business consulting service, mostly in the Federal Government contracting and management consulting industries. I have provided consulting services to both large Fortune 500 companies, and small companies whose names are largely unknown. I have worked with and served some incredibly successful men and women, and others who should have been poster children for how not to run a company. Some of these people claimed to be Christians. Many of them didn't make that claim.

I would love to tell you that the most Christ-like and successful business people I have worked with were devout Christians. But that would not be true. Unfortunately, many of the most successful men and women I served who exhibited Christ-like behavior in at least one discipline, were people who were non-believers. They were business men and women who served various gods, or were without religion. On the flip side, I have seen Bible thumping, charismatic Christians behave in the workplace as I would expect a son of Belial to operate.

That's a sad commentary on success, but it leads us back to the quintessential question. Why wasn't it working for me and other devout Christians that I know? Was success in the business arena reserved for non-believers? Weren't the righteous supposed to flourish? Wasn't good supposed to triumph over evil? Where was the abundant life Jesus promised? Where were the answered prayers promised as part of His abiding presence and our walk with Him? If the Kingdom of Heaven is not in word but in the power of the Holy Spirit, where was the power of the Holy Spirit in our lives and business? Where was this Kingdom of Heaven?

I took this question to my pastors and the most devote Christian business people I knew. I studied many books and messages on "marketplace ministry," how to operate and succeed as a Christian business owner, and become a Kingdom-minded business. I was extremely disappointed in the information and answers I found and felt everyone was ignoring this paradox of success. I started praying for the little boy to come forward and shout, "The Emperor has no clothes!"

Consequently, the purpose of this book is to attempt to answer this quintessential question almost every Christian business owner has asked at one time or another, *"What's wrong? Why isn't it working?"* What do we have to do to start seeing the type of success in our business we would expect to see based upon biblical promises? I don't profess to have all the answers to this question, but I am going to present some of the answers and solutions the Lord has shown me over the years as I have sought Him and His life in my business ventures.

During this quest, I have discovered that most Christian business people operate their business using the same business paradigm and model the world employs. Their reasons for being in business and the purposes they are trying to accomplish are also the same. They chase money without realizing that money is supposed to be chasing them. Their results, not so surprisingly, tend to be the same or worse as the world obtains. But it doesn't have to be that way. It isn't supposed to be that way. But in order to change our results, we will have to make a paradigm shift in understanding the purpose behind our business and start doing business with the Lord, and do it according to Kingdom of Heaven principles.

I have discovered that most well intentioned Christian business people struggle or fail in their business for one of three reasons:

a) They are in the **wrong business** (the wrong Kingdom assignment).
b) They are in the **right business** for the **wrong reasons** (not operating under a Kingdom paradigm).
c) They are in the **right business** using the **wrong business model** (doing the right assignment the wrong way).

In this book, we will address all three disorders and how to right your floundering ship and bring the Kingdom of Heaven into your business.

3

Kingdom Business Success

In addition, we will address:

> ➢ How to position yourself for success by abiding in Him and He in you
> ➢ How to partner with God for success in your life and business
> ➢ How to make the paradigm shift that is necessary to see the Kingdom of Heaven operate in your life and business
> ➢ How to stop working *for* the Lord and start working *with* Him
> ➢ How to determine your Kingdom assignment and the Kingdom purpose for your business
> ➢ How to implement Kingdom principles of success into your business
> ➢ How non-believers have used these Kingdom principles to make them wealthy

If you have ever felt that you were carrying the weight of your business on your shoulders and wanted some help from God, then you have come to the right place. If you have ever believed you were doing "all the right things" but still haven't seen the success you were expecting, or felt like you were a branch disconnected from the vine with very little fruit to show for your efforts, then you have found the right book.

Some of the Kingdom principles of success we will address will surprise you. Others will seem quite trite, until you start thinking about how frequently you and your corporate leaders violate these principles every day. With each principle, I have attempted to provide a scriptural context to support the principle along with real-life examples from my business consulting experiences. I have tried to avoid sermon-like teaching since most business owners want the nuts and bolts and not the theory behind the operation.

Therefore, I have provided enough scriptural content to substantiate that these principles and paradigms are biblically based and sound

4

doctrine, but have also included real-world business examples to demonstrate these principles in action. I have tried to provide a balance between theory and practical application with the emphasis on the latter. Since I am using examples from my personal experiences and expect some of our clients to read this book, I have changed the names of the clients, their company names, and even their respective industries. At the end of each chapter, I have presented some questions meant to invite you to have an open dialogue with the Lord on your life and business. Please do not skip over these questions, but rather meditate on them. Ask the Lord to show you the areas in which you are violating these principles and which areas you can improve upon.

Most books or seminars that deal with Christian business success approach the subject from either a spiritual perspective or a secular one. The spiritual approach tends to sound like a sermon and ignores the basic business activities which are required by any business person. Their message seems to be that if you focus on the spiritual aspect, the secular business activities will take care of themselves. Most Christian business people have already discovered, it rarely works that way.

Those who approach the subject from a secular perspective seem to take secular books and seminars and place a banner of Christianity over them. Their message seems to be that we just need to do the same things successful non-believers do. They refer to those business activities we do in the natural realm as the "practical" side of business. It appears they believe the spiritual activities we need to perform do not have any practical aspect to them. It's ok to worship God and pray, but don't forget there is a practical side to business.

In this book, I espouse a balanced perspective for business success and have put "both oars in the water." In order to be successful Christian business people, we first need to be properly positioned in our relationship with the Lord and with each other. We need to understand what we are called to do, who we are called to serve, where we are called to do it, and the Kingdom purpose behind what we are doing. In order to take our mountain for the Lord and be a bright shining light to the world, we need to be the very best business people on the business mountain. Like Joseph in Egypt, we need to be the people the world thinks of when they are looking for wisdom and solutions to their problems. We need to embrace excellence and shun mediocrity. We need to steward everything we have received from the Lord, especially time and money, as if we will be held accountable for what we did and didn't do with it. We need to excel in both the spiritual and secular aspects of our lives and business.

David was a man after God's own heart and spent considerable time in worship and prayer. But when the time came to fight Goliath, he took his weapons with him and went out to do battle. Get ready to take the mountain you are called to take dominion over in order to bring it into the Kingdom of Heaven. But realize that in order to do it, you will need to do it the King's way, and not man's way. This will require a combination of excellence in both spiritual and secular activities.

Although the intended audience of this book is the Christian business owner or CEO, the principles of success presented here pertain to success and prosperity in any career endeavor or Kingdom assignment. These principles will even work for non-believers. In fact, you will find that successful non-believer business owners already incorporate many of these principles into their lives and businesses. They follow these principles without understanding the scriptural context, simply because *the principles make perfect sense to them.* In Chapter 15, I present ten reasons why many wealthy non-believer business people achieve success and why their success is based upon the Kingdom principles described herein.

But before we talk about Kingdom principles of success, we first need to ensure that our relationship with the Lord and with our brothers and sisters is where it should be. We need to ensure that we are *positioned correctly* for success.

Questions for Reflection

1. Have you ever found yourself asking the quintessential question "What's wrong? Why isn't it working?" What was going on in your life and business at the time you asked?

2. Have you ever felt God let you down and hasn't been doing His part in your life or business? Have you ever expressed your frustrations to Him?

3. In what areas of your life do you feel you could use some divine help or even a miracle right now? Ask the Lord to show you if there is anything you need to do, or stop doing, to receive this provision or miracle right now.

SECTION 1: POSITIONING YOURSELF FOR SUCCESS

Chapter 1

Abiding In Him

"Abide in Me, and I in you. As the branch cannot bear fruit of itself unless it abides in the vine, so neither can you unless you abide in Me. I am the vine, you are the branches, he who abides in Me and I in him, he bears much fruit, for apart from me you can do nothing" (John 15:4-5).

In searching for the answer to the quintessential question, *"What's wrong? Why isn't it working?"* the Lord led me to the above scripture. I wasn't sure what it meant to abide in Him and Him in me, or even how to go about doing that. But I could certainly relate to the analogy of being a fruitless branch and being cut off from the source of provision. I knew what it was like to exert lots of personal effort with very little fruit or success.

In my business experiences, I've often felt like a juggler attempting to keep twenty plates in the air without any of them falling to the ground. It seemed that in my role as the leader, I was carrying the weight of the entire company on my shoulders. Its success or failure was entirely on my shoulders. But I didn't want it on my shoulders. I wanted it on someone else's shoulders. Specifically, I wanted it on the Lord's shoulders, but He didn't seem to be helping very much. Certainly not as much help as I was expecting from Him. Oh, I forgot to mention, in this book we are going to be brutally honest with each other.

For some reason, I was feeling my business was disconnected from the Lord. The cord was plugged in but there was no juice coming from the electrical outlet. Whatever success occurred in my business seemed to be largely hit-or-miss and came from extreme amounts of effort on my part, and a certain amount of luck. In Christian parlance this is often referred to as "works of the flesh."

Kingdom Business Success

There were large amounts of personal effort with very little anointing on those efforts. It seemed like business was all of me and very little of Him. Does that sound familiar?

And yet, I believed I was doing all "the right things." I not only attended church, but I was involved in many ministries ranging from Children's Sunday School, driving the church van, prison ministry, and even Men's ministry. I was faithful in giving tithes, offerings, and alms. I was an avid reader of the Bible, daily devotionals, Bible commentaries, and Christian books. I prayed regularly and attended the weekly church prayer meeting. I felt like I was growing closer to the Lord in my personal life, yet He seemed to be distant and uninvolved with my business life. Wasn't God interested in my business? Wasn't this the message that came from the 7Mountain strategy and marketplace ministry, that my business was my place of assignment?[1] God's interest in marketplace ministry seemed to be a paradox to my experience in business.

All of this is to say, I could certainly relate to the image of being a branch disconnected from the vine with very little fruit to show for my efforts. I could definitely relate to my client's question of *"What's wrong? Why isn't it working?"* Although I did not have the answer to this question, I felt the Lord was leading me to the answer with the above scripture from the book of John, about the necessity of abiding in Him and He in me.

Similar to the results I was receiving, I found that most Christian business owners and CEOs are familiar with the biblical promises of prosperity and success, but have yet to see the manifestation of those blessings in their personal lives and business. Hence, the reason for this quintessential question. Each of us wants to be like Jesus and turn water into wine; or at least into more financial revenue. We want to be able to ask the Father and receive all things we need that pertain to godliness and righteousness - especially those things that pertain to our financial situation.

Why do we believe that something is wrong with our business from a biblical perspective, and why do we believe God is to blame? What are the Biblical promises we feel are not being fulfilled in our lives that cause us to ask this classic question? Why do we believe, dare I say it, God owes us? Why do we believe we should be more successful in business and finances than our non-believer competitors? In order to have this question we must first believe that we deserve better results or we wouldn't be asking this question!

When Jesus said, He came that we would have life and have it more abundantly (John 10:10), He was talking about $z\bar{o}\bar{e}^2$ life or the type of life in God Himself. This was the type of life forfeited in the fall in the Garden of Eden through sin. This was the type of life man had before death entered into our lives through sin. Through His propitiating sacrifice, we now have access again to this $z\bar{o}\bar{e}$ life. Our expectation then, is that we see the manifestation of this $z\bar{o}\bar{e}$ life in our lives and businesses. If we don't see it, then we assume something must be wrong and we start asking the quintessential question. It is the expectation of the abundant life of Christ in our lives and business that causes us to ask this query.

The key to seeing the Lord's $z\bar{o}\bar{e}$ life and fruitfulness in our lives and business is to abide in Him.

> "Abide in Me, and I in you. As the branch cannot
> bear fruit of itself unless it abides in the vine, so neither
> can you unless you abide in Me. I am the vine, you are
> the branches, he who abides in Me and I in him, he bears
> much fruit, for apart from me you can do nothing" (John
> 15:4-5).

The Lord promised that those who would abide in Him would be able to ask for anything in His name. We would be able to speak to the mountains and they would be removed (John 14:12-14; 16:23-24, 26-28; 1 John 5:14-15; Matt 21:21-22).

Kingdom Business Success

I had heard various teachings about abiding in the Vine but most of them focused on the awesome promises the Bible offered for those who did abide in Him; similar to the above scriptures. Very little was said about how one actually goes about abiding in Him. I heard teachings that ranged from simply spending time reading and meditating on the Bible to spending hours with praise and worship music on soaking in His presence. Since the Bible is its own best interpretation, I started studying the scriptures with the intent of understanding what it meant to abide in Jesus and how that was accomplished. I found nine key scriptures that all had a common thread between them. Here are three of them.

> "If you love Me, you will keep my commandments. If anyone loves Me, he will keep my word; and My father will love him, and We will come to him and make Our abode with him" (John 14:15, 23).

> "If you keep My commandments, you will abide in My love; just as I have kept My father's commandments and abide in His love. This is My commandment, that you love one another, just as I have loved you. This I command you, that you love one another" (John 15:10, 12, 17).

> "This is His commandment, that we believe in the name of His Son Jesus Christ, and love one another, just as He commanded us. The one who keeps His commandments abides in Him, and He in him" (1 John 3:23-24a).

From these scriptures, we can see that love and obedience are the foundational requirements for us to abide in Him and receive the provision and blessings promised to those who would become disciples of the Lord Jesus Christ. We are called to love God and love our brothers and sisters. The scriptures go on to say the evidence of our love for God will be measured by our obedience to His commandments.

To be a disciple of Jesus Christ requires us to become like Him (1 John 2:6). Christianity was never meant to be a religious experience but rather a metamorphosis of our total being to become like Him. His thoughts become our thoughts. His words become our words. We become so intertwined with Him that we start looking and sounding like Him to those around us. To abide in Him is to become one with Him, the same way husband and wife become one when they marry.

Modern Christianity has "dumbed down" the Gospel of the Kingdom in order to make it more palatable to the masses. We have removed the part of the gospel that refers to dying with Him in His baptism so that we can be resurrected with Him to a new life. Death always comes before new life in the Kingdom of Heaven. We have removed the part of the Gospel that says we need to pick up and carry our cross, which signifies death to self and the sacrifices we will have to make in order to be followers of Christ. We have also removed the part about the lifelong process of change necessary for us to become like Him in every way.

It is much easier to become a convert to modern Christian theology than a disciple of Jesus Christ. Perhaps this is why modern Christianity has a form of godliness, but lacks the power of Christ (2 Tim 3:5). Perhaps this is why we are all looking at each other wondering why we don't see the divine, abundant life of Christ in our lives (John 10:10).

This concept of abiding in Him and Him in us and becoming like Him in every way is the antithesis of religion, and is even considered blasphemous by some people. However, the Bible says that abiding in Him is becoming one with the Spirit of God. "But the one who joins himself to the Lord is one spirit with Him" (1 Cor 6:17). Christ was sown as a seed in His death so that we would become the "little Christs," or the fruit of His harvest (John 12:24). As Christians, we are called to be little Christs to the world.

Jesus exhorts us to become like Him. "The one who says that he abides in Him ought to walk in the same manner as He walked" (1 John 2:6). "A disciple is not above his teacher, but everyone when he is fully trained will be like his teacher" (Luke 6:40 NKJV). As we abide in Him and He in us, the world should see Him in us. If they are not seeing Him in us, then we need to examine why we are not abiding in Him.

Abiding in Him and He in us is a major paradigm shift from the Old Testament. Under the Mosaic Law, man was separated from God by his sins and served Him who resided in heaven. In the Kingdom of Heaven paradigm, man is the tabernacle of God and God dwells with man and in man. In Him we live and breathe and move (Acts 17:28a). We now become one with the Lord, similar to husband and wife. Like all marriages, we are called to abide in Him 24/7 and not just on Sunday mornings. Wherever we go as the tabernacle of God, we take Him with us. We cannot leave Him at home while we go to work. We will discuss this paradigm shift in greater detail in the next section.

Since love and obedience are the foundational requirements to abide in Him, and abiding in Him is the key requirement to having access to receive whatever we ask for in prayer, we will look closer at these foundational principles in further detail in the next few chapters. We might find that the Lord's definition of love, obedience, and honor are different than ours.

Principles in Practice

Ron was the best example I met of a Christian business person abiding in the Lord. He was the Vice President of a Government contracting company specializing in software development. He was also my boss, which gave me the opportunity to work closely with him and see him handle a wide range of business challenges.

I never heard Ron say anything that I knew was not true, nor exaggerate his or the company's capabilities and experience. This characteristic itself was exceptional in the Government contracting arena. There is no shortage of lies and exaggerations in proposals submitted on Government contracts.

I never saw Ron break any rule or law. I can't imagine that he ever travelled above 55 mph on the freeway. It wasn't in his character to do something he knew was wrong. I never saw Ron gossip or slander any person, even those people who had failed him, intentionally fought against him, or dishonored him. Ron honored everyone, even those who were hard to tolerate and accept.

Ron was unflappable. I have seen him in numerous situations where everyone around him was worried over the potential loss of valuable contracts that could derail the company and put us in the unemployment line. But I never saw him worried or anxious. There was always a calm reserve about him, as if he knew something the rest of us didn't. It was as if he knew that in the end, the Lord would make it all work out for good; even if we did lose the contracts (Rom 8:28).

Victor was the owner of this software development company where Ron and I worked and he was anything but a Christian. Victor would have been a great poster boy for how not to run a company. Victor had very few moral principles and the ones that he did have, he would have gladly compromised to achieve a small measure of success.

Ron provided a stark contrast to Victor's approach to business. Victor often wanted his management team to approach a contract or solve a problem in a manner that was dishonest or immoral. If Victor had his way, we would have stated in our proposals that we had been to the moon and back several times, or something just as implausible. Through the wisdom and favor the Lord gave Ron, he was often able to influence Victor in how he ran the company, and probably kept Victor from doing things which would have landed him in prison.

Herb was a very successful business entrepreneur. But Herb could also have been a politician. I have never known anyone who could work a room as successfully as he could. If there was a contest to see who could go into a crowd of people and come away with the most information on each attendee including names of spouses, children, birth dates, and favorite ice cream, my money would be on Herb. He was the ultimate networker. Along with his networking skills, he was also one of my top candidates for a CEO that lived his life abiding in Him.

Most of the people Herb spent his day with did not know the Lord. The insurance industry is known for brokers, actuaries, statisticians, and people who worship money. Most of Herb's clients would be surprised to know that someone as successful as Herb could actually be a disciple of Jesus Christ. Herb knew that the people he would encounter each day did not know the Lord, so he always started his day with worship time, prayer, and some Bible reading. Herb wanted to make sure he spent some quality time with the Lord at the beginning of each day and hear from Him the plans, strategies, and people the Lord was going to bring into his life that day.

During the day, Herb would steal a few secluded moments to check in with the Lord, pray for his and his client's needs, and listen for course corrections for the remainder of the day. Herb was teachable and would repent when confronted with his sins and mistakes. This might be the most important quality of a disciple of Jesus Christ because, let's face it, none of us were born behaving like Jesus. In order to become like Him in every way, it will take a lifetime of correction. It is only as we let our old ways die and start to think, talk, and act like Him that we reach the point where we are abiding in Him.

The evidence of the success of our discipleship program can be measured by how others see the fruit or results of this metamorphosis program. If they cannot see the change in us as time goes on, are we really becoming like Him? Are we really abiding in Him?

The report we should be hearing from people who know us well is, "*You* are not the same person I used to know." They might not understand what it means to abide in Him or become a disciple of Christ, but they definitely see and recognize the positive changes in us. We are not the same person we used to be (2 Cor 5:17). Herb was that type of disciple.

Bob was a senior manager in a transportation company and came from an Evangelical Christian background. A former Army sergeant

18

with incredible leadership and management skills, he was well liked and respected by everyone who worked with him. Bob seemed to have his life in perfect balance. He was very successful in his professional career and was a good husband to his wife and a good father to his children. He even coached Little League baseball and presented a great role model to the young ball players.

However, Bob came from a religious background that believed in a separation of church and business. Bob believed that when he went to work, he needed to take his Christian hat off when entering the workplace. Granted, he never left his Christian morals at the door but since he did not have a Kingdom mindset and didn't understand the concept of abiding in Him, he went to work but left Christ at the door. Bob did not believe in prayer at work. Bob didn't believe in discussing his religion or his relationship with Jesus at work for fear of being unprofessional or intruding upon other people's lives.

What Bob failed to realize was how much the Lord could have done *through* him at his work, if he had let Him. Bob was still living under the Old Testament model of working *for* the Lord instead of working *with* Him. Although Bob was successful at work using his God given talents and abilities, he never experienced the signs and wonders and miracles the Lord would have done through him, if he had let the Lord work through him.

Abiding in the vine means being connected to Him at all times regardless of where we are and what we are doing. In Him we live and move and have our being (Acts 17:28a). By keeping his relationship with the Lord outside of the workplace, how many opportunities did Bob miss to show the value of his relationship to others who were seeking that type of relationship with the Lord? Can one truly be a disciple of anyone, and hide the One you are attempting to emulate in every way? Although a Christian, Bob failed to grasp the meaning of being a disciple of Jesus Christ.

Questions for Reflection

1. In your experiences, who was the best example of someone that abides in Jesus?

2. What was it about them that made them a good example of His abiding presence?

3. What did you learn from them that you could apply to your Christian walk?

4. Ask the Lord to show you the changes you can make over this next year to do a better job of abiding in Him and letting Him abide in you.

Chapter 2

Love

"This is My commandment, that you love one another, just as I have loved you. Greater love has no one than this, that one lay down his life for his friends" (John 15:12-13).

As we saw in the previous chapter, love and obedience are the foundational requirements for us to abide in Him and receive the abundant life promised to us as disciples of the Lord Jesus Christ. Jesus described love as the summation of the commandments (Matt 22:34-40). Jesus also said obedience to His commandments is the evidence of our love for Him and the Father (John 14:16, 21). Therefore, love becomes the foundational principle of positioning ourselves in the Vine to receive the abundant life that comes from His *zōē* life flowing through us.

The importance of love as a fruit of the Spirit, proving we are disciples of Christ and have become new creatures in Him is well known by most Christians. Then, why don't we see the benefits of walking in love and abiding in Him in our lives and businesses? Why don't we see the benefits of this love in our personal finances and our company's profits? Where's the abundance? Where's the *zōē* life Jesus promised?

The answer may lie in the fact that we really don't understand the type of "love" Jesus was talking about. We may not be fulfilling this love mandate even though we think we are fulfilling this commandment. Is it possible our love is not the type of love Jesus was talking about? Is it possible our love is insincere, insufficient, and ineffective? Is it possible our love is as worthless as Monopoly® money? Let's take a look at the type of love Jesus was describing, as well as how this love is present or absent from our lives and businesses.

21

Types of Love

In the New Testament, love is generally described using one of two Greek verbs; *agapaō*[1] and *phileō*.[2] *Phileō* love is best described as tender affection, approval of, or to befriend. It is used in the New Testament approximately 25 times and is the root word for *philanthrōpia* (love of man, from which we get philanthropy or giving to man), and *philadephia* (love of brothers, from which we get Philadelphia, the city of brotherly love).

Although *phileō* love is a lesser type of love than *agapaō* love, it is certainly a type of Christian love. The apostle John characterized Jesus' love for himself as *phileō* love (John 20:8). After the resurrection, Peter characterized his love for Jesus as *phileō* love (John 21:15-17). But *phileō* love is also the type of love non-believers have for their own (John 15:19).

Agapē, the noun form of *agapaō*, is used to describe God Himself, the love of God for the human race, His love for His Son, and to convey His will concerning how his children will treat each other. Love has its perfect manifestation in God the Father giving His one and only Son to become the propitiating sacrifice for the sins of those who were completely unworthy of His love and perfect sacrifice (John 3:16).

Agapē is not only God's love and His essence, but He commands us to love each other with this same type of love. The New Testament does *not* command us to love each other with *phileō* love, but we are commanded to love each other with *agapē* love. The fulfillment of the "love commandment" as it is known can only be satisfied with *agapē* love and not *phileō* love. *Phileō* love, although scriptural, does not satisfy the love commandment, only *agapē* love fulfills the love commandment!

The unsaved world employs and understands a type of conditional love which is based upon someone pleasing or satisfying them. This can be seen on the Academy Awards red carpet. The fans shout out *"I love you"* to the nominees. This love is generally based upon approval of the acting and lifestyle of those movie celebrities. Once the acting, lifestyle, or causes are no longer approved, the chants of *"I love you"* from the fans will certainly cease, since this love was based upon conditional approval. Remove the conditions of the approval and you remove the expression of love. As Jesus said, "For even sinners love those that love them" (Luke 6:32b).

What type of love do most Christians and CEOs employ? It's probably less than *phileō* love and much closer to the worldly conditional love. Why is that? It's probably because we have never learned or truly understood *agapē* love. Perhaps it's because we know more about how to train dogs than we do about raising children or training employees in the *agapē* love of God. Let us look at the similarities.

The fundamental method to train dogs is through the use of positive and negative reinforcement. When a dog does something unacceptable, the owner pulls on a choke collar to get the dog's attention, physically confronts the dog so the dog can see the body language of the owner, uses a loud, firm voice to show disapproval of the dog's action, and makes the dog feel ashamed and rejected for the poor behavior. Since the dog cannot understand the owner's words, the body language, rejection, and tone of voice become the key components to communicate the owner's disapproval of the dog's actions. In a similar manner, when a dog does something deemed acceptable behavior, the owner pets the dog lovingly, speak in a warm, upbeat, accepting voice, and give some treat or toy as a positive reinforcement.

The theory behind dog training is that through repetition of positive and negative reinforcement to the dog's behavior, the dog will eventually figure out which behavior is acceptable and which is unacceptable based upon the response of the owner. Acceptance and self-esteem are important to human motivation according to Maslow's hierarchy of needs, and apparently important to dogs as well. Therefore, dogs will modify their behavior to be loved, accepted, and feel esteemed. No dog wants to feel rejected.

What's the difference between dog training and the conditional love most of the world employs? With the exception of the choke collar, the difference is probably little. Think about how most parents and teachers raise children. When the child displays good behavior, we use positive reinforcement including cookies and candy, stars on tests, smooth words, and loving kindness to show the child they are good ("Good boy!"). But if the child makes a mistake, we yell and scream, isolate them by making them go to their room, and remove their toys and television as punishment. The positive and negative reinforcements we employ with our children would make perfect sense to any dog watching these events.

What are the long term results of this positive and negative reinforcement training to our children? Our children grow up knowing only conditional love (i.e., my love for you is based upon whether or not you please me) and not the *agapē* love of the Father. Since they've never met their heavenly Father, they assume He must love them the same way everyone else on earth loves, which is conditional love.

Even worse, when these people encounter problems in their life, such as sickness, financial struggles, death of a loved one, failure of a business, etc., they associate these events with negative reinforcement. They assume they must have done something wrong that displeased their Heavenly Father and what they are now encountering is negative reinforcement for their bad behavior. They don't imagine that the problems they are encountering are brought on by demonic influence or the curses already present in the world from the fall in the Garden. Instead, their training teaches them that the negative consequences in their life are simply part of a negative reinforcement training program. *"I must have done something wrong."* Sound familiar?

How does this conditional love affect you as the CEO of a company? When these children who have learned conditional love through positive and negative reinforcement grow up, they will be looking for jobs. Some of them will end up working for you. Some of them might end up on your executive team. In fact, you yourself may be the product of this conditional love training program and have never come to know or understand the *agapē* love of your heavenly Father.

People who only experience conditional love can never understand *agapē* love without becoming born-again *and* receiving a heart-felt revelation of the Father's love. They can read the Bible and achieve mental ascent that God so loved the world that He gave His only begotten Son, but unless they feel or experience the love of the Father, they will never be able to have *agapē* love for God, themselves, or anyone else. How can they fulfill the love commandment if they've never known *agapē* love? Therefore, how can they abide in Him without knowing *agapē* love?

Because there are so many born-again Christians who have come from a conditional love background and have never experienced the love of the Father, there is a great disconnect between understanding *agapē* love and walking in *agapē* love. If we can't feel the love of the Father and walk in that love, how can we ever *agapē* love each other? For this reason, many inner healing and deliverance ministries have sprung up to deal specifically with helping believers receive the *agapē* love of the Father. We'll address the benefits of these inner healing and deliverance ministries and provide some recommendations in later chapters.

How inner healing/deliverance ministries work is beyond the scope of this book, but as the CEO, it is important you understand neither you, your executive team, or your employees will ever be able to *agapē* love each other without first becoming born-again *and* having a true heart-felt revelation of the Father's *agapē* love. Until that occurs, you will be loving each other with the same type of conditional love taught in our finest dog training schools and wondering why you are having relational issues with your spouse, children, employees, customers, and vendors. Additionally, you will find yourself asking the quintessential question *"What's wrong? Why isn't it working?"*

Jesus said the measure of true *agapē* love is based upon one's willingness to lay down his life for those he loved (John 15:13). As disciples of Christ, we are to become like Him in every way and therefore the measure of our love and whether it is *agapē* is based upon our willingness to lay down our life for each other. It is not enough to say, "I forgive you." Our forgiveness must be rooted in *agapē* love. This type of love says, I am willing to lay down my life or rights for your mistakes and sins toward me and others. I will forgo my self-will and emotions to pay the price for the sins and mistakes you have committed against me, so you can be released to live an abundant life. That is an incredibly high call of love. But it is also the type of love the Lord expects from each of us. This is what it means to become a disciple of Jesus Christ. This is the type of love necessary to abide in Him. Anything less than this type of love, and we are deceiving ourselves.

Is it possible, the reason the world calls us a bunch of hypocrites is because they see through us and recognize our love is insincere and basically worthless? Is it possible they, who the Bible calls blind, have seen the deception we have missed? (2 Cor 4:4). It is time to examine ourselves and ask the Lord to show us whether our love is counterfeit or not.

What Would *Agapē* Love in Your Business Look Like?

Without *agapē* love, your company may have a profit but you yourself will not profit. In 1 Corinthians 13, which is sometimes referred to as the "Love Chapter" of the Bible, we see that without love, our best works profit us nothing (1 Cor 13:1-3 AMP).

There are many businesses in the world that know nothing of the *agapē* love of God and do not pretend to operate in love but have significant financial success. However, anything we do without love will not profit *us*. Financial increase without love is rooted in the spirit of mammon and not the Kingdom of Heaven. In Chapter 15, we will look at why and how non-believers succeed in business without *agapē* love .

Jesus said that our obedience to His commandments was the test of whether or not we loved Him. In the next two chapters, we will take a look at the type of obedience Jesus was talking about as well the manifestation of our love, which is honor. Once we learn how to abide in Him, we will position ourselves in Him for success.

Principles in Practice

Sam was the owner of a franchise dealership. Sam found that his responsibilities and duties as CEO of his company precluded him from spending time alone with the Lord and performing the disciplines of worship, prayer, Bible reading, and journaling, that would help him grow in intimacy with His heavenly Father and as a disciple of Jesus Christ.

"I just don't have the time!", Sam would say in frustration. He would then go on to explain where his time was consumed in making sales, following up on invoicing, paying bills, handling employee issues, refinancing business loans, and travelling to and from their various offices and client sites. On top of those responsibilities, there was the time he spent with his wife and children supporting the various activities they were involved with. Sam just couldn't figure out where to fit the Lord into his busy schedule. Sound familiar?

My spiritual advice to Sam was very simple. I explained to him the definition of idolatry. I told Sam that as important as his relationship with his wife and children was to the Lord, those relationships should pale in comparison to his zeal and fervency for his relationship with the Lord. Our greatest delight in life must come from Him or He considers our passions idolatrous. He will not allow us to have other gods before Him. Even if those gods come in the form of spouses, children, or our businesses, which we often consider "our babies."

As for his business, I told Sam it would be better to lose his company and maintain his relationship with the Lord. The Lord could always give him a better business if he failed in this one. But if he failed in his relationship with the Lord, then he will know the true meaning of poverty and failure. As my business partner Judy Sullivan likes to say, "Poverty is not the absence of money. It's the absence of God."

Sam took my admonition seriously and started to organize his calendar to spend time daily alone with the Lord in worship, prayer, and meditation. Additionally, he went through inner healing ministry to deal with issues of rejection and an orphan spirit. He realized he couldn't love others if he didn't love himself first and see himself through God's eyes.

About the same time, we started to see changes in his business and family. People were getting healed and the sales pipeline started to open up. More importantly, Sam's relationship with the Lord started to develop into a more intimate, trusting, Father/son relationship. Peace came to his life and business, and he started to have confidence in the eventual success he would receive, based upon his growing relationship with his heavenly Father.

Travis was a business development specialist in the Federal Government contracting arena. Since business relationships are very important in this "good old boy" network, Travis decided to partner with Doug on a particular Government procurement estimated to be worth $125 million over 5 years.

Doug was not known for his honesty and integrity but rather for his charismatic charm and ability to spin a story. Doug knew many of the key decision makers in the Government Agency who would be involved in this procurement decision. It was Doug's business relationships and inside knowledge that attracted Travis to even consider doing business with Doug. The dollar signs associated with the contract made Travis dismiss the voice of his conscience telling him to stay away from Doug. The finder's fee on this business deal was estimated at $5 million dollars over 5 years, and Travis was willing to split that with Doug for his help in landing the contract for Travis' client.

Travis negotiated a deal with his client for a monthly retainer fee that would be applied to their finder's fee on the contract and promised Doug an equal split of the monthly retainer fee and the future finder's fee. During the next 18 months, Doug collected his monthly retainer fee and pretended to be working on helping influence the decision makers to award the contract to Travis' client. In the end, another company was awarded the contract.

As Jesus promised, there is nothing hidden that will not be revealed (Matt 10:26). Within the weeks that followed, Travis found out through the "good old boy" network that Doug had actually helped steer the contract towards the winning company and away from his client. In fact, Doug had worked out a deal for himself to not only receive financial remuneration, but also a senior executive position in the winning company after contract award. Needless to say, he never told Travis he changed his mind about whose side he was on, but continued to accept his monthly retainer fee coming from Travis' client. To add insult to injury, not only did Travis find out about this betrayal, but Travis' client found out about the betrayal and believed Travis was an accomplice with Doug. The client not only held Travis accountable for Doug's actions, but believed Travis was actively involved in this betrayal. Travis' reputation with his client and in the Government contracting arena was sullied through Doug's betrayal.

It took Travis several years to reach the point of true forgiveness and love towards Doug for what he had done and the resulting damage from Doug's actions. I asked Travis how he was able to come to the point where he could truly say he had forgiven Doug and had *agapē* love for him. I'll never forget Travis' sincere response.

He explained to me that in the years following this betrayal he had significant bitterness and resentment towards Doug and even toward himself for getting involved with Doug in the first place. During those years, Travis found himself living in hell. Nothing was going right with his life, relationships, and business. Everything in his life had the kiss of failure and death on it. Travis found himself living in a self-made prison. To make things worse, Doug seemed to be unscarred by this event and seemed to be prospering quite well from his treachery.

Travis' epiphany came when he realized the prison he was in was self-made, and he held the key in his hand to letting himself out. But he also knew the price of letting himself out of this prison. He would have to release forgiveness and love Doug with the same type of love God loved him. At first, he thought this was an expensive price to pay for letting himself out of this prison. Doug certainly didn't deserve it. However, the Lord reminded Travis he was equally undeserving of the love and forgiveness the Lord had already given him. Although Travis knew what he should do, it was a tough pill to swallow. However, in time Travis realized he was also paying an incredible price for the spirit of failure and death that had come upon his business, his relationships, and his finances. He finally came to the realization that the price to love Doug and give him true forgiveness easily outweighed the price he was paying for being in his self-made prison.

Travis started crying out to the Lord for the grace to love and forgive Doug. Travis told the Lord he was willing to shine Doug's shoes with his own tongue and polish them with his hair if necessary to reach the point of true love and forgiveness. Soon afterwards, the Lord gave Travis the grace to truly love and forgive Doug for his offense. Now, whenever Travis is unsure of whether he has truly loved and forgiven someone, he asks himself this question: "Am I willing to die for this person to pay the price for their sins towards me? Am I willing to shine their shoes with my tongue and my hair to show how much I love them? If the answer to both questions is not a resounding "yes," then he continues to pray for the grace to truly love and forgive them.

Robin was the business owner that provided me with the best example of *agapē* love towards his family, employees, and customers. Before it became vogue, Robin was the owner of a very successful discount warehouse store. Everyone wanted to work for Robin. His wages and benefits were only slightly above average for the industry, but there was always a long line of applicants looking for a job with his company.

When you walked into his store, there was a feeling of love in the air. The employees seemed to love their jobs, the customers seemed to love the store and the deals they could find, the managers seemed to love the employees and treat them as if they were all from the same family. No one seemed to complain, even though the number of shoppers resembled Christmas week at most department stores.

Robin was the hero of the community. If there was a fundraiser going on, they were sure to ask Robin for money, and he always came through and provided something. Robin would close his store on Sundays and major holidays to give his employees some needed rest. At a time when heroes are scrutinized closely, no one could ever find anything bad to say about Robin. He was the husband of one wife, his children were pillars of the community, and he was known for his Christian values. You couldn't study this man and the values he lived and not come away loving him.

Robin was an unassuming and quiet man with a love for people. Unlike charismatic leaders with strong personalities that fill a room, Robin would barely attract anyone's attention in a crowded setting. But once he spoke to you, you couldn't help feel much better. His words seemed to carry life in them. He always made you feel good about yourself. Unlike today's charismatic leaders who force themselves on you, Robin was more like fly paper. People were just naturally drawn to this business leader.

When Robin died, the community turned out in masses for his funeral. The funeral service was standing room only. It's been said that the greatness of a man can be measured by how many lives he touched while he lived. Robin was that type of business man. He had a big heart full of *agapē* love for everyone.

After his death, Robin's very successful discount warehouse store was sold to one of his competitors who didn't share the same values Robin held. Not surprising, what was once blessed and prosperous started to die. There was no more *agapē* love for employees and customers, but simply "business as usual." Within ten years after the sale, Robin's former business was deemed unprofitable and closed for good.

Questions for Reflection

1. How would you characterize your love for a.) God, b.) yourself, c.) your family, d.) your employees, e.) your customers, and f.) your competitors? Would you characterize your love for each of these people as *agapē, phileō*, or conditional love?

2. Who do you know that is the best example of someone who loves the Lord with all of their heart, soul, mind, and strength? What can you learn from their life and relationship with the Lord?

3. Who do you know that is the best example of someone who loves others with the same love Christ loves you? How do they do it? What can you learn from their life and relationships with people?

4. If the test of *agapē* love is your willingness to lay down your life for others who have abused you, lied, cheated, and stole from you, can you say that you truly *agapē* love everyone? Ask the Lord to show you those people you are unwilling to lay your life down for who remain your debtors. Ask the Lord to give you the grace to love them so much that you would be willing to give up your rights, will, and emotions so that they can live the abundant life Jesus promised.

Chapter 3

Obedience

"Therefore, to one who knows the right thing to do and does not do it, to him it is sin" (James 4:17).

I never met a client who thought they were living in sin. You might think that means all of our clients were great men and women of God. I'd like to believe that as well. But I am afraid it probably means many of our clients were living in deception. Let me explain.

As discussed in the previous chapters, love and obedience are foundational requirements in order to abide in Him and receive the blessings promised as disciples of the Lord Jesus Christ. Jesus said obedience to His commandments is the evidence of our love for Him (John 14:15, 23). Therefore, obedience is a foundational principle to position ourselves in the Vine in order to receive the abundant life that comes from His *zōē* life flowing through us.

In order to abide in Him we must become like Him in every manner. "The one who says that he abides in Him ought himself to walk in the same manner as He walked" (1 John 2:6). Jesus was the lamb without spot or blemish. He lived a life without sin. In order to be a disciple of Jesus we must strive to live without sin and walk in righteousness. When we blow it, me must confess our sins, repent, and keep working towards that goal.

We are never permitted to reach a level of comfort because we believe we are "largely without sin." There is no such thing as a little bit of cancer in someone's life and there is no such thing as a little bit of sin in someone's life. As a malignant tumor will grow and spread to healthy cells, so will a little sin leaven the whole lump of dough (Gal 5:9).

Kingdom Business Success

Many Christians are deceived about the importance and necessity of obedience in their own lives because they misunderstand the concept of righteousness, and specifically their own righteousness. They mistake the righteousness we obtain when we become born-again from the righteousness we are called to walk in after we become born-again. Let me explain the difference.

When we are born-again, we become "*the* righteousness of God through faith in Jesus Christ...being justified as a gift by His grace through the redemption which is in Christ Jesus" (Rom 3:22-24). Having been justified (or made righteous) by his Blood "...there is now no condemnation for those who are in Christ Jesus. For the law of the Spirit of life in Christ Jesus has set you free from the law of sin and of death" (Rom 8:1-2). From these scriptures it sounds as if the righteousness obligation of our discipleship walk was taken care of at the time we became born-again. Or was it?

Righteousness is similar to another divisive biblical topic – sanctification. We became sanctified (separated unto God) at the moment we became born again, but we see in the scriptures that sanctification is an ongoing process we are called to walk out daily, and occurs as our old self dies and the spirit of our mind becomes renewed to become like Him (Eph 4:22-24). Our righteousness is similar to our sanctification. We obtain His righteousness at the moment we are born-again, but righteousness (or doing righteousness acts) is something we are called to walk out daily in order to be righteous. "Little children, make sure no one deceives you; the one who practices righteousness is righteous, just as He is righteous" (1 John 3:7).

We cannot walk in disobedience and claim we are walking in righteousness. We cannot use the righteousness we obtained when we became born-again as a license to sin. As disciples of Christ we must walk as He would walk, and He would not sin. The moment we stop obeying God and start believing we are righteous because we have already obtained His righteousness at conversion, we start to deceive ourselves and we start to fake Christianity.[1]

So, why do so many devout Christians walk in disobedience? The reason probably resides in fear and deception. Fear is the motivational force behind almost every type of sin, and deception is the lie that masks the truth of the consequences of the sin. Think about the times you have sinned in the past and then identify the motivational factor behind the sin, and it's pretty much guaranteed it was based in fear. Fear of man's disapproval, fear of lack and poverty, fear of death, fear of punishment, etc. Even sins that may look isolated from fear are typically rooted in fear. For example, why do CEOs get angry and impatient with their employees? Isn't because we are *afraid* we will end up looking bad because of their performance, or we are *afraid* we will not achieve the results and goals we were trying to achieve? Perhaps their failure costs us money and the loss of a customer and we are *fearful* of both the financial loss and the potential damage to our reputation that could result from their mistake.

How does deception come in? Deception comes in the form of misunderstanding the consequence of sin. All sin results in death (Rom 5:12-14, 6:23, James 1:15). Death can come in the form of a physical death, financial death, death of relationships, but there is always some form of spirit of death associated with sin - always. It is a spiritual law that will remain in effect until "the last enemy to be abolished is death" (1 Cor 15:26).

The death caused by sin may not be seen or apparent at first and may not even materialize in your lifetime. It might be passed down to your children or estate as a generational curse. But do not be deceived, at the time we sin, death has an opening into our lives. All sin results in death. But the good news is we can break off the curse that entered our lives through this sin by confessing and repenting of our sins.

> "If we say that we have no sin, we are deceiving ourselves and the truth is not in us. If we confess our sins, He is faithful and righteous to forgive us our sins and to cleanse us from all unrighteousness. If we say that we have not sinned, we make Him a liar and His word is not in us" (1 John 1:8-10).

35

Unlike Pinocchio whose nose grew every time he told a lie, we will not often see an immediate change in our circumstances. We generally do not see an immediate failure in finances, sales, marriages, or relationships from our sins. Perhaps, like Pinocchio, it would be better if we did see an immediate effect. It's during this time when the results of sin in our lives are not transparent, that we become deceived. We forget the door to death has been opened. We must shut it immediately before the seed of death has had time to grow and spread.

Psychologists say that everyone who commits any wrongdoing first rationalizes in their mind that what they are doing is not that bad. If you study the biographies of some of the most wicked men and women of history, you will see that they didn't see themselves as being bad people. Reasoning caused them to see themselves and their actions as permissible and acceptable. They reasoned that what they were doing was an acceptable action and something others would do, if they were in the same circumstance.

I remember hearing a preacher once say, "Reasoning will lead you down the path of disobedience nearly every single time." Reasoning causes us to look at things with our intellect rather than viewing things from the perspective of the revealed truth the Lord has given us in His Word and through His Holy Spirit. We start reasoning with our mind and stop listening and obeying the voice of our conscience.

Our intellect and our thinking will only be correct and truthful to the degree our minds have become sanctified through the washing of the Word and the ongoing sanctification of the Holy Spirit. The Lord gave us our minds and He expects us to use them, but until they become sanctified they are prone to lead us into deception and sin.

It is impossible to walk in disobedience and faith at the same time. One of the greatest miracle workers of the twentieth century was A.A. Allen. Many of his healing miracles were captured on video. Allen believed that "Power is a direct result of faith, and faith comes by obedience."[2] In order to have mountain moving faith, our conscience cannot condemn us for disobedience. Our conscience is the voice of the Holy Spirit speaking to us through our spirit man.

The Holy Spirit examines our hearts and minds (Rom 8:27, 1 Cor 2:10-11) and reveals the truth. When our conscience does not condemn us, we can have faith and confidence our prayers have been heard and answered, because we have the faith of God living inside of us. This will require us to ask the Lord daily to examine our hearts and expose any sin in our lives. By bringing our conduct into the light, it will be exposed for what it is. If it is sin, it will be exposed as such and then we can confess and repent of it. But remember, sin will always attempt to hide in the darkness.

Life in the Kingdom of Heaven is always preceded by death. You cannot be resurrected with Christ until you have first died with Him. This means a death to your flesh and self-will. Along with becoming your Savior, Jesus must become the Lord of your life. Dead men do not lead their own lives. Most Christians are the lord of their own lives. They operate in self-will and ask God to bless the life they have chosen for themselves. Does that sound familiar? To truly abide in Him, we need to let go of the steering wheel of life and allow Him to lead us down the path He has chosen for us. Practice asking the Holy Spirit to lead you moment by moment each day, and let Him guide and direct your footsteps into the life He has already blessed for you.

Does this mean you cannot see success until you first start living a life of perfect obedience to Him? Of course not. The Lord provided for you and blessed you even when you did not know Him. How much more will He provide for you now that you are attempting to abide in Him? But we need to seek His righteousness and seek to be like Him in every way or else we are just playing religion. If He is not the Lord of our lives, then we are simply deceiving ourselves and falsely claiming to be a Christian.

In the next chapter, we will look at the biblical principle of honor, which can be called the manifestation of our *agapē* love for God and man.

Principles in Practice

Gerry was the owner of a construction supply company. Typical of many Christian owners I have met, he knew about God but had yet to experience Him. Gerry's relationship with the Lord was in his head and had yet to come to His heart. He never experienced the love of the Father. Sure, Gerry knew God loved him, but he couldn't feel His love. Without feeling the love of the Father, it is impossible to love the Lord with all of your heart, soul, mind, and strength. Additionally, the time spent in worship and waiting upon the Lord will seem unproductive and fruitless, when you cannot feel the love of the Father.

Without the confirmation in his heart that he was loved and accepted, Gerry struggled to hear the voice of the Holy Spirit when it came time to make decisions. When the revealed will of the Lord cannot be heard, man will always resort to reasoning to figure things out on his own. Gerry made most of his decisions based upon his intellect and his experiences. Unfortunately, his reasoning was imperfect and limited, and so were many of his business decisions.

Struggling to keep a once thriving business afloat, Gerry started to earnestly seek the Lord. Gerry may not have had a personal relationship with the Lord, but he was desperately seeking one. Like many men, Gerry suffered from an orphan spirit caused by his poor relationship with his father and other male authority figures in his life as he was growing up. Since most men suffer from this same malady of not experiencing the love and acceptance of the Father, they are incapable of loving and accepting others. You cannot give something to others you have never received yourself.

You may be asking yourself "What does an orphan spirit have to do with obedience?" The answer is everything. It's a domino effect. Unless you become born-again and have a heartfelt experience of the Father's love, you will never be able to love God or others with *agapē* love. Without *agapē* love, you will never walk in obedience to His commandments or be able to abide in Him. Without abiding in Him, you will never see the manifestation of the incredible promises He gave his disciples who abide in Him. In summary, you will never be able to abide in Him and experience the abundant life of God without experiencing the *agapē* love of the Father.

Along with the issues he was experiencing due to the orphan spirit, Gerry suffered from the effects of his own words. "Death and life are in the power of the tongue, and those who love it will eat its fruit" (Prov 18:21). Gerry's words typically described his problem and not the desired outcome. "We're broke. Our employees are incapable of doing anything right. We can't seem to do anything right." True to the proverb, Gerry was declaring words of death over his business and his employees and he was receiving the fruit of death from the words he was speaking.

Gerry's words were not only destructive to his life and business, but they caused him to walk in disobedience to God. How? The Bible says, "Can two walk together, unless they are agreed?" (Amos 3:3 NKJV). In order for us to walk together with the Lord, our words must agree with what He is speaking over our situation, and He is speaking words of life over us. "I call heaven and earth to witness against you today, that I have set before you life and death, the blessing and the curse. So choose life in order that you may live, you and your descendants" (Deut 30:19).

In time, Gerry went through inner healing ministry to deal with his orphan spirit and he started to change his words. He organized his schedule to spend time each day with the Lord to seek and worship Him. He started to watch over his words and declare the results he wanted, and not decree and agree with the problem. Gerry started to see his business turn around and reach the point where the doors that were once closed to him were now being opened. Prospects who would not return calls were now calling back. When we abide in Him, the door of success opens up for Him wherever He goes.

Oscar and Phil were founders of one of the most exciting business opportunities I ever encountered. They set out to build a kingdom-purposed business (discussed in Chapter 6). Before starting the business, they and their team fasted and prayed to seek the vision, direction, and blessing of the Lord. They carefully screened each potential business partner to ensure they were like-minded in their walk with the Lord and their reasons for getting into this business venture with them.

They set up intercessory prayer teams (discussed in Chapter 11) to seek wisdom, direction, and provision from the Lord as well as conduct spiritual warfare over their personal lives and business. They engaged in identification repentance to release forgiveness for offenses of the past between countries and cultures to ensure the enemy would have no open door to bring a curse upon their business enterprise. Oscar and Phil were determined the enemy would have no open door to harm their business even before they even opened their doors for business.

As Oscar and Phil started to meet with potential investors, customers, and vendors, there was a growing excitement in the air. Doors were opening up to decision makers who were normally too busy to meet with any fledgling business. Business executives were cancelling previously scheduled meetings or somehow having their calendars cleared so they would be able to meet with Oscar and Phil's team. It was great to see the favor of the Lord in action as he put the right business people together in the same room at the same time. At the end of the meetings, everyone came to the same conclusion - this was a God idea and had His signature on it. They all wanted to be involved in this unique business opportunity.

Oscar and Phil knew the Kingdom purpose of their business and knew how the activities and profits of the business were going to advance the Kingdom of Heaven. They carefully sought out and vetted investors to ensure the money they were investing in this company was untarnished. If you were looking to set up a Kingdom-purposed business model, they did everything you could imagine to guarantee the success of this business venture. Oscar and Phil's business story should have had a happy ending, but it did not.

Before the company actually sold any product, Oscar and Phil decided to change their business model from a franchise model to a company-owned model. This change seemed small to them and would guarantee the initial founders were well compensated as the business succeeded. However, the guarantees they were looking for came at the cost of security for the investors and franchise prospects. The new model seemed to turn everyone off. Everyone that is, except Oscar and Phil.

Due to the change in the business model, the unity, peace, and love once present in this business venture were replaced with division, distrust, and anxiousness. The doors of incredible favor seemed to close and along with them, the money needed to complete the launch of this company. What was once considered highly favored and blessed by God and man, seemed to be dying on the branch.

The intercessory prayer team and other leaders of this business venture all believed they were hearing from the Lord that the problems they were encountering were a direct result of the change in the business model. They believed the original economic model was part of God's vision and plan for this business. Oscar and Phil also believed they were hearing from the Lord, but didn't believe the change in the model had anything to do with the change in circumstances. They simply saw the setbacks as spiritual warfare against their business (discussed in Chapter 13). They never imagined they were walking in disobedience to the leading of the Holy Spirit.

Oscar and Phil were blessed with a God idea for a business. They followed it out to the best their abilities and character would permit them. If this was a game of horseshoes, they would have been close enough to win. Their obedience brought the favor of the Lord into their business. Their disobedience brought the spirit of death into their business. Reasoning lead them into deception, and deception lead them to disobedience. It was the same trick the enemy used in the Garden of Eden. One could argue that it didn't seem fair, but who would we be arguing with?

Kingdom Business Success

The prophet Samuel said,

> "Has the Lord as much delight in burnt offerings and sacrifices as in obeying the voice of the Lord? Behold, to obey is better than sacrifice, *and* to heed than the fat of rams. For rebellion is as the sin of divination, and insubordination is as iniquity and idolatry. Because you have rejected the word of the Lord, He has also rejected you from *being* king" (1 Sam 15:22-23).

Lamar was the owner of a retail store and had enjoyed some level of success in business. He was also a single man and attended a local church where he met Patricia. After dating for several months, Lamar and Patricia began to have sexual relations. Although Lamar knew his "occasional" sexual relationship with Patricia was "not right," he allowed himself to become deceived as to the seriousness of this sin and the consequences it would have on his life, finances, and business. Lamar reasoned that both he and Patricia were mature Christians who were involved in their church and community and were doing *most* of the right things. Besides, Lamar and Patricia weren't living together and they weren't doing it "all the time." Lamar knew this occasional sexual relationship with Patricia was not God's best for him, but then again being single wasn't God's best for him either. Certainly God would understand, under the circumstances.

In time, Lamar encountered financial challenges, a decline in his business, employee issues, and complications with his business relationships. Things seemed to be in a slow downward spiral. After receiving counseling, he broke off his relationship with Patricia. He repented from his sins in this area and even went through deliverance ministry to break off any curses associated these sexual sins.

His business started to turn around and things started getting better in his personal life and business. However, this recovery only lasted about 6 months. That is when he met and started dating Janis. Lamar and Janis eventually were married, but unfortunately they couldn't stay away from each other during the courtship period, and the spirit of death once again entered his business through the open door created by their sexual sins.

Once married, they again repented from their past sins and things started to improve in their personal lives and business. Hopefully, they learned their lesson about sin. Keep in mind the destruction resulting from sin doesn't usually appear in one day. It doesn't usually disappear the day after repentance either. It often takes months and sometimes years to see the decay and regeneration associated with opening and closing the door of sin in your life. Keep this in mind when you weigh the consequences of your sins. Otherwise, you will become deceived.

Questions for Reflection

1. Ask the Lord to show you the areas of your life and business where you are walking in less than total obedience to His will.

2. Be honest with yourself and ask the Lord to show you the motivational spirit behind each of these areas of disobedience to His will. Don't be surprised if there is some type of fear associated with the reason for your disobedience. Understanding the motivational spirit behind your sins will help you overcome them.

3. Seek the grace of the Lord daily to overcome these areas of disobedience in your life. Never give in and accept defeat or settle for anything less than complete obedience to His perfect will for your life.

4. Get ministry help if necessary to deal with generational iniquities, sins, curses, and proclivities (discussed in Chapter 13). Hurting people hurt others, and we all need to be healed of past wounds and reach the point of forgiving and releasing in order to walk in *agapē* love with everyone.

Chapter 4

Honor

"Honor all people, love the brotherhood, fear God, honor the king" (1 Peter 2:17).

Would you like to know the secret to achieving favor with God and man? Would you like to be the person who receives unmerited favor in both your business and personal life? The secret to that type of favor is embedded in the biblical principle of honor. Learn to be a person who embraces and lives a life of honor and you and your business can walk in favor with God and man. "The reward of humility and the fear of the Lord are riches, honor and life" (Prov 22:4).

If abiding in Him and He in us is the secret to receive the abundant life promised to us as disciples of the Lord Jesus Christ, and love and obedience are the foundational requirements to abide in Him, where does honor fit in? Biblical honor can best be described as an outward manifestation of our *agapē* love towards God and man.

Today's society and especially Western civilization knows very little about the concept of honor. Eastern cultures still practice honor to a higher degree than we do in the West, but the concept of biblical honor has largely been forgotten in our day. In fact, we live in a society that mocks honor and embraces and creates entertainment around the practice of dishonor. It is very difficult to find a movie or television sitcom where dishonor is not the central theme of the entertainment.

Dishonor is rampant in today's culture, from our government leaders to our spiritual leaders. It seems dishonor has saturated every segment of society to the point where we have become calloused to the principle of honor and aren't even aware when we are practicing or embracing dishonor. When presented with television shows that mock people who should be honored, we laugh along with everyone else at the satire, not realizing we have just added our agreement to the dishonor being portrayed. That is how calloused we have become to the sin of dishonor.

So what is biblical honor and why is the practice of honor so important to God? Let's take a look at the etymology of the word and see what the Bible has to say about the importance of honor, and the promises God has made concerning those who live a life of honor.

In the Old Testament, the Hebrew word for honor is *kābôd* and refers to the weightiness, or wealth, or quantity, or physical weight associated with the presence and glory of God.[1] One of the first uses of this word in the Old Testament is in the Ten Commandments where the Lord admonishes us to "Honor your father and mother that your days may be prolonged in the land that the Lord your God gives you" (Ex 20:12).

In the New Testament, the Greek word *timē* is generally used for honor and is defined as a valuing, a price paid or received, preciousness, honor, or esteem.[2] Taking the Hebrew and Greek together, we see that biblical honor is about esteeming others as being significantly valuable in a tangible way. This is the way God deems us, and He insists that we deem Him and each other in the same manner. Three New Testament scriptures that reflect God's commandment to honor each other are presented below.

> "Honor all people, love the brotherhood, fear God, honor the king" (1 Peter 2:17).

> "Do nothing from selfishness or empty conceit, but with humility of mind regard one another as more important than yourselves" (Phil 2:3).

> "*Be* kindly affectionate to one another with brotherly love, in honor giving preference to one another" (Rom 12:10 NKJV).

From the etymology of the word and the scriptures above, we see that the first definition of honor is to esteem others as being more valuable than ourselves. This is not a self-deprecating viewpoint that says I am nothing and you are everything, but a Christ-centered viewpoint which says, I value you so much that I would be willing to die for you. To put it another way, on a scale from one to ten, I am a ten, but you are an eleven!

It is impossible to value others properly if we have poor self-esteem. In order to honor others as more valuable than ourselves, we must first recognize and understand our own value in God's eyes. We must understand our Heavenly Father loves and values us as much as He loves Jesus. He loves and values us so much that He sent His only Son to die on the cross to win us back to Himself. He is not stuck with us, but rather He chose us and paid an incredible price for us. This understanding of our value in the Lord's eyes must start in our head but then move to our heart in order to feel His love, acceptance, and value in our own lives. Only then can we learn to love, accept, and value others in a similar manner.

The second definition of biblical honor can best be seen in the story of Noah and his three sons. Noah became drunk and passed out naked in his own tent. His son Ham saw this event and informed his two brothers. We may have been taught in Sunday school that Ham laughed, giggled, gossiped, and mocked his father, but the scriptures reflect that Ham's only sin was he told his brothers the truth about what he had seen (Gen 9:22). How often have we felt that stating the truth about a person or situation leaves us blameless? Ham's exposure of the truth, not to those outside of his family but to his own two brothers, dishonored his father and cost him and his ancestors their inheritance in the Promised Land.

The second definition of honor is to make someone look better than they really are, and cover over their weaknesses, shortcomings, and sins. Shem and Japheth, Noah's other two sons, instinctively understood this and walked backwards into Noah's tent to cover him up. The Bible says, they looked the other way in order to prevent them from seeing their father's nakedness. They knew of his sin, but looked the other way to avoid seeing it. They chose to cover over and ignore their father's sin rather than expose it.

Many Christians believe as long as they are speaking the truth about people, regardless of the consequences of the conversation, they are blameless in the sight of God. The Word of God is full of examples where people were either blessed or judged based upon how they honored or dishonored other people – even when they were speaking the truth about a situation. Since the Lord knows everything, the last thing He needs is another fact checker reporting to Him. What He sorely lacks are people who will help make His sons and daughters look better than they really are by covering over, ignoring, and forgiving their shortcomings and mistakes.

Does this mean we should always cover over and ignore people's faults, mistakes, and sins? Of course not. As a business leader you are responsible for evaluating and correcting your employees. As a parent you have similar responsibilities towards your children. If you are in a mentor-protégé relationship, you have a responsibility to provide honest feedback towards your protégé regarding their weaknesses and the areas where they need to improve.

However, the Body of Christ has been largely residing in a ditch on one side of the road where we feel obligated to expose every tiny flaw we see in our brothers and sisters, and feel we are justified to bring exposure to those flaws as long as we are speaking the truth. We need to learn to speak the truth and wrap it in love in order to have balanced teaching. Only bring exposure when necessary, or when you believe keeping silent would be abandoning your responsibility based upon your role in the situation. Otherwise, keep quiet and judge not so you will not be judged (Matt 7:1).

Biblical honor is based upon *agapē* love towards God and man and is not just an external action. The Word commands us to rise up before the gray-headed and honor the aged (Lev 19:32). However, we can perform the external action of rising up without honoring the aged. Unless the heart is based upon the right motivation, *agapē* love, God

48

does not consider the external action one of honor. He considers it hypocrisy.

A perfect example of hypocritical honor is seen whenever the president of the United States stands before a joint session of Congress. The members of Congress stand and applaud, the music plays, and everyone puts on their phony smile. Before and immediately after the session, we see our Governmental leaders "trash-talking" the same president they externally honored with insincere hearts.

True biblical honor starts and culminates in the heart and is rooted in *agapē* love. External actions are the result of a heartfelt attitude of esteeming others more valuable than ourselves. The Lord does not credit external actions of honoring people as biblical honor if our hearts are insincere. The Lord weighs the intention of the heart (Prov 16:2, Jer 17:10). External actions of honor will naturally follow a heart that lives a life of honor.

The opposite of honor is dishonor, which is defined as belittling, mocking, disparaging, being disrespectful towards, or withholding something due to someone else. If you want to understand dishonor, pick up a newspaper. It is often said bad news sells, but what *really* sells newspapers are stories of dishonor. Take the time to examine what you read and hear in the media and start looking for the elements of dishonor embedded in the dialogue.

The more sensitive we become towards recognizing dishonor, the more we will realize just how calloused we have become towards the practice of dishonor in our everyday life. Until we can hear the Holy Spirit telling us how and when we are practicing dishonor, we will not be able to repent and ask the Lord to give us the grace to love these people with the same *agapē* love He has for them. Our *agapē* love will then manifest as honor.

In our western mentality, we generally believe people need to earn our respect and honor. But from a Kingdom perspective, we are mandated to honor all people as well as the Lord, the king (or ruling officials), elders, and those in authority. Many times we fail to give honor that is due and yet wonder why the Lord is not honoring us by answering our prayers.

In summary, *agapē* love and obedience are the foundational requirements in order to abide in Him and He in you. Honor is the manifestation of your *agapē* love for God and man. But before you can enter the Kingdom of Heaven and abide in Him, there is a price you must pay. In fact, it will cost you everything that you have. In the next section we will discuss the price of admission to the Kingdom of Heaven and learn to look at our lives and business from God's perspective, and not ours. I refer to this as *the Kingdom of Heaven paradigm shift*.

Principles in Practice

Deborah was the best example of a leader who employed honor in the workplace that I ever had the privilege of watching and learning from. She was the Senior Vice President of the Technology Maintenance division of a multibillion dollar corporation. Technology maintenance is a highly metric-centered industry. Issues and problems as well as improvements, are generally measured in fractions of a percent. It is also an industry that is largely transparent. This means no one seems to know you exist until something breaks, and then everyone in the world seems to know your first name and is calling you at the same time. In other words, this is a position that has moments of intense stress. It is during these moments of stress we find out exactly how much *agapē* love is inside of us.

Deborah had weekly meetings with her direct reports and leaders who were responsible for preventing and performing triage on the technical problems that occurred during the previous week. As a former project manager, I have seen many people perform leadership in this role and know how challenging it can be to get people to admit to mistakes which could have been prevented and obtain creative solutions to prevent these issues from reoccurring. This manager role is often performed with a Telly Savalas personality (if you can remember the Kojak TV series). Nothing gets accomplished without a lot of shouting, name calling, and insincere threats. There is very little honor associated with the Kojak style of leadership.

Deborah had a totally different style of leadership based upon honor and drawing the best out of people. If Deborah's style of leadership had a tag line it would be "You know, we're better than that!" When challenging people to make necessary changes for improvements, one resistance all managers will hear from their subordinates is "It can't be done." This response is often accompanied by the many reasons the manager's requests are unreasonable and can't be accomplished. Even if they could be done, it's not their responsibility to make those changes. It's some other group's responsibility. Sound familiar?

The tendency for most leaders at this point is to counter each resistance with some type of logical argument. Deborah seemed to avoid those games of deflection by simply pointing out to her subordinates the many times they had actually done these things before, or had done things even more challenging - and done them successfully! She would edify and exhort people based upon their previous accomplishments. She didn't employ cheap flattery but recognition of previous successes. She would then exhort them that they could fix this problem because, "You know, we're better than that." At this point, her team couldn't argue with their own prior successful results. They had no choice but to agree with her that these suggestions for improvements could be done.

Deborah was the only manager I ever met who could take you to the wood shed to correct your mistakes and have you end up feeling better about yourself when it was over. Afterwards, you were excited to go back and retackle the project with a renewed enthusiasm that you really could do better. You really were expecting better results the next time around. Why? Because you found yourself saying, "I'm better than that!" Honor will do this to people even when they are being taken to the woodshed for their mistakes.

Kingdom Business Success

Ron, my former boss, was the best example of someone who honored his competitors. The Federal Government contracting arena is a dog-eat-dog world. There are no awards for second place in the procurement industry and many of these Government contracts are worth millions and sometimes billions of dollars. There are no shortages of unscrupulous business people, men or women, who are willing to sell their souls for one of these big Government contracts.

I never heard Ron make a disparaging remark toward one of our competitors, even when we lost a contract bid to a competitor who had won the contract through lying or cheating. Ron always viewed our competitors in light of their strengths and accomplishments. He focused on what was good about them and did his best to overlook their lapses of integrity.

When Ron would meet our competitors at Bidder's conferences, seminars, or while visiting our client sites (where our competitors were often trying to steal our work), he was always very friendly and respectful toward them. They in turn seemed to love Ron and never hid the fact they would love to hire him to come work for them. Ron seemed to know how to make his enemies his friends simply by honoring them. By honoring his competitors, the Lord would set a table for him before his enemies and give him incredible favor with them (Psalm 23:5-6).

Victor, mentioned earlier, was the owner of this same Government contracting company. Victor had very little good to say about those in authority in his life. This included the Government, the IRS, his customers, his business partners, and even his own corporate Board. He was quick to point out their weaknesses and mistakes, their hypocrisy, and how he would do things differently if they would only listen to him and take his advice. Victor would frequently dishonor these authority figures in his thoughts and words.

When Victor would meet with those in authority, he had little patience for attempting to understand them. It was almost guaranteed at some point in the conversation when they were trying to explain their rationale for their decisions, policies, and actions, Victor would cut them off in mid-sentence. He would then start telling them how he perceived the situation and how he would handle the situation, if only people would listen to him.

As a general rule, most of those authority figures were not offended by Victor's rude interruptions, at least not the first time. They would typically honor Victor and allow him to finish his discourse before attempting to return to the point they were trying to make before being rudely interrupted. But Victor was seldom finished, and this process of not listening and interrupting would repeat until the authority figures realized Victor was not listening to them. The final admonition these people would generally give to those who were accompanying Victor, was to leave Victor at home the next time they met.

Victor never thought he was dishonoring those in authority. He thought these people were ignorant and incompetent and would speak those words to anyone in ear shot. Victor didn't realize his words of dishonor were seeds being sown into his own life. In time those seeds of dishonor would sprout and he would reap the harvest. This harvest included being dishonored by his own employees, subcontractors, and even his own Board members who voted him off the Board and out of the company. They even had a locksmith come and change the locks to the offices. It was a sad day to see Victor standing outside of his own company. He was locked out of his own offices with his employees refusing to let him inside. Eventually, all of his business eroded and the company closed its doors. Remember, when we dishonor those in authority, we are dishonoring the Lord who placed those people in authority.

Those who are under your authority will always be watching to see how you honor those in authority over you. They will look to see where you set the bar for honor to determine how much honor they need to give you (Luke 6:38). Victor never understood this concept and reaped the dishonor he sowed.

Questions for Reflection

1. Who do you know who best exemplifies a life of honor towards all people? What is the secret to their success? What can you learn from them? If possible, ask them how they are able to live a life of honor and what goes through their mind as they interact with the type of people you are normally tempted to dishonor.

2. Ask the Lord to show you the areas of your life and business where you need to repent for failing to live a life of honor. Ask Him to show you how you could have handled those situations differently that would have resulted in you honoring those people.

3. Ask the Lord to show you the triggers that cause you to dishonor people. Is it when you feel you are being dishonored? Ask the Lord to show you how to reprogram your responses so you can always honor others, even when they are dishonoring you.

SECTION 2: THE KINGDOM PARADIGM SHIFT

Chapter 5

The Kingdom of Heaven Paradigm

"But seek first His kingdom and His righteousness,
and all these things will be added to you" (Matt 6:33).

"All in." It's a phrase that has become very popular in today's society. Although best known as a term used when playing poker, it is now being used in corporate America, the military, and even our Government to represent someone who has committed all of their resources to a particular goal. They are holding nothing back in reserve. They are totally committed to the effort. They will win or lose, live or die, based on the results of the endeavor for which they have totally committed everything. They *are* "all in."

In order to become a disciple of the Lord Jesus Christ and abide in Him and He in you, you must be "all in." In order to enter the Kingdom of Heaven and see the Kingdom of Heaven manifest in your life, you must be "all in." If you are not willing to sell all you have in order to enter the Kingdom of Heaven, you will watch it from the distance but not be able to enter into and abide in the Kingdom (Matt 7:21-23, 13:44-46).

What is the Kingdom of Heaven? Is there a difference between the Kingdom of Heaven and the Kingdom of God? How does the Kingdom of Heaven compare to the kingdom of this world? Is the Mosaic Law part of the Kingdom of Heaven? Has the Kingdom of Heaven already come, partly come, or is it coming in the future? What does the Kingdom of Heaven have to do with the quintessential question of *"What's wrong? Why isn't it working?"*

These are all excellent questions. A room full of theologians would have trouble coming to agreement on the answers and would struggle to explain it concisely in ten pages or less. Seriously, this is the type of topic that has made up many doctoral theses for seminary students. I am not going to attempt to provide detailed answers to these questions, but I will provide scriptural support for the definitions and terms I will be using in this book. I am going to attempt to give sufficient scriptural support to provide you with the information necessary to answer a more important question; at least more important in regard to the purpose of this book. That question is "What does the Kingdom of Heaven have to do with my business?"

In order to define the Kingdom of Heaven, we first need to define the Gospel of the Lord Jesus Christ. Ask one hundred Christians to define the Gospel of the Lord Jesus Christ and most of them will struggle to come up with a good response. This a pretty sad commentary given the mandate of the Great Commission that says we are supposed to be preaching this gospel. Ask one hundred preachers the same question and what you will probably get for a response is what is known as *the Gospel of Salvation*.

The Gospel of Salvation is the message of the free gift of salvation only found in Christ Jesus. It is the message that our sins separate us from the God who created us and loves us. His perfect love was manifested by sending His Son Jesus to shed His blood for our sins so we would be redeemed from the kingdom of darkness into the Kingdom of Heaven. This is probably best summarized scripturally by what is referred to as the Romans Road to Salvation (Rom 3:23, 6:23, 5:8, 10:9) along with John 3:16 and Revelation 3:10.

The Body of Christ has done a fairly decent job of preaching the Gospel of Salvation, especially to those who sit in church pews on Sunday morning. But is the Gospel of Salvation the gospel the Lord Jesus Himself preached, or did He preach a different gospel? If you read the four gospels, you will actually find that Jesus spent very little time preaching on becoming born-again, getting saved, or anything that would show He was doing a decent job of preaching the Gospel of Salvation.

Most of what Jesus preached on was the Gospel of the Kingdom. In fact, in the Bible the gospel is actually referred to as **the Gospel of the Kingdom** (Matt 4:23, Luke 16:16). The Gospel of Salvation is part of the Gospel of the Kingdom, but it is only a part of the gospel. Most of the gospel Jesus preached was directed towards those who would become His disciples. He spent significant time describing the Kingdom of Heaven and how it contrasted with the kingdom of this world, and even life under the Mosaic Law. He preached this new message so those who would follow Him would know what it would take to enter the Kingdom, the paradigm shift they would need to make in order to live in the Kingdom, and the new bar for righteous living expected of those who would become his disciples.

The apostle Matthew refers to the Kingdom as the Kingdom of Heaven, while Mark, Luke, and John refer to it as the Kingdom of God. The three synoptic gospels show these two terms being used in the same context. In this book we will use the terms Kingdom, Kingdom of Heaven, and Kingdom of God synonymously. We will capitalize Kingdom to differentiate it from the kingdom of this world and the kingdom of darkness.

What is the Kingdom of Heaven? It is the domain of the King. It's the domain where the King has ultimate authority and power and is Lord over all (Psalm 103:19 NKJV). It's the domain where His laws and decrees are enforced. It's the domain where rebellion to the King is punished and terminated (Luke 19:14, 27). It's an eternal domain (Dan 4:3). It is a spiritual domain (Luke 17:20-21) that includes sovereignty over all other kingdoms including the kingdom of this world (Matt 4:8-9). The Kingdom of Heaven is at hand and is being progressively built up. This will continue until the kingdoms of this world become the Kingdom of our Lord and His Christ, and He will reign forever and ever (Rev 11:15).

We all start with the perspective of the kingdom of this world because this is where we came from before we were born-again. It is because the Kingdom of Heaven operates so differently than the kingdom of this world, and differently than the life they knew under the Mosaic Law, that Jesus spent so much time describing it to those who would follow Him. He wanted his followers to be ready for *the paradigm shift*.

Life in the Kingdom

Here are some of the differences the Lord spoke about regarding how different our lives would be in the Kingdom of Heaven compared to what we experienced when living in the kingdom of this world, even for those who were living under the Mosaic Law. These principles were part of the good news Jesus preached to those who would become His disciples and enter the Kingdom of Heaven. This is the essence of the Gospel of the Kingdom:

"For the Kingdom of God does not consist in words but in power" (1 Cor 4:20).
The Kingdom of Heaven is about the power of the Holy Spirit. The Kingdom of Heaven is not entered into through reasoning, nor does it operate according to religious doctrine. It is manifested through the power of the Holy Spirit so that our faith does not rest in the wisdom of man but on the power of God (1 Cor 2:4-5). Christianity was never meant to be a religion, but a manifestation of the power of God expressed in us and through us through Jesus Christ.

"And I will give you the keys of the kingdom of heaven, and whatever you bind on earth will be bound in heaven, and whatever you loose on earth will be loosed in heaven" (Matt 16:19).
The keys to the Kingdom of Heaven refer to the spiritual authority to open doors no man can shut, and to shut doors no man can open (Rev 3:7). Jesus gave His disciples His authority to exercise so that man's faith in Him would not be a religious experience.

"Behold, I have given you authority to tread on serpents and scorpions, and over all the power of the enemy, and nothing will injure you" (Luke 10:19).
Jesus declared all authority had been given to Him in heaven and on earth and that He was giving His

disciples this authority to allow them to fulfill their assignment, take back dominion of this world, and protect them from the kingdom of darkness.

"But I say to you that everyone who is angry with his brother shall be guilty before the court; and whoever says to his brother, 'You good-for-nothing,' shall be guilty before the supreme court; and whoever says, 'You fool,' shall be guilty *enough to go* into the fiery hell. But I say to you that everyone who looks at a woman with lust for her has already committed adultery with her in his heart" (Matt 5:22, 28).

Under the Mosaic Law, sins were largely categorized by what you did or did not do. They were largely based upon actions and not thoughts or attitudes of the heart. In the Kingdom of Heaven, we see a paradigm shift where the bar of righteousness has been raised. It is not enough to abstain from committing a sin, we are expected to keep our heart attitude and thoughts free from sin as well. Jesus goes on to say it is what is in our hearts that defile us, for all sin originates in the heart (Matt 15:18-20).

"And He was saying to them, "To you has been given the mystery of the kingdom of God, but those who are outside get everything in parables" (Mark 4:11).

The Kingdom of Heaven is a mystery to those outside the Kingdom. Much of the Gospel of the Kingdom was meant to explain those mysteries to those who would become disciples of Jesus. Even after we enter the Kingdom, we are not expected to know and understand everything (Mark 4:26-27). But we are expected to be obedient and act on the revelation we have received. If you are waiting to figure everything out before you step out in faith to do what you already

know you should be doing, then you will be waiting a
very long time, for the Kingdom of Heaven is a mystery
and is being revealed progressively.

Jesus went on to give many more examples about the Kingdom of
Heaven and how it contrasted with the kingdom of this world and the
religious life they knew under the Mosaic Law. He said we must be
willing to give up all we had to enter the Kingdom and leave anything
behind that would tempt us to sin. We must pick up our cross daily and
follow Him (Luke 9:23, 14:26, Mark 9:43-48). This doesn't sound like
cheap salvation to me. Jesus was saying that in order to enter the
Kingdom of Heaven and walk in the abundant life contained therein,
we must be "all in."

Bringing Your Business into the Kingdom of Heaven

Under the Gospel of Salvation paradigm, the Lord was only
interested in you and specifically in your spirit and soul. When you
became born-again, the Holy Spirit came to reside in your spirit man.
Your soul would undergo a transformational process through the
washing of the Word and putting off the old man and putting on the
new man. You were now saved and waiting for...eternity. You were
supposed to go to church, pay your tithes, be a good example of a
Christian, and wait for the return of the Lord, or your death. Whichever
event would come first. Doesn't sound like much of a life, does it? It's
no wonder we weren't smiling in church on Sunday morning. It's no
wonder we had trouble getting the rest of the world to come and join
our team.

Under the Kingdom of Heaven paradigm, when we become born-
again, we don't come empty handed into the Kingdom. We bring
everything with us, including our business. The Lord wants you, and
the price of admission to the Kingdom is everything you have. Before I
lose some of you, let me explain the scriptural basis of being "all in"
regarding the Kingdom of Heaven. In order to understand the concept
of your business and everything you have coming with you into the
Kingdom, we need to look closely at the Greek word *oikos* which is

often translated as house or household. "They said, believe in the Lord Jesus, and you will be saved, you and your household" (Acts 16:31).

In this scripture, the word translated "household" is the Greek word *oikos*. It is used to refer to a house, a household, a family, a family's lineage, and even a nation.[1] In modern translation, it is probably best translated as an estate. Whereas someone's *oikia* would represent their dwelling, their *oikos* would represent their entire estate. In ancient Greece, wives, children, slaves, and even agricultural farms and livestock were considered part of a man's *oikos*. Acts 16:31 literally says "...and you will be saved, you and your household (or estate)." If only the jailer was being saved by his decision to become born-again, there would be no need to reference his household or estate.

When we become born-again and enter the Kingdom of Heaven, the Lord expects us to bring everything with us. This includes all we are and all we have. Do you have a mountain of debt and business failures? Bring it with you. Do you have a broken heart over hurts and offenses from the past? Bring it with you. Do you have harmful addictions in your life? Bring them with you. Do you consider yourself "damaged goods?" Bring the damaged goods with you. The Lord is in the healing and restoration business and He wants to make you whole in every area of your life, not just your soul. In fact, He not only invites you to bring your *oikos* with you, He insists on it. The cost of admission to the Kingdom of Heaven is your entire estate. In other words, the price of admission is all you are and all you have. You must be "all in" to get in.

So what does the Lord want with the estate you are bringing into the Kingdom? Remember, He is on a mission to restore all things. He will bind up the broken hearted, proclaim release to the captives, comfort those who mourn, and give beauty for ashes (Isaiah 61). He will use your weaknesses and foolishness to confound the wise. He will level the mountains and fill in the valleys of your life. He will burn away all sin and set you free from addictions and the chains of anger and bitterness. As the King, it is His decision as to what to use for His glory and what to eliminate from your life. Your job is simply to bring all you have and all you are into the Kingdom and let Him sort it out.

The Kingdom of Heaven is about fruitfulness, increase, and multiplication. *Zōē* life, the abundant life, is found in the Kingdom of Heaven. When you give your business to the Lord for His Kingdom purposes, He is able to do incredible miracles through your business. Two of these business miracles can be seen in His use of Peter's boat to preach to the crowd on the shore and the accompanying catch of fish, and also in the multiplication of the five loaves and two fish to feed the 5,000 with 12 baskets left over (Luke 5:3-7; 9:12-17).

The Lord will use whatever we give Him that is part of our *oikos* including our loaves and fishes, our boats, our business, wealth, talents, gifts, and experiences. The Lord never wastes anything. But He will not use something that has not been given and dedicated to Him. Have you dedicated your business to Him yet? Has your business died in Christ so it can be resurrected as a new creature, one dedicated for His use in any way He chooses? Perhaps it is time you baptize your business to Him. I have included a prayer of dedication in Chapter 17 for those who have never done this before and would like to bring their business into the Kingdom of Heaven.

Most Christians are more familiar with the paradigm of life under the Mosaic Law than in the Kingdom of Heaven. They are taught the laws and commandments, the observance of feasts and sabbaths, the sacrifices of tithes and offerings, and serving the Lord. The Kingdom of Heaven is not about religion but about passion and purpose. It is about restoring all things as if there had never been a fall in the Garden of Eden. It is about a life of abiding in Him and He in us 24/7. No more religion, simply continuous unbroken relationship with the God who loves and created us for His purpose. It's about His life flowing through us and into everything we touch. This was such a radical concept that Jesus spent a great deal of time preaching about this paradigm shift.

Passion and purpose for the Lord and His Kingdom are a key part of the Kingdom of Heaven paradigm. In the next chapter, we will look at discovering your purpose in this life once you have entered His Kingdom. I refer to this as *your Kingdom assignment.*

Principles in Practice

Jeremy and June were the leaders of a successful non-profit organization and two of the most sold out people for Jesus you could imagine. Before knowing the Lord, Jeremy was deeply in debt, with a growing alcohol problem and a wife and two children. Jeremy cried out to the Lord he didn't believe in, and the Lord came into Jeremy's life. His wife had come to the Lord a few months earlier. During the next year, Jeremy and June joined a church and dove into the deep end of the pool. They got involved with Sunday school, Bible studies, children's ministry, and evangelistic outreaches. They started giving tithes, offerings, and alms. Jeremy wore a big wooden cross around his neck and didn't miss any opportunities to let people know they needed to get born-again, or go to hell.

Having a strong teaching gift, Jeremy felt the desire to go to Bible school, so he and June sold the little they had and drove off to Bible school with their two children. June home-schooled the children while Jeremy enrolled in his studies and got a part-time construction job to make ends meet. After Bible school, Jeremy and June relocated back to their prior location. Jeremy got a good job with a technology company and June stayed home with the children. Wanting to get out of debt quickly, they went on an extreme budget that provided them no discretionary spending. However, their hard work and discipline paid off and within three years they were debt free. Using this same level of discipline, Jeremy and June started their non-profit organization on a shoe-string budget to raise up and teach Christian leaders.

Through dedication, hard work, and the Lord's blessing, Jeremy and June were able to build their organization to over 300 members. Since Jeremy and June's gifting was in hard work and discipline and not people skills, the Lord sent them a few strong leaders who could help them build their organization and serve as a buffer between their members and Jeremy's harsh countenance. Eventually, Jeremy and

June lost some of these leaders and when the members dealt directly with Jeremey and June, their hard countenances started turning away the members. The last I heard, they were down to less than 40 members.

Jeremy and June were definitely "all in" regarding the Kingdom of Heaven, but they had yet to learn how to abide in Him and He in them. When people saw and talked to them, they didn't see Jesus, they saw their old man that had yet to die. Without the love of God in their hearts, Jeremy and June became New Testament Pharisees. They created incredibly high standards which they themselves could neither obtain nor sustain, but expected everyone else to meet those standards. Their love for people was conditional and based upon people meeting Jeremy and June's expectations, and obeying the commandments of God. Jeremy and June had become New Testament religious zealots.

Unfortunately, there are many New Testament religious zealots in the Body of Christ. We need to be "all in" regarding the Kingdom of Heaven and our relationship with the Lord, but until we learn to abide in Him and He in us, others will not see Jesus in us, they will only see a bunch of New Testament Pharisees.

Gus and Sylvia are great examples of Christians who are "all in" regarding their relationship with the Lord as well as ones who are constantly seeking to abide in Him. In their personal lives, they live in the presence of God and are constantly seeking His direction for what they should be doing, where they should be doing it, and to whom they should be doing it. Gus and Sylvia look at everything they own as belonging to the Lord and are ready to share or give it all away at a moment's notice. They never fear lack of provision because they know even if the Lord asked them to give away everything, He would bring them more to replace what they gave. They possess what the Lord has given them, but nothing except the Lord possesses them.

As the owners of an industrial services company, Gus and Sylvia's attitude towards the Lord and His Kingdom go with them whenever they enter the office. They see all of the employees, customers, vendors, and business associates as people the Lord has brought into their life. They see their role in these business relationships as one of serving people as Christ would serve them. Whenever someone new comes into their life, they ask the Lord if this is someone He has brought and if so, for what purpose and how He wants them to work with them. If they are unsure if a new person coming into their life is from the Lord, they pray and ask Him to remove anyone who doesn't belong there.

Gus and Sylvia live a life of prayer for their personal lives and business. They do their best to walk hand-in-hand with the Lord over every detail of their lives, including making dinner at night. They never leave the Lord at the door, either at their home or their business. They are constantly doing their best to walk as one with Him.

Although they are "all-in" with the Lord, they still encounter the same challenges and struggles everyone else faces in life. However, they never face these challenges alone. They know He is with them always and their faith provides them the assurance He will successfully see them through. The increase of the abundant life is coming into their marriage, their relationships, their business, and Kingdom assignments. When you are "all-in" and abide in Him, His *zōē* life comes into every area of your life. His life produces more life. This is the type of life we are all seeking.

Questions for Reflection

1. Which gospel have you been exposed to previously? The Gospel of Salvation or the Gospel of the Kingdom of Heaven?

2. Have you ever given everything you have and all you are to the Lord? Have you ever told Him that you are "all in" regarding His Kingdom? If not, I have included prayers in Chapter 17 to help you dedicate your life and business to the Lord.

3. Do you operate your business and your work as if you and your business are part of the Kingdom serving His purpose? Or is

that part of your life separated from Him, since you've always believed your business is secular and not sacred?

Chapter 6

Your Kingdom Assignment

"A plan in the heart of a man is like deep water, but
a man of understanding draws it out" (Prov 20:5).

"So, *why* are you in this business?" My client Larry raised his head somewhat quizzically and replied, "For the money." I could tell from the look on his face that he wanted to say, "Could there possibly be another reason?" I tried not to smile. You see, Larry was chasing money. He had yet to figure out that in the Kingdom of Heaven we are supposed to pursue the King, His Kingdom, and His righteousness. Money is supposed to chase us. Larry was chasing something that was supposed to be chasing him!

In the last chapter, we talked about the paradigm shift necessary to see the Kingdom of Heaven operate in our lives. We talked about entering the Kingdom of Heaven with all you are and all you have. This means if you are a business owner, you brought your business with you into the Kingdom. But now that you have entered the Kingdom of Heaven, what is your assignment in the Kingdom? What is the purpose or role you and your business will play in the Kingdom?

In this chapter, we are going to discuss your assignment in the Kingdom and the role you and your business will play in the Kingdom. In regard to identifying their Kingdom assignment, I have discovered that many well-intentioned business people struggle in their business for one of three reasons: a.) they are in the wrong business, b.) they are in the right business for the wrong reasons, or c.) they are in the right business using the wrong business model. We will look at all three scenarios, but first let's discuss your assignment in the Kingdom and the purpose it fulfills.

Kingdom Business Success

What is Your Kingdom Assignment?

For those outside of the Kingdom, the determination of their career assignment becomes largely a coin toss. It is largely a matter of personal interests, skill sets, education level, determination, and luck. Educational statistics show that 75% of those entering college have not selected a major.[1] After entering college, 50% will change their major before completion of college. Ten years after graduation, 80% of those who successfully graduate are working in a field outside of their college degree. Those statistics probably wouldn't matter if we all eventually ended up in the assignment for which we were created. This would be analogous to putting a jigsaw puzzle together. Keep moving the piece around and eventually you will find the place where it belongs. But understanding our purpose and assignment in life seems to be far more challenging than most jigsaw puzzles.

If you ask the average American if they are satisfied with their career assignment, the large majority will say no. A Gallup poll showed 70% of Americans are either unengaged (mentally and emotionally checked out) or actively disengaged in their work.[2] They have no sense of purpose or meaning from their assignment. They go to work for the paycheck without any passion in what they are doing. Is it any wonder that those outside the Kingdom are still trying to figure out what they want to be when they grow up, regardless of their age? Without any purpose and passion for their work, is it any wonder the average American fails to excel in either their career assignment or their finances?

But what about those of us who have entered the Kingdom of Heaven and are in the process of becoming disciples of the Lord Jesus Christ? Should it be any different for us? Absolutely! But whether we steadily move in the direction of our Kingdom assignment or struggle with the same jigsaw puzzle problem will be based largely upon whether we make the paradigm shift in *how* we seek and pursue our Kingdom assignment.

When we enter the Kingdom of Heaven, the Lord assigns us a place in the Body of Christ (Eph 4:15-16). Unfortunately, we do not get to decide our placement. That is entirely His decision. He reserves the right to move us around as He sees fit. He often orchestrates things in seasons and our assignments can change as the seasons of our life change. Remember, the cost of discipleship is death to oneself. He is Lord over everything including our will. His will must become our will. The cross we are called to carry while we follow Him is death to our will and complete obedience to His will at all times.

As we try to ascertain our assignment in the Kingdom of Heaven, part of our assignment is easy to understand based upon an understanding of whom we have become. We are disciples of the Lord Jesus Christ. We are called to walk as He walked. We are called to become like Him in every way. That is an extremely high calling. This means whatever His assignment is should also be reflected in our assignment.

We are called to be Christians, or "little Christs" to the world. We are called to preach the gospel of the Kingdom, heal the sick, raise the dead, cast out demons, and disciple the nations. Whatever else constitutes our assignment, such as being a business owner, we are first called to be a little Christ and bring the Kingdom of Heaven and the power of Christ everywhere we go and to everyone we meet. We cannot separate our career assignment on this earth from who we have become.

When we show up at work, we cannot leave our religion at the door any more than we could leave our head or our hearts at the door. **What we do is based upon who we are and the two cannot be separated**. If someone hires us to work for them, they also hire Christ in us to work for them. Therefore, whatever our assignment is in the Kingdom of Heaven, we bring *Christ in us* to that assignment. If we know what Christ would do on a job assignment, then we know what we should be doing as well.

Kingdom Business Success

But what about our unique Kingdom assignment? How do we know where the Lord has assigned us? If we brought a business with us into the Kingdom of Heaven, is it still our assignment or could it be a different business or totally different assignment? Obviously, the Lord knows, but how do we discern His will? We will address wisdom and understanding in Chapter 12, but the short answer to this question is that your Kingdom assignment is a gift you will have to find and unwrap. Your assignment is something you will have to passionately seek and pursue. The Bible says, "A plan in the heart of a man is *like* deep water, but a man of understanding draws it out" (Prov 20:5).

Your Kingdom assignment will be something you must seek as if it is buried treasure. Some people intuitively know their assignment at an early age. Some people claim to have had a God encounter when they were young in which the Lord spoke to them or gave them a dream or vision of their future. For the rest of us, we put our hand to the plow and keep seeking the will of the Lord for our lives. We spend time in His presence and listen to the still small voice speaking to us in a loving manner.

Although the Lord can call you to an assignment totally disparate from the ones you have had in the past, it is more likely He has had you on a path leading to your assignment. Therefore, one technique that can help you identify your Kingdom assignment is to look at your past assignments. In what assignments have you had favor and success in the past? Does the mosaic of your life seem to have a common thread? Sometimes it is easier for others who know us well to see those patterns in our life. Seek counsel from those who both know you quite well and know the voice of the Lord. They can sometimes give great insight to your strengths and weaknesses and the patterns in your life you do not see.

Passion

One of the most important keys that will help you discern your Kingdom assignment is to understand what you are passionate about. By passion, I am talking about the type of passion that would give someone the zeal and drive to commit their entire life to a cause or project. I am talking about the type of passion that would make someone willing to die for a cause. This type of passion would drive someone to pursue a cause even if there wasn't any money to be made from that enterprise. This type of passion would cause someone to send His only Son to the cross to die for the sins of unjust men and women so they would be set free from prison. This is the type of passion I am talking about. So, what are you passionate about?

What are *your* deepest heart's desires? What is it you passionately desire to see and be a part of, that it brings you to tears to think you might not be able to see it in this lifetime? What do you want to see accomplished so badly, the very thought of seeing that desire fulfilled in the near future brings incredible joy to your life? What do you want to accomplish so greatly, if you could never make any money from it or get any credit for being able to accomplish it, you would still spend your life pursuing it? Understand the answers to those questions and you are on the way to discovering your Kingdom assignment.

There are two characteristics all successful business people possess, regardless of whether they are believers or non-believers. In fact, I have never heard of any successful business person in any generation who did not possess both of these qualities in abundance. These biblical characteristics are *passion* and *discipline*. I am going to address the importance of passion here and discipline in a later chapter.

Study the biographies of successful business people like Bill Gates, Steve Jobs, Warren Buffet, and Donald Trump and you will find some common denominators. The first and most obvious one is their passion for their career field. They threw themselves into their careers at an early age and determined they would be successful at them. They put in long hours learning their industries and studying their competitors. They became experts in their field before they started to see the financial rewards of their endeavors (Prov 22:29).

As disciples, our passion should be for the Lord, His Kingdom, His righteousness, and our assignment in the Kingdom. Money follows service. Money follows value. When your product or service generates value for others, money will naturally follow that service. The more value you provide, the more money will follow your service. If you have passion for your assignment, you will find new ways to provide increased value to others from that endeavor. In time, you will leave your competitors in the dust, the same way these four men did with their competitors.

Business people who are in the wrong business or wrong Kingdom assignment frequently fail in their business. Sometimes this is due to a lack of passion for what they are doing. The only reason they were in the business was to make money. They were chasing money and not their Kingdom assignment. They didn't see their business as an assignment, they only saw it as a way to make money. That is a sad place of existence and should only occur for those outside the Kingdom.

What many Christian business people fail to grasp is that sometimes God wants them to fail in their business. Why? The faster they fail in this business, the faster He can move them into the right business; their Kingdom assignment. If God blessed everything you worked on, how would He ever get you to abandon your will for your life and start seeking His will for your life? If your business is failing, it is possible God is trying to tell you something. He might be trying to tell you He has something better in mind for you and the sooner you let go of this business, the sooner He can put you into the business He's already blessed for you. Even if business people succeed in the wrong business, good can be the enemy of great. Failing to move from the wrong business to the right business can be the difference between being successful and miserable in life, and being successful and having abundance in every area of your life.

The Right Business For the Wrong Reasons

When I asked Larry why he was in the business he owned, I was seeking to uncover his passion in life and the purpose he believed his business fulfilled in serving the King. Instead, I discovered like many of those outside the Kingdom, he saw his business as a cash cow for putting money into his pocket. He was serving mammon and not the Lord. Without understanding what the Lord wanted to achieve *through* his business, his business was struggling because he wasn't walking in agreement with the Lord's will for his business.

I believe Larry was in the right business for the wrong reasons. His failure was based upon having the wrong paradigm. Like those outside the Kingdom, he saw his business as a vehicle to generate wealth for himself and his family and permit him to give tithes and offerings. Larry didn't realize he was trying to be the lord of his own business. In his paradigm, he and his business were at the center of his world and everything else and everyone including the Lord, revolved around him. Yet, he couldn't figure out why the Lord was not involved in his business.

When I asked Larry if he would still be in this business if there wasn't any money to be made from it, his response was no. He couldn't see how the service he provided was serving the King and advancing the Kingdom of Heaven. He could not see the purpose of his business from the King's perspective, nor was he trying. Like so many others, he was content to ask the Lord to bless his business, instead of giving his business to the Lord and asking the Lord to show him how this born-again business would serve Him and His Kingdom.

Why is it so important to understand the reasons you are in business? Because it defines *who* you are serving, *what* you are serving them, and *where,* or the geographical place of your assignment. To better understand the motivating spirits behind the non-believer's business model, we need only look at the tower of Babel.

> "They said, 'Come, let us build for ourselves a city, and a tower whose top *will reach* into heaven, and let us make for ourselves a name, otherwise, we will be scattered abroad over the face of the whole earth'" (Gen 11:4).

Kingdom Business Success

There are at least three sin natures behind the decisions that motivated the ancient Babylonians to build the tower of Babel. These sin natures can be summarized as greed (a tower whose top reaches into Heaven), pride (make a name for ourselves), and fear (lest we be scattered abroad over the face of the earth). The construction of the tower of Babel itself was not sinful, but the motivating spirits behind the purpose of the tower were rooted in man's basic sin nature (1 John 2:6).

The motivating spirits behind a business not only determine who we serve but will eventually dictate the corporate policies, rules and procedures, and how a company will pursue their objectives. A study of the motivating spirits of mammon, greed, pride, and fear which are behind the non-believer's business model will show us the Lord has something better in mind for us in the Kingdom of Heaven.

There is nothing wrong with a company wanting to become more successful and profitable, but if our faith is in the profitability of the company to provide for us and give us happiness, then we have committed idolatry in our hearts. Only the Lord Himself can provide us with those desires. In the Kingdom of Heaven, wealth and riches have a purpose and a mission. We must look at them as a vehicle to achieve the assignment we have been given. We should never chase wealth. Wealth is supposed to chase us. We are told that we will have wealth and riches when we need them. But, they can never be allowed to possess us.

A business can be successful for the wrong reasons. Those who serve the spirits of mammon, greed, fear, and pride do not care why their businesses are successful. However, for those of us who serve the King and His Kingdom, in order to truly be successful we need to understand why we are in business, what purpose our business is serving to advance His kingdom, and to whom we are called to serve. We must operate our business in a way that glorifies Him and conduct our operations in a way He Himself would conduct the business, if He were the CEO of our company. The Lord will not be lord over our business if the reason we are in business is to serve other gods.

What would the Kingdom purpose for your business look like? It is hard to say because it will be something unique for each business and business owner. Here are three abstract examples and I will include one real life example in the story of Dane & Debbie later in this chapter.

> Perhaps you manufacture ball point pens. Prior to each batch of pens going out to your customers, you have your intercessors pray over each batch so that each person who touches a pen will have dreams and visions of the Lord Jesus; each person will use this pen to dedicate their life to the Lord and write psalms of praise and thanksgiving to Him. You pray these pens will be used to sign contracts to bless people and businesses and shape the laws of our nation.

> Perhaps you have a cleaning business. While your employees are cleaning a home or business, you have them pray over each place and release forgiveness for the sins that have occurred, and pray the grace and peace of the Lord Jesus comes into everyone's life who enters the premises. You pray that each person will feel the love of the Father and turn to Him. You anoint each chair, office, and cubicle and release a blessing over that office and the people who work there.

> Perhaps you have an extermination business and you see the correlation of the spiritual with the natural realm. While your employees are taking out the unwanted critters from the house or business, your intercessors are praying a spiritual cleansing to go along with the cleaning in the natural realm.

Your greatest fulfillment in the business world will come when you find out *where* you are called to serve, *who* you are called to serve, *what* you are to serve, and how providing this service to people serves the King and His Kingdom purposes. When that happens, all the other things you are seeking in life will fall into place. That is when you will know the true meaning of success. You will start keeping score by the number of lives you introduce to Christ and the number of lives you bless by releasing the power of Christ in you, and not by your Financial Statements. When you do that, the Lord will take care of adding to your Financial Statements.

Whatever spirit you serve, you are enslaved to that spirit (Rom 6:16, 2 Peter 2:19). If you are chasing money, you are enslaved to the spirit of mammon. If you are still chasing money and success in the business world, it is time to get off the merry-go-round ride. Start spending time in the presence of the Lord and cry out to Him. He has something better for you. It will be the most thrilling adventure of your life. The next time someone asks you *"Why* are you in this business?" the last answer you will ever give is "for the money."

The Right Business with the Wrong Business Model

Let's assume you have finally figured out what you are passionate about and have a pretty good idea what your Kingdom assignment is. You are starting to see your business as part of a Kingdom assignment and seeing it from His perspective. You now have a pretty good idea how your business serves the Lord and His Kingdom, and you can see the Kingdom purpose for what you are doing. The metrics you are using for success are *not* those of the world but based upon how many people's lives are being impacted for the King with your business. Sounds like everything should be clicking pretty smoothly, right? Don't be surprised if your answer at this point is "No." Many business people struggle in business because they are in the right business, using the wrong business model.

If you go back and study the biographies of great business people, you will find there is a part of their story that tends to get glossed over in the biography. That part of the story is typically their early years in business when they either struggled or had limited success. This is the season before they had the level of success that made them famous. They then describe their eureka moment and go into great detail in the biography on their successful years. But what was going on in their business before their eureka moment? They were probably in the right business but using the wrong business model. Let's look at some familiar examples.

When IBM approached **Bill Gates** about developing an operating system for their upcoming PC, Bill was writing BASIC language interpreters for microprocessors. It was the change in Microsoft's business model from developing software language tools to developing software operating systems, and an industry change in software license models that took Bill Gates from entrepreneur to billionaire.[3] Would we have ever heard of Bill Gates if he was still developing BASIC interpreters for PCs?

Donald Trump started in his father's real estate business that specialized in renovating and renting apartments to the post-war middle class.[4] It wasn't until Trump moved to Manhattan and started to design high end, one-of-a kind real estate projects for the wealthy that he made a name for himself and became successful. Would anyone have heard of Trump if he was still rehabbing middle-income apartment complexes?

Dick and Maurice McDonald's first drive-through restaurants featured only hotdogs, not hamburgers.[5] Later, they founded the McDonald's Bar-B-Q restaurant which included hamburgers on the menu. Eventually they saw the profitability was in the hamburgers, milkshakes, and french fries and not the other barbecue items. Where would they be if they stuck with selling hotdogs? Would anyone have heard of them?

You might be in the right Kingdom assignment but employing the wrong business model. If so, you are probably struggling in your business and asking the quintessential question. How do you determine the correct or best business model for your business? I offer two suggestions: 1.) spend time in prayer in the presence of the Lord seeking wisdom and understanding and 2.) make sure you have a solid business plan.

Kingdom Business Success

Just as it was necessary to spend significant time in His presence to get the revelation of which field or business you are called to, you must spend time in His presence to understand which business model you should be using. You may be called to the computer software industry, but which software product? Is your target market the consumer, business, or government sectors? Is this a niche market product or a product that will be used by everyone? How will you determine how much to charge for the product? Will it be based upon market price or cost of goods sold? What is the unique selling proposition your product offers over other solutions? If the Lord has given you this assignment, then He has answers to these questions. Spend the time necessary in His presence to get the answers and tweak and peak your business model to become successful.

It is unfortunate, but most business owners do not take the time to develop a professional business plan. If they do develop one early in their business, they seldom take the time to update it on a regular basis. If you ask many business owners why they don't have a well thought out business plan, they will tell you they lack the time or money to develop one. They fail to put a cost on the struggles they are facing in their business without a business plan. They are also neglecting to put a price on how much it costs to fail in business.

I believe one "God-idea" is better than 100 good ideas. Many struggling business people tell me the Lord gave them their business idea. That's great. Sometimes a God-idea will be counter-intuitive. However, if it really is a God-idea, a good business plan will show the simplicity and brilliance of this God-given business idea. God-ideas and business plans are not mutually exclusive. If anything, the business plan should show the non-believing world you are onto something so wonderful only God Himself could have come up with the idea in the first place.

If you haven't identified your Kingdom assignment yet, continue to do what you are currently doing, but set aside time each day to get into the presence of the Lord and get your assignment. Stay long enough to get the business model and not just a vague idea of the type of business or industry. Seek to understand the purpose your assignment will serve in the Kingdom. Become passionate about your assignment. Treat it as something you will be held accountable for (you will be). Study your competitors. Do your homework. Become the expert in your industry. Become the King's servant who does not stand before obscure men, but stands before kings to tell them about his King and the Kingdom.

Principles in Practice

Heath (wrong business) was a business broker or business deal maker at best. A less polite description would be an opportunistic wheeler-dealer. Heath sought out business opportunities where one party was in need of something to complete the deal. Through Heath's "connections" of people with various degrees of integrity, he would provide a matchmaking service to connect business parties together to complete the deal. If the deal was consummated, which seldom happened, Heath would receive a commission on the deal.

The type of deals that would fall into Heath's lap included everything from brokering foreign government procurements, railroad equipment, oil tankers, oil and gas rights, software applications, unusual real estate transactions, and non-FDA-approved medicine. Although he was a solid Christian, Heath never questioned why these potential deals were coming to him. He always assumed it was the Lord trying to bless him. Heath never stopped to wonder if perhaps the reason these deals were falling into his lap was that everyone else with better sense was passing them by. He never asked the Lord if this was something he should be involved in, he just assumed it was the Lord and the Lord would bless each deal.

Heath knew that many of the people he was involved with in these deals were not known for their moral integrity or religious beliefs, but he assumed the Lord would protect him from the pack of thieves he was surrounding himself with. Heath had yet to figure out that in the world of business integrity, you cannot be a little bit pregnant.

Kingdom Business Success

Heath knew he was called to the business mountain but hadn't taken the time to seek the Lord to understand his assignment. Additionally, he never sought to understand how these business deals served the King and advanced His Kingdom. He never sought to understand the purpose for these deals from the Lord's perspective. Heath's only interest in these deals was how much money he would make. Like Larry, Heath was chasing money and not the King. Heath was bringing very little value to anyone and doing nothing to serve the King. He had no purpose or passion for these business deals. These deals could not have been his Kingdom assignment.

Francis (right business, wrong reasons) was someone who was born to be a successful salesperson. After graduating from college, he was hired by a major manufacturer and took an entry-level sales position with the company. Francis was an avid student of the business and took many courses after hours to hone his sales skills, product expertise, and industry knowledge. After 10 years of hard work, commitment, and a can do attitude, Francis was able to purchase a dealership position with the same appliance company. Francis was now in a position to start raking in some serious money. This was good, because during those ten years, Francis also accumulated a wife, a family, and significant debt to go along with this new dealership.

Although Francis was a professed Christian, God was external to Francis' universe. At the center of his universe was his family, his business, and his ever growing debt. Francis was trying to get God to have a more active role in his world and would often pray along those lines. He often found himself struggling to make ends meet and success seemed somewhat hit or miss. He tried to fit God into his busy schedule each day, but often found he lacked the time. He was too busy serving his family, his business, and his debt problems.

Francis loved his business but he wasn't too keen on many of the customers. They wouldn't respond to his sales proposals in the timeframe he desired. He would go to great lengths to help them see the benefits of his products and his company over his competitors, but he never took the time to get to know what made his customers tick. He wasn't in love with his employees either. They never seemed to be knowledgeable, dependable, or productive. They were slothful and stole time and money from him. He couldn't seem to attract and retain good help.

You could say people skills were not Francis' forte and that he didn't love his customers and employees the way he should, but the bigger issue was he never understood the purpose his business was intended to fulfill in serving the King and His Kingdom. He saw his business as a cash cow that would allow him and his family to pursue their dreams and get out of debt. Francis was in the right business for the wrong reasons.

What Francis needed was to spend some quality time with the Lord. He needed to dedicate his business to the Lord and ask Him to be Lord over it. He needed to understand the purpose he and his business were fulfilling in serving the King and His Kingdom. Perhaps the Lord wanted to use these appliances as a door opener to share the Gospel with his customers and employees. Perhaps the Lord wanted Francis's employees to pray over each appliance before it was sent to the customer and believe that everyone who touched and used the appliance would have dreams and visions of the Lord. Perhaps, the Lord wanted to use this company to finance other Kingdom ventures. Francis needed to find out exactly what the Lord intended to do with him and the business he was running. Only then would Francis be fulfilled in his assignment and be able to see the type of success that he was looking for.

Louie (right business, wrong model) was the owner of small media company with a goal of building his company to the $5 million dollar annual revenue size. Most of the projects they were working on were in the $5K to $25K dollar size. Additionally, most of these projects were all in the lower end of difficulty to solve and therefore, they had many competitors who were competing for this work from the same client base.

Kingdom Business Success

In time, Louie realized their current business model was not scalable. The production pipeline that included the design, development, quality assurance, and implementation was shaped like a funnel. There were only a few people in the company who could work on each project at the narrow end of the funnel. They would struggle to work on more than 6-10 concurrent projects. However, even if all of their projects were $25K dollar size projects, they would have to work on 200 of these projects in a given year to make their $5 million dollar goal.

Louie came to the realization what his company needed were a few larger projects in the $150K range to serve as their "bread and butter" contracts. The smaller contracts could be added as time permitted and could be used to train new personnel. Once Louie understood the business model necessary to succeed, he and his intercessors started praying and seeking larger project opportunities they might have previously shied away from.

In time, they started seeing, bidding, and receiving projects over $100K in size and are currently bidding on a couple of opportunities of $5 million dollars each. The $5 million dollar goal is now seen as a stepping stone for the $20 million dollar revenue they are currently seeking. But this wouldn't have happened if they hadn't realized their current business model would not get them where they wanted to go.

Dane and Debbie (right business, right reasons, right business model) started a trade industry out of their garage based upon experience Dane received while serving in the military. They developed niche products for both Government and commercial clients which were not commercially available or were being produced by only a small number of competitors. As the saying goes, "there are riches in the niches." They would seek out problems that had no known solution and spend time researching how they could develop a product that would solve their customer's problem.

From the very start of the business, Dane and Debbie were always asking the question "Where is God in all of this?" They knew that unless the Lord builds the house the workers labor in vain (Psalm 127:1). They knew that if the Lord was leading them in this company, there was a purpose behind the business other than to put food on their table. They constantly sought the Lord for direction on how their business was intended to serve His Kingdom.

They started to see opportunities outside of their business where they could align their business to serve the local community and government. They started to see their company as a vehicle to hire those who were unemployable by others. They started to sow part of their profits into other Kingdom opportunities outside of the company as they were led by the Lord, instead of sowing all of the profits back into their company or into their pockets like most business owners.

Along the way, they implemented numerous changes to their business model in how they priced, marketed, designed, produced, performed quality assurance, and even shipped their products. They saw mistakes as a paid education and made sure every time they made a mistake and lost money, they learned from the educational process to improve their business model.

After many years of hard work, Dane and Debbie finally built their company to the point where they could step down from running the company and could now use their time and money to engage in other Kingdom ventures in business, government, and community to serve the Lord. After many years of hard work and believing the Lord for everything they needed to be successful, they were in a position where they could ask the Lord for the next assignment in their life.

Questions for Reflection

1. If you are in business, do you feel like you are in the right business assignment?

2. Are you trying to see your business from the Lord's perspective or are you still content to just make money from it? Do you understand the purpose and role you and your business play in

serving the King and advancing His Kingdom? If not, keep seeking revelation from Him on what purpose your business plays in the Kingdom of Heaven and your role in serving the King and His Kingdom.

3. If you feel that you are in the right business, have you considered other business models for your business? Are you seeking the Lord each day for wisdom and understanding on the best business model for your business assignment?

Chapter 7

Stewardship

"And he called ten of his slaves, and gave them ten minas and said to them, 'Do business with this until I come back'" (Luke 19:13).

Truth and perception are not always synonymous. Our perception of the truth may not be true if it is based upon a paradigm that is incorrect. This has been the theme of this section of the book and the important paradigm shift that needs to take place in order to grasp the concept of the Kingdom of Heaven. Many people misunderstand the Kingdom and attempt to view it from the religious paradigm they knew prior to entering the Kingdom. In this chapter, we will continue to describe the Kingdom of Heaven and the role your business plays in it regarding the biblical principle of stewardship. If you have been waiting for God to bless *your* business, get ready for a paradigm shift.

Stewardship is a principle frequently embraced on the church mountain but is seldom mentioned in the business world. Unfortunately, it is often used to motivate people to give their finances and time into other people's ministries and endeavors. If you are skeptical of that observation, mention the term stewardship to most Christians and they will assume you are looking for their time or money. This is unfortunate, since the biblical principle of stewardship defines God's role and our role in this life and the one to come. Stewardship is one of the basic tenets of the Kingdom of Heaven.

But what is stewardship and why is it important in the Kingdom of Heaven paradigm? Is stewardship a New Testament principle or did it exist prior to the New Testament? What does stewardship have to do with defining God's role and our role in the Kingdom of Heaven? What does stewardship have to do with the quintessential question of *"What's wrong, Why isn't it working?"* In this chapter we are going to address these questions and others. You may come to realize that it wasn't *your* business you were asking the Lord to bless.

Kingdom Business Success

Defining Stewardship

"The earth is the Lord's and all it contains, the world and those who dwell in it" (Psalm 24:1). The foundation of biblical stewardship is the tenet that everything belongs to God and He permits us to manager or steward what belongs to Him. We own nothing. That means nothing at all and including our very lives. Additionally, He promises to hold us accountable for how well we steward what He has entrusted to our care.

The term steward comes from the Greek word *oikonomos* which translates as the manager of the household.[1] We saw that the word *oikos* meant house or household. The Greek word *nomos* means law or rule.[2] An *oikonomos* is the person who rules or runs the household. This was often performed by a trusted free slave who managed the household of their master. Joseph's role in Potiphar's house would be a good example of a household manager and how we are called to be stewards or managers of the Lord's Kingdom. In the story of the unrighteous steward in the New Testament (Luke 16:1-9), we see another example of a steward or household manager. In this parable, we see the Master of the house holding his steward accountable for squandering his Master's possessions (Luke 16:2).

Since the Bible is its own best interpretation, one of the best definitions of stewardship can be seen from Jesus's parable of the usage of money in the Gospel.

> "While they were listening to these things, Jesus went on to tell a parable, because He was near Jerusalem, and they supposed that the kingdom of God was going to appear immediately. So He said, "A nobleman went to a distant country to receive a kingdom for himself, and *then* return. And he called ten of his slaves, and gave them ten minas and said to them, 'Do business *with this* until I come *back*.' But his citizens hated him and sent a delegation after him, saying, 'We do not want this man to reign over us.' When he returned, after receiving the kingdom, he ordered that

these slaves, to whom he had given the money, be called to him so that he might know what business they had done. The first appeared, saying, 'Master, your mina has made ten minas more.' And he said to him, 'Well done, good slave, because you have been faithful in a very little thing, you are to be in authority over ten cities.' The second came, saying, 'Your mina, master, has made five minas.' And he said to him also, 'And you are to be over five cities.' Another came, saying, 'Master, here is your mina, which I kept put away in a handkerchief; for I was afraid of you, because you are an exacting man; you take up what you did not lay down and reap what you did not sow.' He said to him, 'By your own words I will judge you, you worthless slave. Did you know that I am an exacting man, taking up what I did not lay down and reaping what I did not sow? Then why did you not put my money in the bank, and having come, I would have collected it with interest?' Then he said to the bystanders, 'Take the mina away from him and give it to the one who has the ten minas.' And they said to him, 'Master, he has ten minas *already*.' I tell you that to everyone who has, more shall be given, but from the one who does not have, even what he does have shall be taken away. But these enemies of mine, who did not want me to reign over them, bring them here and slay them in my presence" (Luke 19:11-27).

Here are some defining elements of stewardship that can be extracted from this scripture:

> ➤ The Master has gone away to receive a Kingdom but will return.
> ➤ We are called to put the resources the Master has given us to work while He's gone.
> ➤ We will be held accountable for our management of those resources.

> ➢ Those who steward their resources well and bring a good return are commended and rewarded.
> ➢ Those who do not steward their resources well will have the resources taken away and given to someone who is a good steward.
> ➢ The way to receive more resources and more authority is by being faithful with what we have already received.
> ➢ The Lord considers money to be "a very little thing." If we cannot steward money well, how can we steward cities?
> ➢ Not everyone embraces the Master as being Lord over the Kingdom or over their lives, but every disobedience to the King will eventually be brought under subjection.

Stewardship in the Old Testament

Stewardship is not a New Testament concept, but has been in existence since the creation of man. In the Old Testament, we see God creating man and woman and giving them dominion over it. The authority they were given to fill and subdue the earth and rule over every living thing that moves on the earth is a delegated authority (Gen 1:28). It is ambassadorial in nature. The Lord did not give the earth to Adam and Eve, He loaned it to them. They were called to steward the creation on God's behalf. "Then the Lord God took the man and put him into the Garden of Eden to cultivate it and keep it" (Gen 2:15).

Along with Psalm 24, Psalm 50 contains the Lord's declaration of ownership and Lordship over His creation:

> "For every beast of the forest is Mine, the cattle on a thousand hills. I know every bird of the mountains, and everything that moves in the field is Mine. If I were hungry I would not tell you, for the world is Mine, and all it contains" (Psalm 50:10-12).

In the book of Leviticus, the Lord gave regulations pertaining to the use and transference of ownership of the land. The Lord summarizes the law by saying "The land moreover shall not be sold permanently, for the land is Mine" (Lev 25:23a).

The concept of tithing which was required by the Mosaic Law, was a test in stewardship for the Israelites. When the Israelites entered the Promised Land, they would be required to give a tenth of their increase in produce and animals to the Lord. This did not mean they owned 90% of their possessions and God owned 10%, but rather the tithe served as a reminder that everything belonged to the Lord and He was the one who gave life, land, families, and increase to His children. It all belonged to Him. Tithing would serve as a reminder of His role to His creation, and creation's role to the Creator.

As for the 90/10 paradigm, let me also clarify for the theologian's sake, the Mosaic Law required the Israelites to give more than 10% of their increase to the Lord. There were actually multiple tithes the Israelites were required to give at various times and places. In addition, there were other offerings they were required to make. Therefore, the Mosaic Law wasn't a 90/10 or even a 70/30 paradigm. Exactly how much was required is a subject of controversy that I'll avoid. The point I'm making in this book is that under the Mosaic Law, after you have given what was required by the Law to the Lord, the rest was yours to spend as you please. Since most people are only familiar with one tithe and believe 90% of the money is "theirs," I will call this false perspective *the 90/10 paradigm* in this book.

In the Old Testament, man is separated from God due to his sin nature. Fallen man soon developed a paradigm of God being external to his life and his world. The more sin-depraved man became, the farther away and less involved God appeared to man in his paradigm. Man started to see the creation as something that was his by default. Man had his life, his home, his family, his business, and his possessions. The Mosaic Law should have corrected that paradigm, but instead, probably served to define a different paradigm where man gave God what belonged to Him with the remainder belonging to man. This could be viewed as the 90/10 paradigm. If man gave 10% of everything to God, he could keep the remainder for himself. This is the false paradigm of ownership many people come from when they become born-again. This is the false paradigm many born-again Christians still possess.

Stewardship in the New Testament

As discussed previously, many Christians came into the Kingdom after hearing the Gospel of Salvation and not the Gospel of the Kingdom of Heaven. They believe God is only interested in their souls and everything else in the world is irrelevant regarding their relationship with God. They give their life (or at least a part of it) to the Lord, but never give all they are and everything they have to the Lord. Therefore, their initial paradigm after becoming born-again is that God is only interested in spiritual things and is disinterested in the material world.

The next paradigm shift occurs when these new believers start attending church and are taught the concepts of paying tithes and giving offerings and alms. They now embrace the Old Testament 90/10 paradigm. If it isn't part of the 10% they give God, then it must belong to them. Part of their 90% would include their business. Even more dangerous than being a false paradigm, these new believers can start focusing on the principals of giving without focusing on their relationship with God. They may start giving out of a religious obligation and look prideful at those who do not. They are now in danger of becoming New Testament Pharisees.

At some point, these new believers may start hearing the concept of stewardship, but it is generally focused on getting the new believers involved in their local church. They are exhorted to steward their time and finances to sow into local church and parachurch ministries. Their business is seen at this point as a vehicle that allows them to give their time and money to the Kingdom. They now have a paradigm which includes some aspects of stewardship.

Hopefully, these believers will eventually hear the Gospel of the Kingdom and realize Jesus didn't die only for their sins, but to bring restoration to everything lost in the fall in the garden. He came to bring the year of Jubilee to everyone and everything. He died to restore things to the way they were meant to be if there had not been a fall in the garden. Jesus came to restore all things and establish His Kingdom here on earth as it is in heaven.

But in order to enter the Kingdom, we must be "all in," and this means surrendering all we are and all we have to Him. We now own nothing. We have become stewards of His Kingdom. We must be willing to sell all we have and pick up our cross daily and follow Him. We make the divine exchange by giving Him all we are and all we have and receiving all He is and all He has in return. The authority we now have as believers is a delegated authority that comes from Him. As stewards, we get to exercise His authority here on earth.

What we are Called to Steward

The New Testament has much to say about what we are called to steward. This encompasses much more than our time and finances and includes:

> - Our relationship with God – We must love Him with all of our heart, our soul, our mind, and our strength.

> - The Gospel – We are called to be stewards and ministers of the Gospel of the Kingdom (1 Cor 4:1).

> - Family – "But if anyone does not provide for his own, and especially for those of his household, he has denied the faith and is worse than an unbeliever" (1 Tim 5:8).

> - Time – We have no time of our own. Our time has become His time. "Poor is he who works with a negligent hand, but the hand of the diligent makes rich (Prov 10:4).

> ➤ Talents – Each of us has already been given certain talents in accordance with our abilities and we will be held accountable for how well we use those talents in this world.

> ➤ Property and Other Resources – Everything we have belongs to God (Luke 14:33).

> ➤ Finances – We don't make any purchases, personal or business, without checking with the Master.

> ➤ Employees – We will be held accountable for how well we treat them.

> ➤ Customers/Clients – Did they see Christ in us, or did they only see someone looking to make a sale from them?

Stewardship of Our Kingdom Assignment

The most memorable and emotional decision in my Christian walk did not occur when I became born-again. That was an easy decision. When I came to the Lord I had nothing. Giving all I was and all I had to the Lord in exchange for all He was and all He had was a no-brainer for me. The most memorable point came to me 14 years later. It was when I came to realize that all my life I had been asking the Lord to *bless my plans*. Sound familiar? Like many of my clients, I had my life planned out with a long laundry list of things and goals I wanted to achieve in this life. I was waiting for the Lord to put His blessing upon my plans for my life.

But like Abraham, the Lord was calling me to follow Him without knowing where I was going. All of a sudden, I had an image of being on *Let's Make a Deal* and Monty Hall was telling me that I could keep the prizes I had already accumulated in life or take what was behind Door Number 2. I knew what was behind Door Number 2 was the Lord's perfect will for my life, but I had no idea what that included. I did know what was on my list of plans for my life and I started to review them one by one. The thought that my plans might not be on the Lord's list and I might be walking away from them for the rest of my life brought me to tears. Did this mean I couldn't have the successful businesses I always wanted? Did this mean I would be single my entire life and go to some mission field in a part of the world that I had no interest in? I started to imagine how completely different my life might look compared to the dreams I had pursued for many years.

I weighed the cost of complete surrender to the Lord and His will for my life. "For which one of you, when he wants to build a tower, does not first sit down and calculate the cost to see if he has enough to complete it? Otherwise, when he has laid a foundation and is not able to finish, all who observe it begin to ridicule him" (Luke 14:28-29). I told the Lord I would lay everything on the altar of consecration and take what was behind Door Number 2 sight unseen, as long as what was behind Door Number 2 was His perfect will for my life. *That* was the most memorable and emotional point of my Christian walk.

Sixteen years later, I look back at that moment with a bit of embarrassment. Why am I embarrassed? Because I realize now that I didn't really know the One who I made the exchange with at the time. If I had, it would have been another no-brainer. You see, I have come to know my Father and know He is perfect in every way. His love is perfect, His plans are perfect, His decisions are perfect, His way is perfect, and His timing is perfect. Everything about Him is perfect. Whatever His perfect will is for my life, there is nothing else in the world that will bring me the happiness and fulfillment His plans will bring.

Something else I have learned about our Father over the years is that He never asks someone to give up something without offering them something better in return. Whatever He asks you to give up, know He has something better in mind for you. Our cross that Jesus charged us to pick up and carry each day is meant to lead us into joy and not misery. Certainly there will be a sacrifice (it wouldn't be a cross if there wasn't). But as we follow Him, we will know the joy of abiding in Him and He in us, which will make the sacrifice seem worth the cost. If you are willing to trade in your life for what God has for you behind Door Number 2, I assure you that you will never regret the decision. For those who are ready follow Him, I have included some prayers in Chapter 17 to help you dedicate your life and business to the Lord.

Principles in Practice

Steve and Melodie were the best examples of good stewards of the Kingdom. They saw everything they did and everything they owned as belonging to the Lord and serving His Kingdom. As much as they loved each other, they saw their personal relationship with the Lord as their greatest joy and their number one responsibility in their lives.

Steve and Melodie had a very busy calendar encompassing their family, business, church, and the leadership positions they held in the community. But their first commitment to time always revolved around their personal relationship with the Lord. They would schedule time alone and together to fast and pray and seek the presence of the Lord. They were careful about what they watched, what they listened to, and what they said, to ensure they did not defile the temple of the Holy Spirit (1 Cor 3:16-17). Like many successful people, they seemed to get more out of a 24 hour day than most people.

Before money came into their business or personal finances, Steve and Melodie were always seeking the Lord to understand where He was in those business deals, where He intended the finances to go, and for what purpose. They saw their finances as already allocated by the Lord even before the finances actually showed up. They gave generously to their church and ministry needs, but their giving was not out of compassion or obligation, but based upon hearing from the Lord on how and when He would have them give. Sometimes, it was based upon a seed sown in faith, other times it was based upon the harvest that came in. They never saw the money as belonging to them; it all belonged to the Lord.

Steve and Melodie were often led by the Lord to give of their personal property, their jewelry, art, and memorabilia. They never saw anything they had as belonging to themselves. It all belonged to the Lord and they were just temporary possessors of His belongings. They would frequently honor people with the best of their personal possessions. These would include personal treasures that most people would never consider giving away to anyone except their children.

As well as they stewarded their time, money, and possessions, perhaps what Steve and Melodie stewarded best was their relationships. This included relationships with those in authority, their friends, and even their employees and customers. They treated each person with love and honor. They saw everyone as someone the Lord had brought in to their life for some reason. Their job was to find out the reason and then honor the Lord by honoring each person.

There's no doubt that promotion and increase will come to Steve and Melodie's personal life and business. After all, that was the promise of the Master when He said, "I tell you that to everyone who has, more shall be given, but from the one who does not have, even what he does have shall be taken away" (Luke 19:26).

Spencer was a faithful steward of his time. He held to a very rigid calendar. He was up early, had his devotional time with the Lord, went to the gym and then arrived at work by 7:30AM. He never left the office before 6PM. He would go home to dinner and spend time with his family. He would watch over his children to ensure they did their homework and their music lessons. Spencer was very disciplined in time management as someone who would be held accountable for how he spent each moment.

Unfortunately, Spencer believed everyone should be as diligent and productive with their time as he was. He was intolerant of employees who did not possess the same zeal for stewarding time. Like many employees, they came in late and left early. Their lunch breaks averaged 1.5 hours instead of 1 hour. They were often doing personal chores or surfing the internet when they should have been working. In a nutshell, Spencer was hiring his employees from the same place you may be finding yours.

Kingdom Business Success

Spencer would often harshly criticize his employees for their unproductivity and theft of company time. Unknowingly, he would speak word curses over them by saying they were lazy, useless, incompetent, and unproductive. They were a bunch of idiots wanting to get paid for doing nothing. Spencer didn't realize he was cursing his employees by his words and attitude towards them and abusing the trust the Lord had given him to steward those employees. Spencer forgot that his employees were God's children and the Lord was listening to Spencer berating His children.

Spencer was a good steward of his personal time but a poor steward of his employees. He first needed to learn to love his employees the way he loved his own children. He needed to learn to be a good example and raise them up in the admonition of the Lord. Rather than cursing his employees, Spencer needed to spend time training and counseling his employees on the importance of stewarding their time properly. Spencer should not have expected children to behave as adults. Most people are never instructed about the importance of stewarding time or finances, or stewardship in general for that matter. They come into the work force as children who don't know about the Kingdom, and of course they waste time. Like children, they do not know any better.

The role of a father or a shepherd is to raise their children in the admonition of the Lord. We are to teach biblical principles to our employees regardless of their spiritual beliefs or religious affiliations. We don't need to include chapter and verse from the Bible. The biblical principles contain truth in themselves. In time, with the proper instruction and exhortation given in love, we can expect our employees to become better stewards of time and company resources. For those who will not make the paradigm shift, we may eventually need to let them go and pray the Lord provide them something better down the road. The role of terminating employees who are unteachable and refuse to be corrected is also part of being a good steward.

Questions for Reflection

1. Are you still living in a 90/10 paradigm or have you come to the point where you have given the Lord all you are and all you have? Are you "all in?" If so, keep in mind from this day forward, you own nothing. It all belongs to the Lord.

2. In what area are you strongest in your ability to steward what God has given you? Do not allow yourself to become proud of your stewardship ability in this one area and look down on others who may be weak in this area. You may find these same people are strong in stewarding areas of their life in which you are weak.

3. What is the one area you have the most difficulty stewarding properly? When the time comes to give accountability for everything you have stewarded for the Lord, what is the one area you will be the most embarrassed to review? Ask the Lord to give you grace to become a better steward in this area.

SECTION 3: KINGDOM PRINCIPLES FOR SUCCESS

Chapter 8

Truth

"Therefore, rejecting all falsity and being done now with it, let everyone express the truth with his neighbor, for we are all parts of one body and members one of another" (Eph 4:25 AMP).

Growing up in an Irish-American home, I quickly learned the adage that any story worth telling was worthy of some embellishment. This made perfect sense in light of the fact that the term "blarney" which is excessive and insincere praise, originated with the Irish. Blarney is an embellishment of the truth. Embellishing the truth was a way of life in our family. We didn't see anything wrong with it, nor did we consider that we were actually telling lies.

It took me a while, but I finally figured out that my Dad didn't walk five miles to school each day, uphill, both directions, in three feet of snow. Actually, he lived only four blocks from his school. It was up hill, but only in one direction. But it was a good story and would be considered "puffery" in today's society. In regard to puffery, isn't it fascinating we have laws that legally permit sellers to embellish on their product descriptions and claims, provided the claims are so ridiculous "a reasonable person would not take them literally." This means it is fraudulent for a company to exaggerate a little about their company's products or services, but it is acceptable to lie a lot about them.

It has been my experience that understanding and speaking the truth is one of the hardest principles Christian business leaders face in their challenge to abide in Him. Lies and deception come from satan whom Jesus described as being the father of all lies (John 8:44). If we are abiding in lies and deception, we are not abiding in Jesus. As Christian business people, we need to learn that we can abide in the Truth or we can abide in the father of all lies, but we can't abide in both at the same time.

Kingdom Business Success

As I write this chapter, a news anchor man and a news commentator are in hot water with their respective television stations for having been caught embellishing on their news stories. My experience with news stories is that they generally contain large amounts of incorrect information. I have never seen a news story, of which I had intimate knowledge, where the news station reported accurately on the situation. They tend to shoot from the hip and are more interested in reporting drama than truth. However, it appears that even the producers of news stations get offended when news reporters claim to have been eye witnesses to events they could not possibly have seen, because they were found to have been elsewhere at the time of the news event.

Our society seems to be in love with reality shows. We will watch people surviving on an island, singing for a music contract, pursuing a modeling career, and designing clothes for fashion models. We love relationships and it doesn't matter if the relationships are working or not. We will watch couples courting each other, getting married, having marital fights, and even getting divorced. It seems we will watch anything that is called a reality show.

In theory, reality shows are supposed to show unscripted scenes of everyday life. The attractiveness of a reality show over a sitcom is based upon the premise that the truth of everyday life is more entertaining than the scripted life of a sitcom. However, most viewers understand the paradox of reality TV. There is very little that is real in reality TV. It is far more scripted than the parts not scripted. The contestants are coached in what to say and not to say, the scenes are staged and restaged until they get it right. The winners are often picked in advance by the show producers, and anything not approved or wanted is edited out.

After all that manipulation and control, how much of the reality show is actually...real? How much is true? Even though viewers understand the extent of the falsehood that exists in reality shows, they are so popular that Hollywood keeps on making new ones. What does this say about the American people? Does this mean we don't care about the difference between truth and falsehood as long as you give us a good show?

What is Truth?

"What is truth?" That is the million-dollar question Pontius Pilate asked Jesus in the Praetorium when He was brought before him for judgment. It's the question that an educated Roman Prefect asked Jesus when He said, "You say *correctly* that I am a king. For this I have been born, and for this I have come into the world, to testify to the truth. Everyone who is of the truth hears My voice" (John 18:37-38).

Pilate was a provincial ruler who had been educated under a Greek-Roman society where philosophy and knowledge provided the meaning of life. To Pilate, truth was an idea based upon one's philosophy, knowledge, or experiential perspective and was always debatable. Truth was a concept, a quality, a state, a fact, an idea, or a belief. Pilate couldn't grasp the concept that Truth was a person. Many in today's society, Christians and others still haven't come to the realization that the truth is not subjective. There are no shades of grey in truth. Truth is not an option, it is a person - the person of Jesus Christ. Many people claim to know the truth. Many claim to speak the truth. Only one person claimed to be The Truth (John 14:6).

If the truth is God Himself, then anything that is not true or a falsehood should be quite conspicuous. That should be the case, but after six thousand years of man's existence on the earth, we have been exposed to so many lies and deception that many of us have lost the essence of reality. Instead of there being a very fine line between truth and falsehood, we live in a society where there are plenty of shades of grey, and few absolutes regarding truth and falsehood. From fallen man's perspective, it was a very reasonable question Pilate asked Jesus, "What is truth?"

But what is truth? In the Bible, the Greek word *alēthia* which is translated as truth, is defined as something not hidden, not escaping notice, and not being an illusion.[1] In today's jargon, we would say the truth is something that is "real." The antithesis to the truth is the Greek word *pseudos* which means falsehood, a lie.[2] Even in today's vocabulary, a pseudo prefix indicates something that is false, artificial, an imposter, and not the real thing. An actor's stage name or pseudonym is a perfect example of something *pseudos* or false.

If the truth is something real, evident, and legitimate, and a lie is something fake, hidden, and a false illusion, what is deception? It seems most people believe deception is not as bad as lying. Most people consider the act of lying to be a breach of moral character, but the practice of deception seems to be more acceptable and less dishonest than lying. But what does the Bible say about deception? To deceive is the Greek word *apataō* which means to deceive, to cheat, beguile, to give a false impression.[3] In the Bible, deception is the practice of lying. There is no difference between lying and deception. If someone gives information to another person with the intent of presenting a false impression of the truth, then that person has lied.

Many times deception comes in the form of what we call partial truths. If you have teenagers or have been a teenager yourself, you know what a partial truth entails. For example, on Saturday morning, you ask your teenager what they did the night before. They tell you they went over to one of their friend's home and hung out with him. What they told you is true. The part of the story they left out is that they left that friend's home and went and met some other friends and smoked a joint. After learning there was a party going on at the home of someone else, whose parents just happened to be away, they went and attended the party and did some things you would probably not want to know.

What your teenager told you was true. However, they deceived you by intentionally leaving out part of the truth. What they did was create a false illusion of what happened the night before. They lied because they presented an illusion of the truth. They wanted you to believe the illusion was the truth. That is falsehood. That is lying. All partial truths are a lie because they are meant to deceive someone by creating an illusion that is not true.

Why Do We Lie?

In order to break this cycle of falsehood that is so easy to succumb to in the business world, it is important for us to understand the underlying spirits causing us to lie. As I mentioned in the Obedience chapter, the motivational force behind almost every type of sin is fear and deception and this is certainly the case with the sin of falsehood.

Let's take a look at some of the common business functions that entice good Christian business people to engage in falsehood:

Marketing material: The motivating fear is that our prospective customers are looking for the biggest and the best and if we aren't in that category then our prospects will take their business to our competitors. Therefore, we embellish our qualifications and experience. Isn't it interesting, Walmart the biggest retailer in the world, didn't become the biggest by trying to become the best? No one shops at Walmart to purchase the best products. They shop there to buy the lowest priced products. The corollary is no one buys a Rolex watch because they are looking for an accurate timepiece. We need to learn to express an honest image of our strengths and weaknesses and trust the Lord to show us how to use our strengths to obtain the business He wants us to have.

Proposals: This is a temptation similar to our marketing materials. The added temptation in proposals is to tell the prospect what they want to hear. It is tempting to embellish on our qualifications to match their solicitation requirements. I have written many of these proposals myself, which I dubbed "science fiction." I considered them science since they were technical proposals and fiction because they contained so much…creative imagination. We need to learn how to turn these proposals around and state, "We don't match up perfectly to what you are looking for, but let us tell you why you should consider hiring us for this job."

Loans: The fear here is if we tell the truth about the size of our company, then we won't get the financing. We embellish on our revenue and use projected numbers instead of actuals. We need to realize the banks need us as much as we need them. They have very few perfect loan applicants and we are probably the norm and not the exception to their applicants. If the Lord wants us to get a loan, He will make a way to get us the financing without telling any falsehoods.

Taxes: Since our taxes are generally based upon our revenue and number of employees, we will look for ways to present ourselves to be as small as we can. The motivating fear is we will not have enough money to pay the tax man and ourselves. The temptation is to have two sets of numbers or books. One set to show the tax man and one to show our bank and stockholders. If all revenue and profit belong to the Lord, then all the expenses are His as well. This means He is responsible for paying the tax man.

Employees: Not all the temptations to lie in business are financially motivated. Other temptations arise because of pride or embarrassment. When writing performance reviews of good employees, the temptation is to flatter their accomplishments and minimize their weaknesses. The temptation is the opposite for poor employees. When dealing with employee mistakes, our pride in ourselves and *our* company can create a fear that we will look bad due to our employees' mistakes and shift the blame from us to them.

The spirits of fear and deception are so strong in the business marketplace that we will discuss these motivating spirits further in the next chapter when we address the principle of becoming Fearless.

Abiding in Truth is to Abide in Him

We are called to abide in Him and He in us. If Jesus is Truth, then we are called to abide in the truth at all times. Any time we depart from the truth, we are not abiding in Him. If we engage in any type of falsehood, then we are no longer abiding in Him. If we speak falsehoods, but still believe we are abiding in Him simply because we are born-again Christians, then we have deceived ourselves. We must repent of all falsehood and embrace the truth even when it is challenging to do so in order that we can abide in Him.

The Holy Spirit is called "the Spirit of Truth" and is given to us to lead us into all truth (John 14:17, 15:26). The Holy Spirit is given to us as our advocate, our guide, our comforter, and our mentor. He is called to lead us and guide us on a daily basis and remind us of everything Jesus said. "But when He, the Spirit of truth, comes, He will guide you into all the truth; for He will not speak on His own initiative, but whatever He hears, He will speak; and He will disclose to you what is to come" (John 16:13).

Since the Holy Spirit is leading us into all truth, if we are departing from the truth and speaking falsehoods, then we are not being led by the Holy Spirit. We are being led by another spirit; the father of all lies. We are called to be mature sons and daughters of the King. We are called to walk in the Truth and abide in Him. "For as many as are led by the Spirit of God, these are sons of God" (Rom 8:14 NKJV).

I am ashamed to admit the many times I have lied as a born-again Christian in the business world. But it is from those experiences that I know how challenging it is to walk in truth and avoid all lies and falsehood. I am also intimately familiar with the reasons we engage in lying and deception, and it is almost always rooted in the spirit of fear. There is something we are afraid of that is causing us to lie. It may be fear of man, fear of failure, fear of lack, fear of embarrassment, fear of one of our previous lies being discovered, or fear of something else. I am also intimately familiar with how the enemy uses our lies to get a hook in our lives to prevent us from walking in the abundant life Jesus promised. Satan lies to us by showing us a short cut to success that can be ours through speaking falsehoods. Instead, it turns out to be a short cut to failure. Satan lied to us. I guess we should have seen that one coming.

Kingdom Business Success

But I'd like to tell you about a time when I did it correctly. I was given an opportunity to be a consultant in a prime contractor role to a Fortune 500 company. However, in filling out their voluminous services agreement, I noticed one potential issue. They were requiring I carry large amounts of several types of General Liability insurance. Additionally, the insurance couldn't be from any insurance company, but one that was rated very high. At the time, I didn't have this type of General Liability insurance and I estimated it would cost me at least $17,500 per year, payable in advance, to get this insurance.

Rather than play games over this insurance issue or say anything that would be deceptive, I simply told the Contracting Officer that I lacked the insurance. I could get the insurance, but it would take some time. I knew they wanted me to start immediately, and I assumed the result of telling the truth would prevent me from becoming a prime contractor. They would simply bring me onboard as a subcontractor to one of their primes. There was also the possibility they would not hire me due to this disclosure, and I would miss out on this opportunity all together. The Contracting Officer replied after a very pregnant pause and said, "Let me get back with you." That is never a promising response in contract negotiations.

The Contracting Officer did get back with me the next day and told me to simply leave that section of the services agreement blank and forward the completed services agreement to him. Surprisingly, I ended up getting a prime contractor role without being required to carry that insurance. Over the next three years, the issue of this insurance never came up. I certainly didn't bring it up. Since this insurance is renewed annually, I was saving myself at least $17,500 per year in insurance expenses. My competitors at the Fortune 500 company often asked how I was able to get this prime contract position. My answer was always, "It was the grace of God."

Some of the best stories I have heard about people and companies being favored and promoted, come from situations where people were tempted to lie about their qualifications, experience, or assets. Instead of giving in to the spirit of fear and engaging in falsehood, they made

110

themselves vulnerable and transparent and decided to speak the truth and nothing but the truth, not matter the cost. In the end, they were rewarded for telling the truth.

Be bold enough to be transparent. Never create a false illusion of who you are and what your company has done. Go and ask for the loan and speak the truth about the lack of your revenue and assets. Instead, tell them of your strengths and what you have going for you. Ask for the sale or the contract, and don't exaggerate about your qualifications and experience. Instead, tell them about your strengths and experiences, and tell them why it is a good idea for them to give you their business. Abide in Truth Himself and let the Lord help you with the part that is out of your hands.

Principles in Practice

As mentioned in a previous chapter, **Victor** was the owner of a company where I was previously employed. Victor was the type of business person who told so many lies, he started to believe them himself. Therein resides one of the dangers of lying. When people hear a lie enough times, they start to believe it is true.

Victor often encouraged his employees to lie about the company's prior contract experience, finances, employee resumes, and just about anything he needed to massage in order to win new business. Victor would not write the proposals or marketing material himself, but he would have his employees write the falsehoods as he directed. This way, he could pretend to be ignorant of any errors at a later date. One of the lies that still stands out in my mind was a claim we frequently put in our proposals stating that we possessed three different versions of a particular software tool. However, people intimately knowledgeable of these software tools knew there were only two versions of the tool in existence at that time. Oops.

I spent considerable time with Victor on business trips and got to know him pretty well. Victor never considered himself a liar or one who spoke falsehoods. He even passed a polygraph for a Government security clearance. They must not have asked him about the degree on his resume he never obtained. Victor believed the lies he was speaking were true to some degree. He had lost his compass for the Truth. Even in situations when he knew he was deviating from the truth, he would justify that "everyone does that" and he was only trying to be a good businessman.

Victor was selfish and looking at everything from his perspective. He never considered the effect his lies were having on other people's business. He never thought about the consequences his lies were having on other people lives. People who lie seldom see it from other people's perspective. Eventually the lies he told caught up with Victor, and his company suffered a decline in business for several years before finally closing the doors.

Neil was the owner of a technical services company that I supported at one time. A fellow Irish-American, Neil could spin a story that did the Irish justice for their use of blarney. Neil was also a very shrewd man when it came to signing contracts. In fact, I learned a trick from Neil that I incorporated when signing all future contracts, which is make sure the person signing the contract has authority to sign the contract!

Whenever Neil wanted to engage in a business deal he might want to renege on at a future date, he would tell his Vice President of Operations, who did not have authority to commit the company, to sign the contract. This way, he could back out of a deal at a later time if necessary. Neil didn't consider this deception a lie. In his reasoning, he was just being a clever business man. Neil would claim that the blame was on the other party for not doing their due diligence before signing the contract. But Neil was intentionally presenting a false illusion to the people who were trying to do business with him. He was creating an illusion that the person who was signing the contract had authority to sign it. Neil didn't understand that all false illusions are lies.

Not long after I learned of Neil's trick, I found myself negotiating a contract with a medium sized Government contracting company with revenue in excess of $70 million. Early in the negotiations, I asked the Director of Contracting if he was a corporate officer. He said he was not. I then informed him that as part of the contracting process, I would need to see the letter authorizing him to sign contracts for the company. He quickly responded saying this request would not be a problem.

A week went by without hearing from him. When he finally called me, he said he had been looking for documentation to substantiate his authority to sign contracts for the company. After all, as the Director of Contracts this was his job. However, he couldn't find any substantiation. He then said to me "Jeff, I sign contracts all the time with Government Agencies and large Government contractors and no one has ever asked me to show them evidence that I have authority to sign contracts. You are the first one." I told him that if he had ever met Neil, he would be as guarded as I was about signing contracts.

Eventually, Neil's falsehoods caught up with him and he found himself in trouble with the U.S. Government over his deviations from the truth on Federal Government contracts. As Jesus said, there is nothing hidden that will not be revealed (Luke 8:17).

Elliot was the owner of a small management consulting company. He suffered from a problem all small business owners would like to have, an explosion of new work. However, as all business owners know, a large increase in new work has a negative impact on a company's cash flow. Elliot was becoming work rich and cash poor.

Cash was tight and he didn't have enough money to make payroll. Elliot started to open additional lines of credit with his banks but it appeared his efforts were taking longer than he anticipated. Payday would be one day late to his employees. He could have handled this situation many ways to disguise the problems he was having with "growing pains," but he decided to take the honest route. Two days prior to payday, Elliot sent out an email to the entire company explaining the situation. He apologized profusely for the error and took personal responsibility for it. He stated that payroll would be one day late this week. He also offered to financially help any employee who might be adversely affected by this late payment. He explained the situation causing the problem and promised that the company was taking measures to ensure this never happened again.

During that time period, I never heard one employee make a comment about the delay in payroll. Not even one sarcastic comment. The employees seemed to understand the situation and believed the sincerity of the owner. Whatever fears Elliot may have had about how his employees would view this situation were apparently unfounded. To the best of my knowledge, Elliot never had this problem again. Even better, Elliot never had to carry the burden of fear that a lie which he told previously would come to light, which would then require telling new lies to cover the old lies. As Jesus promised, His yoke is easy and His burden is light (Matt 11:30). If we will embrace the truth, the Truth will set us free (John 8:32).

Questions for Reflection

1. In what areas of business have you been the most tempted to lie?

2. Think about the situations where you have lied in the past and identify the motivating spirits that caused you to lie.

3. When you lied, did you think about the consequences of your lie? Did you think about the repercussions and impact to the lives of those you were lying to?

4. Whenever you are tempted to lie in response to a question, try to obtain a time out. If possible say, "Let me think about that one" before giving a response. Try not to shoot from the hip. Be very deliberate in your response. Ask the Lord to give you the correct answer to the question. Keep in mind, your response to questions in which you are tempted to lie will have ramifications.

Chapter 9

Fearless

"There is no fear in love; but perfect love casts out fear, because fear involves punishment, and the one who fears is not perfected in love" (1 John 4:18).

Similar to walking in the Truth, in order to abide in Him and He in us, we need to walk in the same manner as He walked, and Jesus walked without fear. Fear is the antithesis of the abiding presence of the Lord and opposes the Gospel of the Kingdom of Heaven. Jesus came to set us free from the kingdom of darkness, and fear is a major attribute of that kingdom.

Fear will hold you in bondage to the kingdom of darkness while Jesus is trying to set you free to live the abundant life in the Kingdom of Heaven. Like a python, fear will choke the life out of you and steal the peace and joy Jesus came to give you. Your ability to live the abundant life will be determined in part by the extent you overcome and die to the spirit of fear, and the associated demonic spirits it will usher into your life. You must learn to abide in His peace and be fearless, even while the storms of life are raging against you.

What is Fear?

In order to understand the nature of fear and how it prevents you from living the abundant life, let us take a look at how the spirit of fear showed up in the Garden of Eden. Prior to Adam and Eve's sin in the Garden, there is no mention of fear, anxiety, or worry mentioned in the Bible. Adam and Eve had an abiding relationship with God. God breathed His breath or His Spirit into Adam and gave him life, His *zōē* life. God gave man his assignment in the Garden and told him, "Be fruitful and multiply, and fill the earth, and subdue it; and rule over the fish of the sea and over the birds of the sky and over every living thing that moves on the earth" (Gen 1:28).

After Adam and Eve sinned, we see the entrance of the spirit of fear in their lives. "Then the eyes of both of them were opened, and they knew that they were naked; and they sewed fig leaves together and made themselves loin coverings" (Gen 3:7). Spiritual death and separation from God was occurring just as God promised them. After sinning, when God came to walk in the Garden in the cool of the day, Adam & Eve heard Him and hid.

When Adam & Eve were abiding in God, they had no cares or worries. But after leaving His abiding presence, the spirit of fear entered Adam & Eve's mind. Man was now worried about how he appeared to God, his spouse, and even to the animals. Man knew he was separated. Orphans always see themselves as standing alone. When Adam & Eve heard the Lord walking in the Garden, they hid themselves from God among the trees. Man's own explanation of his actions was, "I heard the sound of You in the garden, and I was afraid because I was naked; so I hid myself" (Gen 3:10). The spirit of fear was present in man's life, where there had been no fear before.

The spirit of fear causes man to be anxious and worry. The Greek word translated to be anxious or worry is the word *merimnaō* which means a careful thought, to be distracted, or overly concerned with.[1] The spirit of fear will cause us to take our thoughts off of the Lord and put them onto the object we fear, or are concerned about. This fixation of our thoughts on something other than the Lord prevents us from abiding in Him and He in us. This fixation on ourselves and our circumstances causes us to enter into idolatry, since we are now putting our focus on the spirit of fear and our surrounding circumstances instead of on God.

An orphan spirit produces many types of fears and concerns. Who is going to provide for me? Who will protect me? What if someone finds out about my weaknesses and who I truly am? Without the abiding presence of God, man believes he is all alone and responsible for providing for himself and taking care of his own life. Without the abiding presence of God, man learns independence and self-will. Our souls and our bodies become programmed to live without God. After we are born-again, these programmed mindsets of an orphan spirit, independence, and self-will are hard to break and reprogram to get us back to the abiding state with God we are called to reside.

Since fallen man has an orphan spirit and is susceptible to the spirit of fear, is it any wonder God admonishes fallen man over and over again not to be afraid? He told them not to be afraid of their enemies, not to be afraid of provision, and not to be afraid of the future. The only thing He told them they were supposed to fear was Himself. It is debatable how many times the admonition "Don't be afraid," or "Fear not" exists in the Bible, but it's a lot! If God said it that many times, it must be important. Perhaps, He said it over and over again because He knew without the admonition to keep our thoughts fixed on Him, our thoughts would naturally drift apart and start to be anxious and worry about the cares of this world.

The business owners we serve frequently encounter fears associated with making payroll, insufficient sales to stay in business, lawsuits from business associates, penalties and taxes from regulators, hiring the right employee, and losing key employees. These are all legitimate business concerns. The answer to these real-life issues lies in our relationship with God and trusting Him to provide and protect us, and not giving into the spirit of fear. Jesus died to set us free from the spirit of fear and the torment and punishment that comes with it. But we must learn to die to the spirit of fear in order to abide in Him and enter into His *zōē* life.

If anyone was truly living without any type of concerns, they would be living recklessly. We need to be concerned about the things that are important in our lives. We need to keep our eyes on important issues, to stay on top of them and make sure they don't come back and bite us. The balance in teaching comes when we learn to keep our eyes and our minds on the Lord *more* than we do on the concerns of life that have the potential to harm us. In fact, this is a prerequisite to understanding the fear of the Lord.

The Fear of the Lord

In the Old Testament, the Israelites were commanded to fear only the Lord their God (Deut 6:13). The Hebrew word *yārē* means to revere, to stand in awe, to be afraid.[2] If you can understand how the Israelites felt when they passed through the Red Sea and saw a wall of water on each side as they walked through the sea on dry ground, or how they felt when they saw the top of Mount Sinai on fire and full of smoke and the mountain itself trembling violently, or how Zacharias would have felt when he saw the angel Gabriel in the Holy of Holies, then you can understand the reverential fear of the Lord. Our God is an awesome God and to have an encounter with Him is to come away saying, "Oh, my God!" That is the reverential fear of the Lord.

In the New Testament, Jesus tells us that we should fear God and Him alone.

> "I say to you, My friends, do not be afraid of those who kill the body and after that have no more that they can do. But I will warn you whom to fear: fear the One who, after He has killed, has authority to cast into hell; yes, I tell you, fear Him! Are not five sparrows sold for two cents? *Yet* not one of them is forgotten before God. Indeed, the very hairs of your head are all numbered. Do not fear; you are more valuable than many sparrows" (Luke 12:4-7).

As born-again children of God who are trying to regain our position of abiding in Him and He in us, we need the proper balance of spousal intimacy and the fear of the Lord in our relationship with the Almighty. We need to grow up and become like Him in all respects, but never forget the awesomeness, the holiness, and the power of the One we have been called to become one with. This is the reverential fear of the Lord. Having been separated from Him once before and now engrafted into the Vine, the fear of being separated from Him again should give us the proper perspective of the reverential fear of the Lord.

Fear Will Keep You From Doing What You Need to Do

The spirit of fear will keep you from doing what you know you need to do. Like a deer in headlights, you will see the objects of concern coming at you, but you will not take the appropriate actions to prevent or limit their impact. When you do take action, they will often be the wrong action. You will solve these problems according to your flesh and your reasoning instead of following the leading of the Holy Spirit.

Fear will affect your decision-making process, and the decisions you make today will determine whether or not you are successful tomorrow. Fear will cause you to become impatient and make decisions based upon mental reasoning and ignore the leading of the Holy Spirit. Fear will cause you to stand still when you should be moving forward. Fear will cause you to move ahead prematurely and attempt to promote yourself, when you should be waiting for the Lord to open the right doors at the right time. Fear will bring the spirit of confusion and distraction to your decision-making process, when what you really need is to hear the voice of the Lord for your next steps.

Fear will feed off of things hidden. Light always displaces darkness. We are called to bring those things we are ashamed of out into the light. Once in the light, darkness becomes light (Eph 5:13). In the end, the Lord promises there is nothing hidden that will not be revealed (Luke 12:2). Empty your closet and expose the hidden object fear is feeding on.

There is no compromise with the spirit of fear. It won't accept part of your life. It wants to choke the very life out of you. Like a python, it will take a grip on you and wait until you surrender more territory, and then increase its grip on you. It wants all of you and will not give up until it has choked the life out of you, or you have broken free of its grip. Never try to compromise with the spirit of fear; it is a waste of time.

Kingdom Business Success

Overcoming the Spirit of Fear

If we are going to abide in Him and He in us we must learn to cast down the spirit of fear and be anxious for nothing. God is love and there is no fear in love because His perfect love casts out fear (1 John 4:18). Therefore, in order to walk without fear, we must first learn to walk in *agapē* love. We must learn to walk in perfect love towards God and perfect love towards our fellow man. In this environment of *agapē* love, fear cannot exist.

The Lord has shown me there are at least three spirits that need to be conquered in order for believers to get back to the abiding presence of the Lord after they become born-again. These three spirits are an orphan spirit, the spirit of independence, and self-will. These are three strongholds that will prevent a believer from abiding in Him and walking in the abundant life.

As mentioned previously, the orphan spirit was a state man was left in after the fall in the Garden. Man suffered a spiritual death and was no longer able to be in communion with the Spirit of God. All the fears, loneliness, isolation, rejection, and lack of resources associated with being an orphan came upon fallen man. He truly was an orphan in his fallen state.

However, when we became born-again, the Holy Spirit came and took up residence in our spirit man and brought assurance that we became children of God and heirs to His inheritance in Christ (Rom 8:15-17a NKJV). Jesus promised the Spirit of Truth would abide with us and be in us. Jesus also promised that He would not leave us as orphans, but He would come to us. He promised that the Father and He would come to us and make their abode in us (John 14:17-18, 23). We would no longer be as orphans in the world but would become children of God living in His presence and abiding in Him.

If you are a Christian business owner and struggling with an orphan spirit or a spirit of rejection, you need to meditate on the scriptures that deal with understanding whom you have become in Christ Jesus to break off this orphan spirit. If this has become a stronghold in your thinking, then I suggest you seek some inner healing and deliverance ministry to help you overcome this mental block. Until you break off this orphan spirt and isolation mentality, you will never be able to abide in Him and walk without fear.

A spirit of independence is kindred to an orphan spirit. An independent spirit comes from a paradigm that sees God as external to us. If you remember, that was the paradigm under the Mosaic Law and the paradigm non-believers possess. An independent spirit looks to serve God instead of seeing themselves serving *with* God, or more accurately, seeing God serving through them.

It has been said often that the Lord is not as interested in what you do *for* Him as what you allow Him to do *through you*. This idea of doing business and life together with Him is the foundation of abiding in Him and He in us. The Lord considers it an affront to attempt to do life without Him. Imagine how your spouse would feel if you set off on a great adventure and forgot to take them with you? They might feel offended. To attempt to do life without Him is to risk having Him say, "I never knew you. Depart from me, you who practice lawlessness" (Matt 7:23).

One of the keys to overcoming fear is through death. Fear has no control over a dead person. When we are led by the Holy Spirit, the enemy can attempt to control our actions through the spirit of fear, but if we resolve to follow His will and not our will, the Holy Spirit will lead us through the event we are facing. However, most of us are led by our self-will more than we like to admit. We avoid things we don't want to do and focus on the things we want to do. We prefer to take the course of action that we are comfortable with rather than follow the direction of the Holy Spirit.

Similar to Naaman the captain of the Aram army, we swear our allegiance to do anything the Lord directs us to do in order to receive our deliverance (2 Kings 5:13). And if the Lord directs us to do something great like selling our business and moving to a third world country, we would do it. But we tend to ignore any instruction that sound insignificant, since we assume an insignificant act of obedience can only bring an insignificant result in our lives. We forget that God seeks obedience and not sacrifice from us (1 Sam 15:22).

A friend of mine once said, "Jesus isn't trying to save you, He's trying to kill you." I would be careful who I repeated that to for concern they might misunderstand his statement, but there is some truth to what my friend said. More accurately, I would say Jesus is trying to save you, but the way to salvation is through death to your flesh and self-will. In the Kingdom of Heaven, before there is a resurrection, there is always a death and burial.

As we will see in Chapter 15, successful people overcome fear by overcoming inertia. They are always moving towards their goals and refuse to move away from their destiny. They set their faces like flint and stay focused on their destiny. They develop a thick skin and learn to ignore the naysayers and those who are in opposition to their goals. On a daily basis, they are willing to do the things unsuccessful people are not willing to do and therefore achieve the results others do not achieve.

Jesus is referred to as the Lion of the tribe of Judah. When lions roar, they put fear into the other animals in the kingdom. As little Christs, we are called not to live in a spirit of fear or timidity, but to put the fear of God into the enemies of Christ. It is time we stop trembling with fear over the cares and worries of our life and business, and start roaring like the One we are called to abide in.

Principles in Practice

Andrew was the owner of a technical services company but lived in fear of what his employees might do and how their behavior would affect his reputation and his business. Andrew never seemed to hire the right employees. Although he hired only experienced technicians, they all appeared to be incompetent and lazy. Nothing ever seemed to get done right or on time unless Andrew was personally watching over the operation.

Andrew was afraid the mistakes his employees made would reflect badly on him and his business. These mistakes could result in losing clients to a competitor, which would in turn affect his revenue and profits. Although his concerns were legitimate to some degree, these concerns of Andrew had increased to a point where they were strongholds of fear in his life and business.

The fear of loss of reputation is rooted in the fear of man. The fear of loss of business is rooted in the fear of poverty. Since Andrew couldn't trust anyone else, he was limiting the growth of his business to a level where he could supervise everything going on in the company. His fears caused him to become a "control freak." Andrew was carrying the load of his business on his own shoulders and didn't realize he had developed a spirit of independence. "If it is to be, it is up to me." Andrew was doing business *for* God but had yet to learn how to do business *with* God.

Andrew needed to hire good managers to help him oversee his work force as well as hire, train, and retain good technicians. But what he really needed was to learn to do business with God. He needed to trust God to help him hire the right people and remove the wrong people from his workforce. He needed to realize his own reputation died the day he died in Christ. He was now a beloved child of God stewarding His business for Him. He no longer had anything to lose since everything he could have lost had already died. Even if the business failed, the Lord would continue to provide for Andrew through another business or other means.

When we feel like we are carrying the weight of our business on our shoulders, it is often because we are doing just that. We need to put the burden on the Lord's big shoulders and let Him carry the weight of the business.

Kingdom Business Success

Terrence owned a dealership with a Fortune 500 company. Although he made an excellent income from his company, he had increased his expenses and standard of living to the point where his income was being used entirely to pay bills and pay down the debt he had accumulated over the years. Whoever said we are all broke at different levels of income was probably talking about Terrence. Since the dealership income is dependent on sales that fluctuate from month to month, Terrence lived in fear of not being able to pay his bills and maintain his standard of living. Terrence was living hand-to-mouth, from paycheck to paycheck.

Although Terrence made a good income, he was living beyond his means and then some. Terrence had ignored Kingdom financial principles. We will look at many of the Kingdom financial principles that Terrence violated in the Financial Abundance chapter. I mention Terrence's mistakes because often the Lord is looking for us to patch the holes in our bucket before He pours more financial blessings into it. Frequently, the Lord is more than willing to help us out of our financial dilemma, but He first wants us to repent of the mistakes that caused our financial situation, so that the new financial blessings will not fall through holes in the bucket.

Compounding his financial problems, his orphan spirit, independence, and self-will caused him to make many mistakes regarding the handling of his personal and corporate finances. Even though he was a born-again child of God, Terrence saw himself as the servant outside the house instead of the heir of the promise living in his Father's house. His orphan spirit had become a stronghold and was keeping him from trusting his Father for provision. This lack of trust in his Father attracted a spirit of independence. He saw himself carrying the load all by himself instead of seeing the Lord involved in everything. The spirit of independence caused Terrence to attempt to be the lord of his own life and craft a plan to deliver himself, instead of seeking the Lord's plan for deliverance from this situation. Terrence was asking the Lord to bless his plan instead of seeking the Lord's plan for his life.

The path out of this type of financial dilemma normally does not happen overnight, and it didn't happen that way for Terrence either. The way to solve this problem is to spend time with the Lord, repent of poor financial stewardship that led to the problem, fix the root causes, and turn over all worries and concerns about the problem to the Lord. Typically, the Lord will give some immediate relief in the way of "grace money" while at the same time requiring us to earn the bulk of the money to pay the debt by implementing Kingdom financial principles. These Kingdom financial principles are explained in greater detail in the Financial Abundance Chapter.

Rick was the owner of a professional services consulting company who suffered from fear of failure and fear of man. Although he had a proven track record with his clients and peers as someone who could always be counted on to get the job done on time, Rick lived in fear of not being able to deliver on his next assignment. Rick was carrying the load of running the company entirely on his shoulders and lived in fear of loss of reputation should he fail or make a mistake on his next assignment. Rick only knew conditional love and believed people would only love and accept him if he was able to succeed in all his assignments.

Although Rick was very proficient in his work, he liked his work load to come to him at a steady pace. As long as he was able to stay on top of and ahead of business, he was comfortable in his delivery. But if the pace picked up, Rick would panic for fear he might make a mistake and look bad to his clients and others around him. This fear caused him to become impatient, angry, bitter, resentful, critical, and judgmental of others. Although others might see him as moody and having a bad day, what they didn't understand was they could trace his bad days directly to his workload. His bad days were indicative of his fear of failure.

Fear of failure is a sign of someone who sees themselves as an orphan and has developed an independent spirit when it comes to doing life and business without the Lord. They carry the load of the business entirely on their own shoulders, and there is only so much they can carry. When the load is comfortable, they are able to carry it independently without the Lord. But when the load increases beyond their comfort level, they realize they need help.

People who have an independent spirit don't realize the Lord is giving them exactly what they want. Like the child who insists on tying their own shoes, they often find that getting what they asked for is not the same as getting what they wanted. Rick was choosing to do life and business without the Lord and the Lord was allowing Rick to do it his way. It is not until we repent of doing life without Him and learn to abide in Him, that He will start carrying the load for us.

Once Rick realized this principle, he repented and started to do everything with the Lord. He began to see the Lord's hand involved in his life and business. Now, when the workload and pressures of life increase, instead of worrying and walking in fear, he looks to the Lord to give him the grace to do what he needs to do, and leaves everything else in the Lord's hands.

Questions for Reflection

1. What are your greatest worries and concerns? What are the fundamental fears these worries and concerns are rooted in?

2. Do you have any fears or concerns that have become strongholds in your life and limit your spiritual growth or walk with the Lord? Have you ever sought professional help through an inner healing/deliverance ministry for these strongholds?

3. On a scale of one to ten, how much of an orphan spirit do you have? Same question for an independent spirit (doing life without the Lord) and a self-will spirit (led by yourself instead of the Lord)? Ask the Lord to give you the grace to die to these spirits so you can truly live life abiding in Him, and He in you.

Chapter 10

Discipline

"But I say, walk by the Spirit, and you will not carry out the desire of the flesh" (Gal 5:16).

In Chapter 7, when discussing your Kingdom assignment, I made the statement that there are two characteristics all successful people share. Those characteristics are passion and discipline. I have never heard of any successful person who does not possess both of these qualities in abundance. We have already discussed the importance of passion as it pertains to successful business people and their Kingdom assignment, now it is time to discuss one of the more challenging qualities to achieve, and that is discipline.

"There is *one* special quality that you can develop that will guarantee you greater success, accomplishment and happiness in life. Of a thousand principles for success developed over the ages, this one quality or practice will do more to assure that you accomplish wonderful things with your life than anything else. This quality is so important that, if you *don't* develop it to a high degree, it is *impossible* for you to ever achieve what you are truly capable of achieving. The quality that I am talking about is the quality of self discipline. It is a habit, a practice, a philosophy and a way of living. All successful men and women are highly disciplined in the important work that they do. All *unsuccessful* men and women are *un*disciplined and unable to control their behaviors and their appetites. And when *you* develop the *same* levels of high, personal discipline possessed by the most successful people in our society, you will very soon begin to achieve the same results that they do."

– Brian Tracy[1]

Kingdom Business Success

You will never be able to walk in the fullness of your Kingdom assignment without having both passion for what you are doing and discipline over yourself and the resources the Lord has given you. Even non-believers, new agers, and self-help motivational gurus understand this principle. Most Christian business people understand it as well, so why aren't they more disciplined? It turns out self-discipline is more difficult to achieve than most people realize, and can even be considered a battle for your soul.

Self-discipline is supposed to be difficult. I am going to explain why it has been so challenging for you from a biblical perspective. You will find that you are not the only one struggling in the area of discipline. You will find your challenge with mastering self-discipline is as ancient as the battle between the Kingdom of Heaven and the kingdom of darkness. But we will also discuss how you can achieve victory in self-discipline through the power of Christ and the leading of the Holy Spirit.

In this chapter, I am going to use the term *discipline* instead of *self-discipline* intentionally. Self-discipline is the term motivational speakers and non-believers use simply because it is the only type of discipline they understand. They do not have a Kingdom of Heaven paradigm, so they envision God to be external to their lives and their world. In the Kingdom of Heaven, Christ is at the center of our paradigm, so we will discuss self-discipline but we will also discuss a type of discipline that goes beyond what man can produce through his own will power. This is Holy Spirit led discipline.

What is Discipline?

Self-discipline is the ability of a person to exercise control over their mind, will, and emotions to affect a desired behavior, conduct, and outcome. Since self-discipline is rooted in our soul, discipline is often associated with our decision-making ability. Our success in life is attributable to the decisions we make. Where we are in life today is based largely upon a summation of the decisions we have made throughout our life. It takes discipline to make the right decisions each day. As we will see, making wrong decisions comes quite naturally.

In order to understand why discipline is so difficult for most people to achieve, we need to understand the part of us the Bible refers to as our *flesh*. The Greek word *sarx* is translated as *flesh* and has a wide variety of meanings in the New Testament, but is generally used to describe the sin nature of unregenerate man (Rom 7:5, 8:8).[2] The term *flesh* is often coupled with the soul of a man and specifically the mind of the unsaved man.

When we were born-again, the Holy Spirit came to live in our spirit man. Our spirit man joined with the Holy Spirit. Our spirit man became the "new man" the Bible refers to in the new birth. But our soul, which is our mind, will, and emotions, was largely unchanged. Any immediate change to our soul was based upon the connection of our soul to our spirit man. If you understood how that worked completely, you would be the smartest doctor in the world!

Once born-again, we start to think differently, behave differently, and relate to people differently since our soul is somehow connected to our renewed spirit man. But the flesh, or the sin nature of man, is still there inside of us. This is the "old man" the Bible tells us we have to put off by the reading of the word (Rom 12:2, Eph 4:22-24, 5:26-27). We have to renew our mind, will, and emotions in accordance with the Word of God. As we listen to the Holy Spirit speaking through our renewed spirit man, we discipline our mind, will, and emotions to become Christ-like and crucify our fleshly desires which are sinful.

Our job is to subdue or to crucify our flesh daily. The apostle Paul said, "I die daily" (1 Cor 15:31). The death he was referring to was the death of the sin nature still in him, the part of him that had yet to die in Christ. The great apostle Paul still had some of that flesh, or sin nature of man inside of him. He had to subdue his flesh each day. This is the battle we face when trying to exercise self-discipline. There is an ongoing struggle between our desire to follow the part of our mind that has been renewed and wants to be led by Holy Spirit, or to follow the leading of the mind of our flesh.

There is a war raging inside us. Until you are perfected and become like Jesus in every way, there will still be some flesh inside of you. Your flesh is fighting your attempts to exercise self-discipline over your soul, your body, and your life. This is why self-discipline is an uphill battle. It is supposed to be difficult because it involves death to your flesh. That screaming sound you hear is your flesh crying out while you are trying to crucify or subdue it to the will of your mind.

Whereas temperance or self-control is considered a fruit of the Spirit, the flesh is an opposing force that would prefer excess, unrestrained passion, gluttony, lasciviousness, intoxication, fits of anger, impatience, chaos, disorder, and greed. To whatever area of your life you are trying to bring control, boundaries, purity, order, and restrictions, your flesh is an opposing force that wants unbridled excess. If you have struggled with self-discipline in an area of life, this is why it has been such a battle. This is the part of the discipline story the self-help gurus never told you about.

Four Discipline Focus Areas

There are at least four areas most business people tend to struggle with that prevents them from living an abundant life and achieving the success they desire. These four areas are time, money, food, and sex. If you can crucify your flesh in these four areas and draw boundaries and restrictions around these four areas, you will be well on your way to performing at a level that will allow you to achieve success in your business.

Time

Many of the business leaders I have worked with were weak or poor in the use of their time and never looked to be held accountable in their use of time. This is one area we need to be open to receive feedback from those we work with. Am I spending time wisely? Am I doing the right thing or am I just being busy? Remember, there is a big difference between being busy and being productive. Successful people focus on the tasks that give the greatest return on investment (ROI), the biggest bang for the buck. They are highly productive people. Unsuccessful people tend to work on tasks that are easy, fun to do, and give them the most personal satisfaction. They tend to be busy, but unproductive people.

Successful people always seem to get much more accomplished in the same time frame as unsuccessful people. These accomplishments may include running several businesses, learning to become fluent in multiple languages, becoming accomplished musicians, achieving academic degrees, writing books, holding office, raising several children, and reading far more books and periodicals than the average person. How do they do it? Discipline is the obvious answer. They were given the same 24-hour time period the rest of us were given. However, they were highly disciplined in how they managed their time. They didn't waste it.

An argument could be made that some of these successful people lived before the age of television and modern electronic devices that take so much of our time these days. They didn't have as many distractions as we face each day. But keep in mind, many of those who lived prior to the age of modern electronics worked six days per week at careers that were far more physically demanding than our modern high-tech jobs. They didn't sit behind a computer all day and then come home at night to sit in front of a television. They were disciplined in how they used and accounted for their time.

Money

In Chapter 8, I mentioned a concept I referred to as the 90/10 paradigm and stated that many Christians are managing their finances under this paradigm that came from a misunderstanding of the Mosaic Law. This paradigm believes that if I give 10% of everything I have received to the Lord, then the remaining 90% is mine to spend as I please. I also stated that this paradigm is false and contrary to the

Kingdom Business Success

Kingdom of Heaven paradigm. In the Kingdom of Heaven paradigm, we have no money. It all belongs to Him and we are simply stewards of the money He gives us.

Since most business people see their money as theirs and not the Lord's, many of them feel the need to spend it. However, if you were a manager of other people's money, you wouldn't spend their money as if it was your own. If you did, you would eventually be in prison for embezzlement. The truth is we are all guilty of embezzling God's money at one time or another. If we are going to abide in Him and He in us, then we have to stop committing this crime.

In order to be disciplined in our stewardship of money we need to develop a budget and manage to it. How much of the money we receive are we allowed to use on personal expenditures? This would include our house, cars, food, vacations, private school for the children, etc. The answer to that question is between you and the Lord. There is no single answer that fits everyone. Jesus said, "the laborer is worthy of his wages" (Luke 10:7). Seek the Lord for wisdom on your budget. Manage to it, but keep in mind that He might ask you to do something that runs contrary to your budget. Be flexible and obedient each day to steward His money as He directs.

Food

Food is a gift from God and is meant to be enjoyed. But like all gifts, it needs some temperance. Left unchecked, overeating will lead to high blood pressure, heart disease, stroke, diabetes, sleep disorder, fatigue, mood swings, stress, depression, feelings of hopelessness, and withdrawal. Being overweight results in the deterioration of bone and cartilage, which leads to the wearing out of feet, knees, hips, and back. In other words, overeating can destroy the temple of the Holy Spirit. Your body is the same vessel you need to serve the Lord and complete your Kingdom assignment. Therefore, the successful completion of your assignment is dependent on your body and your health.

Fasting is one of the best tools for disciplining your body and putting your appetite under submission. Fasting used to be a way of life for many Christians but is now considered to be unnecessary, a religious formality, or legalism. However, if you study the great men and women of God, you will find that fasting was one tool they all employed during their walk with the Lord. The subject of fasting and how to successfully do it are beyond the scope of this book, but I highly suggest everyone give serious consideration to employing this tool to help you walk a life of discipline. Fasting will not only help curb your appetite for food, but will help curb your fleshly appetites. For more information about how fasting can curb your fleshly appetites, read Franklin Hall's book *Atomic Power With God Through Fasting and Prayer*.[3]

Our goal with food, similar to all areas of discipline, is to be led by the Holy Spirit in our food intake. We look to Him to provide guidance as to when to eat, what to eat, and how much to eat. Imagine how much you would weigh if you only ate as directed by the Holy Spirit? Imagine how much energy you would have and how good you would feel? This is where the Lord wants to lead us so we can live the abundant life. Self-discipline is great. Fasting is great. But being led by the Holy Spirit in everything we do, including our eating patterns, is our real goal in life.

Sex

The list of men and women of God who have succumbed to sexual temptations is long - too long. The media has had a field day publicizing these sins. Our enemy is actively engaged in trying to steal, kill, and destroy us, and one of his favorite weapons is to tempt us through our sexual appetite. The sexual appetite is one of the strongest appetites and left without discipline will lead us down the path of spiritual death.

Based upon my personal experiences and what I have seen in the lives of other business people, I know of no other sin guaranteed to destroy someone's finances the way *sexual immorality* (and all forms it comes in) and *covenant breaking* will accomplish. If you want to keep the spirit of death away from your finances, your marriage, your life, and your business, then stay away from all forms of sexual immorality and covenant breaking.

Sexual immorality is one of the sins mentioned in the outcome of the Jerusalem council (Acts 15) which provided admonishment for the Gentiles who were becoming Christians. Jesus declared that those who practice sexual immorality would not enter heaven. Instead, these people will have their place in the lake that burns with fire and brimstone (Rev 21:1-2, 7-8).

I believe one of the keys to success in dealing with sexual temptation is to draw boundaries around your life. Ask the Holy Spirit to illumine your weaknesses and how to avoid the temptations around you. The level of boundaries needed to avoid sin will differ for each person. What is a temptation to one person would not be to another. Don't be concerned with other people's boundaries. Focus on the boundaries the Holy Spirit leads you to employ in your own life.

Where are you weak? Where do you need to draw boundaries? Ask the Holy Spirit to show you where and how to shore up the boundaries in your life, but especially the ones pertaining to sexual immorality.

Discipline Is Getting Scarce

If the flesh is at enmity with God, it shouldn't come as a surprise the world is rejecting discipline and embracing fleshly desires. The world is embracing the deeds of the flesh. The world abhors boundaries, restrictions, order, sobriety, decency, community, and submission to authority. The world embraces and promotes chaos, sexual preferences, debauchery, independence, and lawlessness. This is true in all areas of society including the business and Government arenas, but it can even be seen in the local churches.

In most churches today, anything that looks uniform, connected, regulated, or has any type of boundary around it is considered legalism, control, formality, prideful, and contrary to the freedom we are supposed to have in Christ Jesus. But the freedom that Jesus referred to was not a freedom to do whatever we feel like doing. That type of unrestraint will eventually lead us to follow our own flesh, which is guaranteed to lead us into sin. Of those who would become His disciples, Jesus said:

> "Take My yoke upon you and learn from Me, for I am gentle and humble in heart, and you will find rest for your souls. For My yoke is easy and My burden is light" (Matt 11:29-30).

Jesus never promised a life without restraint, responsibilities, or accountability. A life without any type of restraint is a life of sin. He simply promised that when we abide in Him, we would be connected or yoked to Him in our assignments and that His restraint (or discipline) would be easy. It would be easy compared to the yoke sin puts on people. Our burden would be light, compared to the burden sin puts on people. It is time for the body of Christ to wake up and come back to the middle of the road on the subject of discipline and stop behaving like non-believers.

A biblical sign that we are approaching the end times is evidenced by a society and its Government that calls the deeds of the flesh "good" and the righteous fruit of the Holy Spirit "bad." The Bible says, "Woe to those who call evil good, and good evil" (Isaiah 5:20a).

With society embracing unrestraint and abhorring discipline, is it any wonder you are struggling with self-discipline in some area of your life? The flesh of man is at war with the Spirit of God.

> "The sinful nature wants to do evil, which is just the opposite of what the Spirit wants. And the Spirit gives us desires that are the opposite of what the sinful nature desires. These two forces are constantly fighting each other, so you are not free to carry out your good intentions" (Gal 5:17 NLT).

135

Kingdom Business Success

But the good news is Jesus has given us victory over the flesh. Where the world knows only self-discipline, we have a form of discipline that gives us an edge over non-believers. This believer's edge provides assistance to us in every facet of our life including our minds, our bodies, our businesses, and our finances. It is called the Spirit-led life; being led moment by moment by the Holy Spirit.

The Spirit-Led Life

In order to help us abide in Him and He in us, He has given us His Holy Spirit to live in us. The Holy Spirit is called our Advocate. He leads us, guides us, protects us, and reminds us of everything our Master has told us. The Christian walk was never meant to be walked alone, but an adventure where we walk closely joined with Father, Son, and Holy Spirit. "For all who are being led by the Spirit of God, these are sons of God" (Rom 8:14).

What does being led by the Holy Spirit have to do with discipline? Everything. It is the same paradigm shift. To those who do not have a Kingdom of Heaven paradigm, God is external to them and they are left to use their willpower to create self-discipline in their mind, bodies, and activities. But if we are led by the Holy Spirit, our will is submitted to His will and **He gives us the will to do what He wants us to do**. "For it is God who works in you both to will and to do for *His* good pleasure" (Phil 2:13 NKJV).

The Holy Spirit gives us the grace of discipline to do His will. We just need to seek His will and be obedient to everything He asks us to do. This is easier said than done, especially for new Christians who are used to walking in accordance with their own will. But as we die to our flesh daily and learn to submit to His gentle nudging, we will realize His yoke is truly easy and His burden is light. He gives us the grace to want to do His will and also to do it. He will give us the grace to do the things that we have struggled to achieve using self-discipline alone. Let me give you an example from my own life.

About 20 years ago, I struggled with alcohol consumption. I was drinking about twenty ounces of gin per day; except on days when I drank heavily. There were days when I probably drank an entire bottle of gin. I was what they refer to as "a functioning drunk." I was the first one in the office in the morning and performed as much work with the same quality, as those that did not drink. I was even leading children's Sunday school at that time. Most of the people who knew me, never knew I had this problem. Like a secret agent, I lived two lives.

I told myself numerous times that I would quit drinking entirely or severely regulate my drinking consumption. As much as I tried to take control over this issue through self-discipline, I always failed. As Jesus said, my spirit was willing but my flesh was weak (Matt 26:41). If I had great self-discipline, I never would have reached the point I was at, but my current level of discipline was not giving me victory over this issue.

One day, I turned this issue over to the Lord and asked Him to give me the grace to walk away from alcohol completely. I swore I would never touch another drop of alcohol and asked Him to give me the grace to keep this covenant promise. He answered my prayer and gave me the grace to walk away from it. The desire to drink left me. For the next six months, I was still around alcohol and other "power drinkers" each day, but I was never tempted to have another drink. I never went to any meetings and never went through any withdrawal treatments. In fact, I probably broke every rule the recovery programs provide as guidance to people who are withdrawing from alcohol. I was only able to do that because I had been miraculously delivered from alcohol. My self-discipline was not behind the victory, but simply the power of Christ.

Twenty years later, I consider this deliverance from alcohol a miracle. Since then, many people who are struggling with addictions have asked me how I did it. My response to them is always "It was simply the grace of God." I take no credit for it. Self-discipline had nothing to do with it. If I had any self-discipline in this area, I never would have had this problem. As many times as I tried to win this battle using self-discipline, I failed. It was only when I came to the end of myself and realized I was totally dependent on Him and His grace, that His grace was made available for me to walk away from this problem.

> "Concerning this I implored the Lord three times that it might leave me. And He has said to me, 'My grace is sufficient for you, for power is perfected in weakness.' Most gladly, therefore, I will rather boast about my weaknesses, so that the power of Christ may dwell in me. Therefore I am well content with weaknesses, with insults, with distresses, with persecutions, with difficulties, for Christ's sake; for when I am weak, then I am strong" (2 Cor 12:8-10).

Your weakness might not be alcohol. What do you struggle with that you have yet to conquer using self-discipline alone? Perhaps it is time for you to boast about your weakness and turn it over to the Lord. Ask Him for His grace to crucify your flesh and subdue the part of your will that has yet to die in Christ. Let Him give you victory over this issue. You will never know the fullness of the power of Christ in your life until you reach the end of yourself and find you are totally dependent on Him for your success.

What would your life look like if you were led moment by moment by the Holy Spirit?

> ➢ Imagine what your calendar would look like if you allowed the Holy Spirit to schedule your day. Do you think you would be more productive? Do you think you would have time to learn that language, play that instrument, or read that book you've wanted to do?

> ➢ Imagine if you were led by the Holy Spirit in when you eat and what you eat. Do you think that you would be in better health? Do you think your overall health would be better and have more energy?

> ➢ Imagine if you never spent a dime without seeking direction from the Lord about what to purchase and when to purchase it. Do you think you would have more money and wealth than you have now? Do you think there would be any financial lack in your life? Do you think you would know what and when to invest in?

The Holy Spirit is our Advocate, our helper, and our comforter. When we submit to His leading, we remain joined to the Master and He is able to give us the grace to will and obey His desires for our lives. We just need to learn how to listen to His voice and walk with Him moment by moment each day, while crucifying the voice of our flesh.

As stated previously, there are no successful people in the world who are without an abundance of passion and discipline in their life. But the great edge believers have over the self-help, motivational gurus is that we are not dependent on our self-will to create self-discipline. We have the power of Christ in our lives. "And this is the victory that has overcometh the world, even our faith" (1 John 5:4 KJ21).

Principles in Practice

One of **Ron's** strengths was his people skills. If you remember, everyone loved him and respected him, even our competitors. Ron would always make time to listen to anyone who needed him regardless of what was going on around him at the time. It was this open door policy that made Ron so likeable and allowed him to exercise his people skills. It was his ability to deal with the chaos around him and bring peace to every situation that made him such a great leader, and caused his time to be in great demand. But it was this same open door policy that prevented Ron from focusing and prioritizing his work tasks.

Anyone who has studied time management knows the importance of prioritizing your work load and focusing on one task at a time. Even when you are interrupted on one task for a more urgent task, your focus is then on the second task. Prioritization and focus are the key elements of all time management systems, regardless of which one used. Ron could prioritize his work load, but he couldn't stay focused on the immediate task he was working on. Ron needed to learn to draw boundaries around his time and availability.

If Ron had learned to block out certain times of the day on his calendar for personal work, or post a "Do Not Disturb" sign on his door when necessary, or let his telephone calls roll to voice mail, he would have been a more productive manager. Ron needed to learn to say "Not now" to the well-intentioned people and distractions that would seek his time. Having time management skills does not mean you will never have distractions, changing priorities, or increasing work load, it just means you know how to manage those changes.

For those who think being a good Christian means we always have to make time for people regardless of who they are and what we are doing, keep in mind Jesus didn't make time for everyone. On one occasion, His family attempted to see Him but after being told they were outside, He stayed focused on His current task of teaching and preaching the Kingdom of Heaven (Matt 12:46-50). The Bible says Herod, the Governor of the Judean province, tried to see Him for a long time but was unable (Luke 23:8). Most Christians would jump at the opportunity to meet with and evangelize their Governor. Jesus didn't. Jesus would leave his disciples and depart to have quiet time alone with His Father. Talk about a "Do Not Disturb" sign!

Brice was a Christian business entrepreneur with great people skills but sorely lacking discipline. He probably lacked discipline in several areas of his life, but the areas that prevented him from succeeding in business were lack of discipline in time and money. Brice had great moral integrity. He was a person who was quick to openly confess and repent of his sins to another Christian brother (James 5:16). I would even say he was led by the Holy Spirit in many areas of his life. But when it came to time and money, he seemed to follow his own lead and that is where the train would always derail.

Part of Brice's problem with managing time and money came from unrealistic expectations. Brice always assumed best case scenarios. He seemed to think walking by faith meant that he should always assume everything would line up and fall into place at the optimal time. No two bills should ever come due at the same time. Customers would always pay their bills on time. County inspectors would never come at an unexpected time, and wouldn't find any issues needing to be resolved before moving forward. In other words, if all the stars lined up correctly, then Brice's plans should have worked. But as most business people know, the stars rarely line up perfectly.

Brice never completed his work on time, since he always assumed optimal conditions with no distractions. He had significant trouble focusing on one task at a time. Similar to a child, if he needed to go into another room to get a pencil, he would get distracted with something else and spend 30 minutes or more before coming back to the task at hand. If Brice was supposed to drive somewhere, he would always plan on optimal driving conditions. He never seemed to factor in rush hour traffic, traffic accidents, the lack of gas in his tank, or the need to stop for coffee. It's no wonder he always showed up late for meetings.

Brice could not hold onto money. It didn't matter how much he had. Whatever money he had, he felt the need to spend. Brice thought people who were frugal with their spending were lacking faith in finances. He thought they had a "poverty mentality." He seemed to believe living "hand to mouth" was an expression of faith. It took Brice many years to learn that "a good man leaves an inheritance to his children's children (Prov 13:22) and "the rich rules over the poor, and the borrower becomes the lender's slave" (Prov 22:7).

In order to manage any project in life or business, you must have good estimates of time, money, and resources. Bad estimates will cause extensive delays and can even prevent a project from completing successfully. Brice was terrible when it came to estimating time and money because he always had unrealistic expectations. Even worse, Brice was confusing walking by faith with walking presumptuously.

It is faith when you act upon the Word of God or when you believe the Holy Spirit has led you to do something. It is presumption and foolishness to think you can do things your way and assume God will cover your mistakes and pay all the bills associated with those mistakes, just because you are His son. That is not faith, that is tempting God. Even the Son of God did not tempt God (Luke 4:9-12 NKJV). Brice was a man of faith, but he had gone past faith into presumption and foolishness.

Henry was one of the most disciplined CEOs I have ever worked with. Disciplined in every area as far as I could tell, but his discipline was especially evident in the areas of time and money. This discipline allowed him to grow his business at an unheard of rate, while maintaining a balanced life with his family. What seemed paradoxical, Henry's discipline in time and money allowed him and his employees to have more fun than any other company I have worked with.

When Henry was in the early stages of growing his business, he would serve his Fortune 500 client to the best of his abilities. He would get to the office about 7AM and spend the next hour walking the halls and getting to know the various leaders and managers in the company. Henry had discovered that most leaders in any company either get to the office early to have quiet time for their own work, or stay late at night to get it done. By coming an hour earlier and staying an hour later, Henry was always around to discuss business with the leaders of this Fortune 500 company.

By getting out and talking to the leaders, Henry was finding out where their "pain points" were. He was discovering the problems they had and seeing where he could help them. Henry would even volunteer his time and always asked "Hey, can I help you with that problem in any way?" Sometimes these helpful efforts were done for free. I have seen Henry help clients copy, collate and staple presentations just as a favor to them. He would endear himself to them by serving at no charge. Frequently, these offers to help people led to new projects his company would perform, for a very generous management consulting fee.

Henry was also disciplined in his use of money. He stayed on top of cash flow on a daily basis. I have never known any CEO who had a detailed knowledge of the cash flow situation in his company as Henry had. Although he paid his employees well and the compensation was above average for the industry, Henry watched every dime that came in and went out of his company. He invested a sizeable amount of the company's money on training seminars and team building events for his employees. Henry believed in sowing into his people to make them more valuable. He saw the money that he spent on his employees as a good investment. Henry figured the more valuable his employees were, the more he could bill for their time, which in turn increased the company's profits.

In case you thought any business person who is so highly disciplined in time and money must be boring, Henry would certainly break that stereotype. He knew how to have fun and insisted his employees have fun as well. Henry would hold monthly team building events that would include go cart racing, wine tasting, mountain climbing, golf, sporting events, etc. Although some of these events were after hours, many of them were held during normal business hours. This meant his employees were not billable to his clients during these team building events. Henry believed in these team building events so much, he not only paid for these costly events, but he sacrificed revenue from the hours which were not billable during those events.

Henry was a business CEO who had so much passion for his vision, he was willing to be disciplined in time and money to see the fulfillment of his dream. Henry was the best CEO I have known in the areas of passion and discipline.

Questions for Reflection

1. Who is the most successful person you know? How would you rate their discipline in the areas of time, money, food, and sex?

2. In what areas do you struggle to achieve discipline in your life?

3. Can you achieve victory with self-discipline or is this something that will require the grace of God for you to see the victory?

4. Bring the areas you are struggling with to the Lord, and ask Him to give you the grace to both will and do His will for your life in those areas. When you ask, believe you will receive, and that His grace will be sufficient for you.

Chapter 11

Prayer

"Pray then in this way...your kingdom come. Your will be done on earth as it is in heaven" (Matt 6:9-10).

Let's face it. The reason you don't spend more time in prayer is you haven't seen the type of success you were expecting from prayer. If you are like most people, you have prayed all of your life and seen some answered prayer. But answered prayer seems more hit or miss than predictable. You are looking for a prayer life that is both predictable and powerful. The kind of prayer life Elijah had.

"Elijah was a man with a nature like ours, and he prayed earnestly that it would not rain, and it did not rain on the earth for three years and six months. Then he prayed again, and the sky poured rain and the earth produced its fruit" (James 5:17-18).

Have you ever read this scripture and said to yourself "Hire that man!" After all, who wouldn't want Elijah working for them? Whatever you paid him, you knew he would be worth it. But where can you find Elijahs in this day and age? The truth is, you shouldn't have to look too far. As Christians, we are called to walk in the power of Elijah. The promise of the Gospel is if we will abide in Him, then we would have access to this power. We just need to abide in Him and learn how to release the power of Christ into our everyday situations. After all, this is our calling as Christians; to become little Christs.

Miracles, by definition are meant to be a sign and a wonder to the world and reflect the power of the Holy Spirit in operation. "For the kingdom of God does not consist in words but in power" (1 Cor 4:20). Miracles are God's way of getting the attention of a non-believing world since they represent something that could not have occurred without divine intervention. I mention this up because *I* believe in miracles! I believe in miracles in everyday life and in business. I believe God wants us to see signs, wonders, and miracles in our everyday life and business in order to be effective witnesses to the world.

I do not use the term "miracle" loosely, although some of these answered prayers may not be considered a miracle to some. Many times we have had clients who have needed $50K or more to make payroll in less than 48 hours. We pray for money to come in and generally, it comes in as needed. Was this a miracle or would that money have come in anyway without divine intervention? Regardless of whether it constitutes a miracle, there will always be skeptics. If they were skeptical of the miracles Jesus performed, they will still be skeptical today.

I pray for miracles every day. I pray for miracles in my life and ministry but also in our client's lives and businesses. I believe in miracles not because I'm praying for them to occur or want to believe in them, I believe in miracles because I know the love and faithfulness of our heavenly Father. Once you know His heart, you will never question whether or not He wants to answer your prayers. At times, He will even answer prayers that are contrary to His perfect will for your life. If it's important to you, it is important to Him. And He promises to perfect those things in your life which concern you (Psalm 138:8).

As a business owner, I know you are not concerned with the definition of a miracle or the theology of prayer. You simply want your prayers answered. You want to see the abundant life Jesus promised manifest in your life and business. Prayer is the vehicle to getting those needs met. Prayer is the spiritual force that affects things in both the spiritual and physical domains. It is the language of heaven and one recognized by angels and demons. With our prayers we can bring life to situations and with our prayers we can bring death to situations. Prayer is that powerful!

The subject of prayer would fill many books. In this chapter, I am going to attempt to give a reader's digest summary to this multi-faceted subject as it pertains to bringing the Kingdom of Heaven into your business. We will discuss different types of prayer and why we use them, who should pray, what we should pray for, and why we even need to pray. Prayer is not optional. *You* are called to be a warrior in a Kingdom battle. Prayer is *your* preferred weapon over the enemy. Prayer is the tool that makes the resources of heaven available to you to complete your Kingdom assignment and advance the Kingdom of Heaven here on earth. Make the decision today to become an expert marksman with the weapon of prayer in your personal life and in your Kingdom assignment.

What is Prayer?

What exactly is prayer? I believe it is important to understand *what* we are going to be doing before we get into the mechanics of *how* and *when* to do it. In Hebrew, the word *pālal* means to pray, to intervene, to mediate, and to judge. It also implies a two-way form of communication.[1] In Greek, the word *proseuchomai* means to pray to God.[2] Both of these definitions make up the type of prayer we refer to as "petitioning prayer." This is the type of prayer that most people are familiar with and is the most mentioned type of prayer in the Bible. But there are other types of prayer that are biblically based and we will discuss their role as well. What all these types of prayer have in common is that prayer involves communication with the sovereign God of the universe. Since God is a Spirit, prayer is also a *spiritual* energy or force.

"It is the Spirit who gives life; the flesh profits nothing; the words that I have spoken to you are spirit and are life" (John 6:63). Jesus said His words are spirit and they are life. This means the words we speak are spirit as well. Since they carry the power of life and death, our words are a spiritual force that has the ability to bring *zōē* life into a situation. When we pray, we release energy, a spiritual force into the heavens that causes things to happen. Our prayers are that powerful.

One of my favorite definitions of prayer was penned by R.A. Torrey, a famous evangelist, pastor, and superintendent of the Moody Bible Institute:

"Prayer is the key that unlocks all the storehouses of God's infinite grace and power. All that God is, and all that God has, is at the disposal of prayer. But we must use the key. Prayer can do anything that God can do, and as God can do anything, prayer is omnipotent. No one can stand against the man who knows how to pray and meets all of the conditions of prevailing prayer and who really prays. The Lord God Omnipotent works for him and works through him." – R.A. Torrey[3]

Before looking at the various types of prayer and how they are used, there is a more fundamental question which needs to be addressed and that is why pray at all? If God knows what we need and has truly made provision for us, why doesn't He just give it to us? If your business is a Kingdom assignment from the Lord, why doesn't business just come to you? Doesn't the Lord want you to succeed in the assignment He's given you? Why do you have to fight for something He has already given you? If the Lord promised to protect us, why would we need to engage in spiritual warfare? These are great questions. The answer to these philosophical questions lies in the Kingdom paradigm shift.

Why Pray?

"When all else fails, pray." Whoever started this proverb, it seems to be well known throughout the world. Perhaps it originated from a quote made by E.M. Bounds in the 19th century when he said "Prayer succeeds when all else fails."[4] The logical conclusion of this thought would be "when all else fails, then pray." Regardless of who originated the proverb, it seems to have entered into the mindset of many Christians. But it wasn't supposed to be that way.

Even in the Old Testament we see that prayer was meant to be a way of life. We see the patriarchs of the Bible calling on the name of the Lord and praying for spouses, children, food, water, shelter, forgiveness, revelation of God's will, protection from their enemies, a blessing, success in their endeavors, and prayers of praise, thanksgiving, and worship to God. The patriarchs understood the necessity of prayer and its importance in their life. They understood they were totally dependent on God for everything, and that prayer was the vehicle to bring the resources of heaven into their life.

The subjects of Deism versus Theism and Determinism versus the Free Will of Man are the subjects of philosophers and theologians. The bottom line is mainstream Christianity embraces the concept that God is actively involved in the lives of His children and although sovereign over the universe, He limits His involvement in our affairs to ensure the free will He gave man will never be violated. He therefore needs to be "invited" to perform certain acts that if performed without invitation, would violate the inherent free will of man. Prayer is the official invitation that invites God to get involved in our lives. If this sounds oversimplified, keep in mind I am attempting to reduce to one paragraph concepts that have filled many theological dissertations.

> "It seems God is limited by our prayer life – that He
> can do nothing for humanity unless someone asks Him."
> – John Wesley[5]

This is the simplified answer to the question of "Why pray?" This is why we must pray for wisdom and understanding, provision, protection, favor, and assistance. God wants to be involved in our lives and business and provide divine help, but He will never violate the gift He has given man called "free will." Never confuse the appearance of the lack of God's involvement in the affairs of man, with His lack of interest in getting involved. God might be waiting for His official invitation to come in the form of someone's prayer. You could be the person who sends the invitation to God through your prayers. We don't need to beg God to get involved in our lives. He's begging us to ask Him to get involved so that He can bring the Kingdom of Heaven into our lives and businesses.

Prayer brings the involvement of the Father, Son, and Holy Spirit into our daily lives and business. Prayer is a two-way communication between us and our Master whom we are yoked with in our Kingdom assignment. Prayer is the mechanism that allows us to hear His voice to know when to turn left or right, to know when we are to move forward and when to stop. Everything we need to complete our Kingdom assignment has already been made available to us, but prayer is the mechanism that releases this provision at the appropriate time.

Types of Prayer

There are many types of prayer. Here are some of the more common types every business person should be familiar with and using in their everyday prayer life. Regardless of where you are right now in your prayer life, determine to become a person who lives a life of prayer. Let prayer become as natural and comfortable in your everyday life, as breathing air.

Petitioning Prayer

This is the most common type of prayer and the one mentioned most in the Bible. This is the type of prayer Jesus was referring to when He said "If you abide in Me, and My words abide in you, ask whatever you wish, and it will be done for you" (John 15:7); and again when He said "Ask, and it will be given to you; seek, and you will find; knock, and it will be opened to you" (Matt 7:7). In the book of Philippians, the apostle Paul reminds us to "Be anxious for nothing, but in everything by prayer and supplication with thanksgiving let your requests be made known to God" (Phil 4:6).

The "Lord's Prayer" is a model or pattern for petitioning prayer. This is a prayer model every Christian has been taught and used at one time or another. In this prayer model we are reminded to pray to our Heavenly Father, and to come to Him with an attitude of praise and worship acknowledging that His very name is Holy. We ask Him for our daily needs and for forgiveness for our sins while at the same time promising to forgive those who have sinned against us. We also ask for His protection against the evil one.

What is sometimes overlooked in the Lord's Prayer is that we are to pray His Kingdom comes and His will be done on earth as it is in heaven (Matt 6:10). The implication is that we have a part in ensuring this happens. If you have been waiting to see the Kingdom of Heaven operate in your life and seeing God's will done in your business, perhaps the Lord is waiting for your prayers in order to give Him the invitation He needs in order to make it happen.

Petitioning prayer is simple prayer. Jesus said unless we become like children, we will not enter the Kingdom of Heaven (Matt 18:3). If you are making petitioning prayer complicated, you have lost sight of how easy this is supposed to be. This is supposed to be as simple as a husband and wife asking each other for help. This is as simple as two co-laborers joined together asking each other for help. Whatever you need, simply ask for it and believe your Father in Heaven will provide for you, just because He loves you.

Declarative Prayer

Whereas petitioning prayer is the type of prayer most mentioned in the Bible in both the Old and New Testaments, declarative prayers are the type of prayer most often associated with Jesus' ministry, especially when He performed miracles. Since He is our role model and our King, it only makes sense that this is a type of prayer we should be using to bring the Kingdom of Heaven into our business.

There are three recorded instances where Jesus raised someone from the dead. In each situation, our Lord spoke an authoritative decree. These decrees included "Young man, I say to you arise" (Luke 7:14), "Little girl, I say to you get up" (Mark 5:41), and "Lazarus, come forth" (John 11:43). Although He prayed a petitioning prayer before raising Lazarus, when it came time to raise these three people from the dead, notice that Jesus did not pray a petitioning prayer. He spoke or released a declarative prayer.

God creates with His spoken words. Jesus said His words are spirit and they are life (John 6:63). Some might say this is how God creates, but we are not God. This is true, we are not God, but the ministry Jesus performed on the earth was as the Son of Man and *not* as the Son of God. If everything He did was as the Son of God, we could only marvel at what He did. But since He did it as the Son of Man, He is our example of what a Spirit-filled Christian should look and behave like. We are called to become like Him and when He speaks, worlds are created.

When we release declarative prayers, we are releasing life or death into situations. Choose your words very carefully and ensure you are only releasing death into something that has no place in the Kingdom of Heaven (i.e., sickness and disease, poverty and lack, lies and deception). Speak only words of life to people regardless of their behavior or nature. Never speak words of death or witchcraft control over people. Remember, you will be held accountable for every idle (unprofitable) word you speak. The principles of stewardship apply here. To those who are faithful with their words, they will receive greater authority in their words.

I like to combine petitioning prayer with declarative prayer. I will first ask the Lord for what I need, but then I pray a declarative prayer and decree the release of that provision from the Kingdom of Heaven into my life. I find this works well regardless of whether I am praying for someone's healing or for money to make payroll.

Praying in the Spirit

If there is anyone who knows how to pray, it is the Holy Spirit. Since He lives in us, He knows what we need. Since He is Lord and God, He knows the heart of the Father. He also knows the Son, the One who lives to make intercession for us. We couldn't ask for a better advocate to pray for us. With Him praying for us to the Father, and Jesus interceding for us, the cards are all stacked in our favor.

The subject of the baptism of the Holy Spirit and praying in tongues is beyond the scope of this book. It is also one which will bring schisms very quickly in theology. This is not a book on theology, but one on the practice of applied Christianity. Rather than discuss this subject, I will just say if you haven't received your heavenly prayer language yet, then I highly suggest you seek out ministries that specialize in helping people receive the baptism of the Holy Spirit and can help you release your heavenly prayer language.

There is an old saying in the Body of Christ, some things are easier caught than taught. I believe praying in tongues is one of these things. Many people are great at riding bicycles, but relatively few people are good at teaching novices how to ride a bicycle. Find someone who is very good at helping other people receive this very powerful gift of the Holy Spirit.

When praying in tongues, I like to combine this type of prayer with the power of visualization, which is a spiritual technique in itself. If I am praying for a client to receive $50K in cash in order to make payroll, I will visualize the $50K in cash or check while I am praying in tongues. This helps keep my mind focused while my spirit man is praying. My mind doesn't know what my spirit man is praying, since it is a mystery, but I know that my mind and my spirit man are working together with a common cause. How does that work? I don't have the faintest idea. But I know it works! The great thing about not being a theologian is I don't have to have all of the answers. If you are like my clients, you are looking for results and not explanations.

Prophetic Prayers

When we pray in tongues, the Holy Spirit prays for us. But sometimes, the Holy Spirit shows us *how* to pray. He will give us revelation on how to pray for a particular situation. This revelation may come in a vision, a dream, a prophetic word, our conscience, or His still small voice. When we pray in accordance to this revelation, we call this type of prayer a prophetic prayer.

Sometimes these prophetic prayers are meant to encourage people. The Lord may give a vision of someone who is struggling in their faith to believe their business will increase due to weariness caused by being in a lengthy "dry season." The vision may show hard ground being broken up and water coming from below the surface and watering the desert place. When we pray this prophetic vision, we are releasing something from the spiritual world into the physical world. In this case spiritual water or refreshing is being released into the business.

Prophetic acts are a type of prophetic prayer. A good example of a prophetic act is the battle of Jericho. The Lord told Israel to march around the city once per day for six days but to keep quiet while they were doing it. On the seventh day, they were to march around the city seven times and then let out a shout of victory. The Lord promised when they did this, their enemies' walls would fall down (Josh 6:3-5).

In the business world, I have seen prophetic acts that included dancing over bills spread out on the floor, drawing a line on the ground and then stepping over it to signify stepping into a new season, honoring people with gifts signifying submission to their authority, and creating symbolic checks that signified future pay checks.

Keep in mind you can't manufacture prophetic prayers. Prophetic prayers and prophetic acts work quite well when the Lord shows you how to pray. I have seen many people attempt to recreate someone else's prophetic prayer or acts and hope to see the same results they received. I am guilty of this myself. However, as a general rule it only works as originally directed. This is why it's called a prophetic prayer. The Lord told you how to pray for a particular situation and that is why it worked. When you try the same prophetic prayer over a different situation, it seldom works. When someone else hears about your success and attempts to use it on their situation, it also seldom works. Why? I don't know. Perhaps God does this so that we keep going back to Him with our prayers and don't become dependent on methodologies or ourselves for the answers.

Prayer of Agreement

"Again I say to you, that if two of you agree on earth about anything that they may ask, it shall be done

for them by My Father who is in heaven. For where two
or three have gathered together in My name, I am there
in their midst" (Matt 18:19-20).

The Greek word for agreement is the same word we use for a
symphony, when all musical instruments are playing in harmony. In
order for two or more people to be in agreement, they must not only be
praying for the same end result, but they must be walking in love,
unity, and peace with each other. It must reflect the same type of
agreement the Father, Son, and Holy Spirit have. You cannot pray with
people you are in strife with or hold in unforgiveness, and call that the
prayer of agreement.

In order to pray this way, we must know what we are praying for in
order to be in agreement. Our prayer must also be in agreement with
the revealed will of God. Additionally, our prayer must not violate the
free will of another person. We cannot pray for the failure of a
competitor's business in order for our business to succeed. This violates
the love commandment. We cannot pray a customer or prospect will do
something that benefits us but violates their free will of choice.

One of the most powerful type of prayer of agreement comes when
a husband and wife pray together in agreement. If you are a married
business owner, I highly suggest you and your spouse come together
each day to pray for each other, your marriage, your health, your
family, your finances, and your business. This could be for as little as
15 minutes each day, but the effectiveness of this type of prayer will be
seen quickly. However, this will also require husband and wife first
forgive each other and wipe the slate clean from previous hurts and
offenses that could hinder their prayers. The good news is this will
force you to get your relationship with your spouse right each day
before you start praying together.

Praying with intercessory teams, described later in this chapter, is
another type of prayer of agreement. Some of the greatest revivals in
the last few centuries were generated by a small number of people who
came together to pray for revival in the land. It doesn't take a large

number of people. Quality is better than quantity here. It is better to have a few people who walk in obedience and righteousness to the Lord and also walk in love, unity, and peace with each other. These few people will be able to move mountains with their prayers. The Lord has shown me that there is a multiplication of the anointing that takes place when people walking in agreement pray together.

Fasting Prayer

Most Christians are far more knowledgeable about fasting than they are experienced with fasting. Let's face it, fasting is tough. If it wasn't tough, they wouldn't call it fasting. They would call it something else. However, fasting has been proven to bring breakthrough in prayer when nothing else seems to work. When the disciples asked Jesus why they could not cast a demon out of a man, Jesus' response was "This kind can come out by nothing but prayer and fasting" (Mark 9:29 NKJV).

It has been said that fasting doesn't change God, it changes us. Fasting serves to strengthen our spirit man while crucifying our flesh. The screaming sound you hear when you fast is the sound of your flesh being crucified. Fasting also serves to cleanse your spirit, soul, and body. It removes the toxins from your body while removing the toxins from your soul. Fasting will lessen any doubt and unbelief you have and supercharge your faith at the same time. Fasting will allow you to hear the voice of the Lord more clearly and generally opens up more dreams and visions in the spirit realm.

Intercessory Prayer Teams

There is a growing trend in the business world of employing intercessors to pray for companies, their families, health, and finances. This is one of the core services our company provides to our clients, so I am going to explain why there is such an excitement and trend towards implementing intercessory prayer teams, how they work with business owners and CEOs, and some of the success stories we have seen as a result.

Regardless of the size of your company and your current position in it, you have probably reached the point where you don't have spare time. Your plate is full and you do not have the bandwidth to take on new roles and assignments, even in your own company. You do not have hours to spare each day to pray for yourself, your family, your employees, and your customers. If you are spending 30 minutes per day alone with the Lord in your personal worship time, 15 minutes per day praying for your needs, and an additional 15 minutes per day studying your Bible, you have already devoted more of your day to the Lord than the average business person.

This 60 minute daily goal of worship, prayer, and Bible reading is a goal I believe every business person should set. But even if you are successful at disciplining your time this way, this is probably not enough time to see the type of success in your business and personal life you are looking to achieve. It is certainly not enough time to engage in the spiritual warfare that will be needed to win the battle. This level of prayer will probably keep you in a defensive position and not allow you to take the offensive battle into the enemy's camp and take back everything he has stolen from you. Even if you are gifted in all spiritual aspects, you lack the time to do everything yourself. You might be able to do everything, but you don't have the time to do everything.

However, the chances are you are not gifted in all spiritual aspects and you cannot do everything. The Bible says we see in part and we know in part (1 Cor 13:9-12). Each of us has spiritual gifts that are distributed to us according to the Holy Spirit. No one is equally gifted in all of them. God has arranged the Body of Christ so **we need each other to succeed**. Just as we hire employees who have business skills we do not possess ourselves, it makes perfect sense to hire intercessors who flow in spiritual gifts that we do not possess ourselves.

Keep in mind that intercessors are not intended to replace your own prayer life and devotional time with the Lord. They are intended to *augment* your prayer time. Good intercessors should be praying with you and teaching you how to pray. Your own personal prayer life should be strengthened and enriched from what you will learn from them. The greatest success we have had in prayer is when our clients pray together with us on a weekly basis, and together onsite as much as possible. Where we have seen the least success is when our clients email us a list of things to pray for and leave the praying to us.

Intercessors are not meant to be a "Get Out of Jail Free" card. You cannot live a life of sin and expect the righteousness of your intercessors will keep you from experiencing any troubles in life. We once had a client who was looking for more of a magic genie than an intercessor. He wanted to live his life according to his terms and do whatever he wanted to do and expect his intercessors to keep him on good terms with the Lord. It doesn't work that way. Intercessors work best when the business owner is walking with the Lord and is obedient to the leading of the Holy Spirit on a daily basis.

As an example of how intercessors work with companies, we had a client that was getting ready to graduate from the Small Business Association's (SBA) 8(a) program. The rules of the 8(a) program say that in order to be awarded an 8(a) contract, the bidder must be certified as an 8(a) contractor on the day of the contract award. It doesn't matter when the proposal was submitted for the procurement solicitation, it only matters that they are qualified on the day of award. Since many of these Government procurements take months or even years to award, proposals turned in within the last year of the nine-year qualification period always have the potential for being a wasted bid.

Our 8(a) client was approaching their graduation date but still had three outstanding bids to different Government Agencies that had been submitted many months prior. Time was running out for them to be eligible to win these contracts. As we approached six weeks of the graduation date, I reminded our client that although we were praying these contracts would be awarded to them before their graduation date, it was imperative we keep our eyes on the Lord and not on the SBA for our provision. The Lord promised to provide for us, but He never promised to do it through the SBA 8(a) program. Win or lose these 8(a) bids, our faith needed to be in the Lord and Him alone for our provision. As long as we kept our hearts right, He would provide for our increase through contracts of His choice and His timing.

In the end, our prayers and faith were rewarded. The day before their 8(a) graduation date, our client was awarded all three contracts. Three awards in one day on three different bids. How's that for a batting average? If those contracts had been awarded just two days later, this company would not have been eligible to win those contracts. How is that for answered prayer!

Over the years, I have had the privilege of seeing many people receive answers to their prayers. Some were answered almost instantaneously and some took years to see the manifestation. Some answered prayer seemed almost mundane such as healings for headaches and sickness, hiring the right employees, and timely receivables in order to make payroll. Some of the answered prayers were more miraculous and include homes, businesses, contracts, restoration of family relationships, and babies for couples unable to conceive.

But the best answered prayer is always when the Lord gives us more of Himself. He has already given us Himself. And if He has already given us the best He has to give, how much more is He ready and willing to give us all things that pertain to godliness and righteous. He is ready to give us everything we need to fulfill our Kingdom assignment. He is ready to provide for us. He is just waiting for our prayers to invite His involvement.

> "We tend to use prayer as a last resort, but God wants it to be our first line of defense. We pray when there's nothing else we can do, but God wants us to pray before we do anything at all. Most of us would prefer, however, to spend our time doing something that will get immediate results. We don't want to wait for God to resolve matters in His good time because His idea of 'good time' is seldom in sync with ours."
>
> - Oswald Chambers[6]

Kingdom Business Success

Principles in Practice

Gary and Sue were a young couple who met in college and married soon after graduation. Like many young couples, they were trying to raise a family but seemed unable to receive God's best for their lives. Sue had several miscarriages. At one point, she received prayer from an internationally known minister for healing from those miscarriages. But even after prayer, she had another miscarriage.

Then, the Lord spoke to a business intercessor who knew Gary and Sue and gave specific instructions how to pray over her womb and release a prophetic word. The prophetic instructions included a prophetic prayer declaring Sue's destiny as someone who would be a spiritual mother to many and that she would have many children in the natural herself. Included in the prophetic prayer was the declaration "at this time next year, she would give birth to her first child."

Gary and Sue received and believed the prophetic prayer and approximately 11 months later, Sue gave birth to her first child. Since then, she has given birth to two more children. This is an example of a prophetic prayer. You could attempt to replicate it on other barren couples, but it probably would not work for them. As a general rule, you cannot manufacture prophetic prayers or borrow someone else's prophetic prayer.

Joel and Alice owned a small company with 30 employees and leased their facilities. They were also heavily in debt and had employee problems. They were struggling to keep their heads above water financially and to compound matters, their business loans were secured by their home. One day, they had a revelation that debt no longer had a hold on them. Debt was under their feet. As children of God, Jesus had died to set them free of the curse of debt. Of course, the bills and invoices that sat on their desks did not confirm this revelation, but they knew they were supposed to walk by faith and not by sight for their finances.

Joel and Alice decided to pray over their debt using a prophetic act. They placed their bills on the floor of the office and started to sing and dance over the debt as a prophetic act of victory. They decreed that they were debt free. They started praising and thanking the Lord for giving them the finances and business revenue increase to be totally debt free. During this same time period, they partnered with some business intercessors to help pray for them and their company.

Within one year of partnering with the intercessors and the prophetic act of praising the Lord for the unseen victory, they started to see increases in revenue and profit and the employee issues they had been facing, disappeared. Additionally, they were able to pay down their business debt to the point that they could remove the lien on their home. Their home was now debt free of their business. Within two years, they had increased their revenue and profits to the point where they were able to purchase their own building. Doors started opening for new customers. The Lord started bringing key people into their lives to help them go to higher levels of success.

It's easy to thank and praise the Lord after you start seeing success in your business. This takes no faith at all. But it takes faith to speak words of life into your business when you are heavily in debt, and to praise and thank the Lord as if that new life had already manifested in your business.

Roger and Pam were owners of a company that experienced a significant downturn during the recession of 2008. Over the next six years they struggled to stay afloat and had to lay off many good employees. In addition to their business, they also had another business/ministry and a non-profit ministry. The second business had a negative cash flow and the non-profit ministry was on hold pending an increase in their financial situation.

Looking to end this downward spiral, they partnered with some business intercessors to pray over their businesses and ministries. Within the first few months, they started to see significant success.

They started seeing their monthly revenue increase to pre-recession levels. Their business/ministry also started to show a profit.

During the first year, Roger, Pam, and their intercessors prayer-walked the land surrounding their non-profit ministry. The Lord renewed their vision and purpose of the land and began showing the next steps they would need to take in order to get their ministry off the ground and bring in the harvest. They prayed over the prophetic words and visions they had received over the years and began working on the tasks required to see this vision come to pass. They had renewed excitement about the future of their ministry.

At the end of the first year partnership with their business intercessors, Roger and Pam's business revenue increased approximately 40%. They were able to hire back many of the good workers they laid off during the recession. They went from a negative Net Income to a positive income and were able to pay bonuses for the first time in many years. The business/ministry continued to increase and for the first time, they had to consider what to do with the profit from this business/ministry. Perhaps one of the best blessings they received during this timeframe was a new sense of excitement over the dreams and visions the Lord showed them about their future, and the increase He was planning to bring in their lives.

Carl and Barbara owned a construction company and hired a business intercessor to pray for their company. They had bid upon one construction project and won the contract. However, between the time of the proposal bid and the contract award, the price of steel had gone up significantly. The difference between their proposal bid price and the current price of the steel meant they would not only forgo any profit on this project, but it also looked like they were going to lose money even before the work began.

Carl and Barbara's business intercessor started to pray over this construction project and sought the Lord for wisdom on what to do with this business opportunity. Should they perform the contract at a loss, back out of the contract, or was there another solution to this problem? The intercessor received a revelation from the Lord to "declare the price of steel under the contract price." Carl and Barbara and their management team started to pray that the price of steel would drop well below the current price of steel and down to the price bid on the project. Within a couple of weeks, they were able to find another source for the steel that was below market price and much closer to the price they had bid on the contract. They were able to complete the project and make a profit on the contract.

We have the Wisdom of Almighty God living inside of us. He has the answers for any problem we can encounter in our lives and businesses. We just need to seek Him and hear His voice on how to resolve these problems. He wants us to win. He wants us to succeed. He delights in the prosperity of his servants (Psalm 35:27).

Questions for Reflection

1. Does prayer tend to be something you do only when all other efforts fail, or do you pray throughout the day as if you were working with the Lord?

2. On a scale of one to ten, how much faith do you have that God will answer your prayers? Does the amount of time you spend each day in prayer reflect your faith, or lack of faith, that God will answer your prayers?

3. How much time do you spend each day in your personal worship/devotional time with the Lord? Same question for your daily prayer time and Bible reading? Are you alone when you pray or do you pray with your spouse, intercessors, or management team?

4. Have you considered employing a team of intercessors to pray for you, your family, and your business success?

Chapter 12

Wisdom, Understanding, and Knowledge

"How blessed is the man who finds wisdom and the man who gains understanding. For her profit is better than the profit of silver and her gain better than fine gold" (Prov 3:13-14).

Decisions, decisions, decisions. It has been said that where we are in life today is based upon the decisions we made yesterday[1]. Imagine, if every decision you ever made in your personal life and business was based upon hearing from God. Do you think you would be more successful in your business, marriage, relationships, and finances than you are today?

What if there were some techniques you could incorporate in your everyday prayer life that could help you discern the voice of the Lord more clearly than you have ever heard Him before? Now imagine your future based upon this new "hearing" capability. How successful would your future look now?

If there is a believer's edge in the Kingdom of Heaven over our non-believer competitors, it should be in the area of divine revelation. If we are truly led by the Holy Spirit in all of our decisions, we cannot help but be successful in our business and personal lives. The fact that we have struggled for so long is a sign we have not been making our decisions based upon the leading of the Lord. Sadly, we have been making decisions the same way non-believers make them and then wondering why we don't get better results than they do. Isn't that absurd!

In this chapter, we are going to look at the various ways the Lord speaks to us so you can better discern how and when the Lord is speaking to you. We will look at some practical techniques you can use to present your questions to the Lord, how to wait for the answers, and to discern when those answers are presented back to you by the Lord.

Kingdom Business Success

In addition, we are going to learn the difference between wisdom, understanding, and knowledge as it pertains to your business and how the Holy Spirit, your spirit man, and your soul interact to give the answers and solutions you are seeking.

Defining Wisdom, Understanding, and Knowledge

In the Kingdom Assignment Chapter, I referred to finding your Kingdom assignment as "doing the right thing." I stated that many times, business people are doing the right thing but using the wrong business model. I referred to this plight as "doing the right thing the wrong way." I gave examples where Donald Trump, Bill Gates, and the McDonald brothers changed their original business model and how the change in their business model made the difference between doing well and becoming wealthy.

But how do you know your Kingdom assignment? How do you determine the correct business model? How do you become the best at what you are doing? The answer lies in seeking wisdom, understanding, and knowledge.

In the English language, we often use the terms wisdom, understanding, and knowledge synonymously. However, in the Bible these terms have different meanings both in the Greek and in Hebrew. Since there are many scriptures in the Old Testament where wisdom, understanding, and knowledge are mentioned separately, I am going to use the Hebrew definitions for these terms. But first, here are two examples which use all three terms in the same scripture, showing they mean different things biblically:

> "And He has filled him with the Spirit of God, in wisdom, in understanding and in knowledge and in all craftsmanship; to make designs for working in gold and in silver and in bronze" (Ex 35:31-32).

"By wisdom a house is built, and by understanding it is established; and by knowledge the rooms are filled with all precious and pleasant riches" (Prov 24:3-4).

In Hebrew, wisdom or *hokmāh* is the knowledge and ability to make the right choices at the opportune time.[2] Wisdom is knowing what to do and when to do it. It is the key to decision making and making the right choices that will affect your future. Understanding or *rbûnāh* is the ability to come to understand and to reason, perceive, or discern the fruit, increase, or revenue from wisdom.[3] Knowledge or *da át* is the ability to know intimately and experientially.[4]

I know it sounds like I am splitting hairs here, but let's go back and look at the Bill Gates/Microsoft story to understand how wisdom, understanding, and knowledge pertains to figuring out what you should be doing (your Kingdom assignment), how you should be doing it (your business model), and how to become the very best at what you are doing (experience) so that you can take the mountain of influence the Lord has called you to rule.

If you remember, when IBM came to call on Microsoft, Bill was developing BASIC language interpreters for PCs. When IBM asked Bill if he would also develop an operating system for their upcoming PC, he had several choices to make. He could have said "No, that's not our expertise" and left IBM to solve their own problem. He could also have referred them to another company, or he could have said "Yes," which is the answer he finally gave IBM.

Wisdom told Bill an opportunity existed in developing this PC operating system. But was this opportunity something Microsoft should be pursuing? Understanding told Bill there were only a few companies that had a PC operating system at the time. The fact IBM refused to develop one themselves, even though they had developed operating systems for mainframe and minicomputers, told Bill that even though he lacked knowledge and experience to build this operating system, there were very few people who did. Should he stay in his current area

167

of software expertise or venture out in the unknown? Making this decision is what wisdom is all about.

Once Bill decided to take on the challenge of building a PC operating system, how would he go about doing it? He could have developed one from scratch. After all, he was a very smart programmer with a keen mind. However, that keen mind gave him the understanding to purchase an existing PC operating system already proven and modify it to meet IBM's requirements. That decision involved his reasoning and intellect. This is what understanding will do. Understanding will combine God-given wisdom with reasoning to gain a deeper level of wisdom than is generally available without the use of the mind. Wisdom will often give a big picture but understanding will often provide the details of how to execute the wisdom.

Since Bill did not have intimate knowledge or experience with PC operating systems, along with purchasing the existing PC operating system, he also hired several of the key people from the developer to come work for him. These key people gave Bill the experiential knowledge he would be lacking if he only purchased the software product. Bill was smart enough to know it would take years to catch up on the knowledge of PC operating systems even if he had one himself. In order to become great at something you must leave the classroom and become intimately knowledgeable and experienced in your field. There is no substitute for the type of knowledge which comes from years of trial and error.

If you are going to take your mountain for the Lord, you are going to have to go beyond a big picture revelation of what God has called you to do. It is great to reach the point where you can say you have discovered your purpose in life and know what you should be doing. This is the wisdom which is needed to know your Kingdom assignment. However, in order to figure out *how* to do what you are called to do, it will require a more detailed level of wisdom and require you to engage your mind and intellect in this project to figure out the details of your assignment. You will then have to combine hard work and good stewardship of your assignment to get the type of intimate and experiential knowledge which will distinguish you from your competitors. We often talk about how we need wisdom for our decisions, but what we really need is wisdom, understanding, and knowledge. Now, let us look at how God sends us this wisdom and understanding and some practical exercises to increase our ability to hear from God.

How God Speaks to Us

Spiritual Ears to Hear

If you are having trouble hearing God speak to you, perhaps you are listening with the wrong ears. As the omnipotent God of the universe, God is not limited in how He communicates. He could speak to you in a voice which would be audible to your human hearing, but that is a mechanism He seldom uses. Although the Bible does record people hearing the audible voice of God (Matt 3:17, Luke 9:35, John 12:28) and people in current times have told stories of having heard His audible voice, don't count on that being the major source of your divine revelation. God is a Spirit (John 4:24) and the primary way He will speak to you is through your spirit man.

Before discussing the various ways God speaks to us, it is necessary to understand who we are to understand the type of ears or antenna we have been given. It is often said that man is a triune being: spirit, soul, and body (1 Thess 5:23). We are a spirit, we have a soul, and we live in a body. When we became born-again, the Holy Spirit came and resided in our spirit man. Our spirit man is somehow connected to our mind and the Holy Spirit speaks through our spirit man. However, the god of this world has blinded the minds (or spirit man) of unregenerate man (2 Cor 4:4). While in our fallen state, our conscience (our spirit man) has become seared (1 Tim 4:1-2). After becoming born-again, it takes time to learn how to hear the voice of our conscience or spirit man speaking to us.

Kingdom Business Success

There are some who believe that in addition to our five physical senses we possess five corresponding spiritual senses. I also agree with this theory but it is hard to make a scriptural case for it. But regardless of whether or not man has spiritual eyes and ears which we have yet to rediscover and learn how to use, **the primary channel you will receive revelation from God will be through the Holy Spirit – your spirit man – your soul connection**. This will require you to maintain a tender spirit in order to ensure you can hear what the Spirit is saying through your spirit man.

> "But the natural man does not receive the things of the Spirit of God, for they are foolishness to him; nor can he know *them,* because they are spiritually discerned" (1 Cor 2:14 NKJV).

Man's original sin led him to eat of the tree of the knowledge of good and evil. Since then, man has worshipped knowledge over Truth. Knowledge is discerned through our five physical senses while Truth is discerned through our spirit man. Man has given greater credence to the information he receives through his five physical senses than the information he receives from his spirit man. The laws of stewardship apply here and eventually, fallen man largely lost his ability to hear his spirit man.

Where does the mind fit into revelation? The mind is part of the soul. The spirit man *receives* revelation while the mind *processes* the revelation. The reasoning faculties of our mind are necessary to work with our spirit man in order to get understanding and to experience knowledge. Now, here are some of the more common ways God "speaks" or provides revelation to us.

The Word of God

Everyone is looking for wisdom from God, but few have the time to seek His revealed will contained in the Bible. This is ironic, since the Word of God is not only the most common way the Lord speaks to us, but it is also the most trusted way of receiving revelation of His will.

Why? Many of the other communications channels described below which the Lord uses to speak to us, can also be counterfeited by the enemy. The Bible tells us not to believe every spirit but to test the spirits to see whether they are from God (1 John 4:1). The primary way we test the spirits is to see whether or not they line up with the Word of God. But in order to do this, we need to be intimately familiar with the Word of God.

Since the Bible is its own best interpretation, the best way to understand one scripture in the Bible is to understand every other scripture in the Bible. This requires studying the entire Bible and not just a few favorite passages. I highly recommend every Christian business person use a daily reading Bible plan such as the one available in The One Year® Bible.[5] This is also available online and can be downloaded to a smart phone in a pdf or audio version. By reading approximately five pages per day, this plan will allow you to read the entire Bible in one year's time. If you fall behind in your reading, and we all do, you'll know exactly how far you are behind and how much doubling up you need to do to catch up. You can change the translation each year to help you get a deeper understanding of the Word and to keep your reading fresh. I have personally used The One Year® Bible plan for thirty years and have not heard or seen any other plan that has as much success for keeping people engaged in reading the Bible on a regular basis.

One common way the Lord will speak to us about our current problems and situations is through a *rhēma* word. The *rhēma* word is referred to as the sword of the Spirit (Eph 6:17) and is also considered a "quickened" word,[6] and the word that builds our faith (Rom 10:17). When God speaks a *rhēma* word through the reading of the Bible (His *logos* word), it will often seem as if the scripture is in bold type font. Even if you are familiar with the scripture, you will find yourself going back again and again reading the same scripture as if this was the first time that you have seen it. Sometimes, it seems like the hand of God is pulling my face down to the Bible to take a closer look at the scripture. However this *rhēma* word comes to you, this is probably the Lord speaking to you about a current situation in your life for which He is

171

trying to give you the answer to a question you have been asking. It is also a very safe way of receiving revelation. You are receiving a word from God through the Word of God. But, if you are not reading your Bible, you will miss this "voice" of God.

The Inward Witness or Conscience

As mentioned earlier, the most common way God will speak to you is through the Holy Spirit – your spirit man – your soul connection. When you became born-again, it was your spirit man that was regenerated and became "the new man." The Holy Spirit came to abide in your spirit man (John 14:17, 1 John 2:27). Your spirit man hears the voice of the Holy Spirit and communicates with your soul (mind, will, and emotions).

This communication with your spirit man will often lack any words but have a feeling or sense to it. When you don't feel right about something and have a "check in your spirit", you might feel unsettled or even in extreme cases nauseous. It doesn't feel right even if you don't know why you feel that way. On the other hand, you may feel very good about something. There is a good feeling and you have peace about the idea. When you feel good about it, you have an inward witness that this idea is from God.

I like to describe the voice of my spirit man, the inward witness, as "a knowing." I will frequently know something and not know how I knew the information. When people ask me "How did you know?" I respond, "I just knew." There are some techniques I will describe later in this chapter which will help you develop your ability to "hear" the voice of your spirit man. You want a tender spirit so you can always sense the right direction to turn when you are making the decisions which will affect the success of your life and your business.

One final admonition about this inward witness is that this is a communications channel which can be counterfeited by the enemy. You see, everyone has a spirit man; even the non-believers. Their spirit man has not become regenerated but is still in the fallen state and the

Holy Spirit has not come to abide in their spirit man. The unrenewed spirit man tends to focus on the mind of the flesh and not the mind of God. Demonic spirits can speak to their spirit man and provide revelation which can be either correct or incorrect, the truth or a lie. This is the communication channel used by psychics, fortune tellers, and wizards.

I mention this counterfeit communications channel since these demonic spirits can also communicate with *your* spirit man. So how do you know whether your spirit man is receiving communications from the Holy Spirit or demonic spirits? We are admonished to test the spirits to see if they are from God (1 John 4:1). This is why it is important to be well versed in the Bible. Does the revelation you are receiving line up with the Word of God? If not, reject it. Additionally, the Bible tells us "the wisdom that is from above is first pure, then peaceable, gentle, willing to yield, full of mercy and good fruits, without partiality and without hypocrisy" (James 3:17).

Lastly, make sure you are walking in *agapē* love and peace. Be very suspicious of what you hear from your spirit man when you are tired, angry, irritated, or upset with a person or a situation. Allow yourself time to calm down, get some rest, and allow the Lord to show you His perspective on what is going on in your life. When you are in a peaceful state and walking in love, then you can trust the revelation you are receiving from your spirit man.

The Inward Voice or Still Small Voice

While the inward witness can be characterized as a feeling or a knowing, what it lacks is an actual voice. But your spirit man *does* have a voice and sometimes you can hear it. This is often called the "still small voice" which comes from the story of Elijah running to Mount Horeb after fleeing Jezebel:

> "Then He said, "Go out, and stand on the mountain
> before the LORD." And behold, the LORD passed by, and
> a great and strong wind tore into the mountains and

broke the rocks in pieces before the LORD, *but* the LORD *was* not in the wind; and after the wind an earthquake, *but* the LORD *was* not in the earthquake; and after the earthquake a fire, *but* the LORD *was* not in the fire; and after the fire **a still small voice**. So it was, when Elijah heard *it,* that he wrapped his face in his mantle and went out and stood in the entrance of the cave. Suddenly a voice *came* to him, and said, "What are you doing here, Elijah?" (1 Kings 19:11-13 NKJV).

The inward voice works similarly to the inward witness; through the Holy Spirit – your spirit man – your soul connection. However, instead of a feeling or a knowing, you hear a still small voice that will probably sound like …your voice. That is the voice of your spirit man speaking to you.

Similar to the inward witness, this still small voice can be counterfeited by the enemy. When people are demonized and they "hear voices," they are probably hearing an inner voice through their spirit man which is originating from a demonic spirit. The same admonition for hearing the inner witness applies here. Make sure you are in a peaceful state and walking in love, then you can trust the inner voice you hear coming from your spirit man.

Mental Images, Visions, and Trances

The common denominator of these three sources of revelation is that all three communications channels involve receiving revelation through pictures or sight. Additionally, many times people talk about having received a "vision" from the Lord when they may be referring to a mental image. Let us look at the similarities and differences.

Mental images are the most common way God will speak to someone through a pictorial revelation. If you want to know what a mental image looks like, remember when you were a child and someone read you a bedtime story. Children's stories are written in a way to encourage children to imagine or see mental images of the story being described. If that is too long ago to remember, read the description of a thick, juicy, perfectly marbled, sirloin steak, seared to perfection and served alongside sautéed mushrooms and glazed onions. The mental image that came to the screen of your mind came from your mind. You mind created that mental image after processing the description of the steak. Over the years, you have had many mental images so this one should be easy to understand.

However, your mind can also receive revelation through your spirit man through the Holy Spirit – your spirit man – your soul connection. Your spirit man can speak to you not only through an inner witness and an inner voice, it can also speak to you through mental images. How can you tell the difference between a mental image from the Lord and one that is created by your mind? Good question. Where was your mind before receiving the mental image? If it was on the Lord or you were praying for someone you loved, it's pretty safe to say this image was the Lord speaking to you. Similar to the other communications channels, you will learn you can trust these mental images when you are walking in peace and love.

Whereas a mental image will show up on the screen of your mind, a vision will show up on ...another screen. This screen will often look somewhat off-center to the screen of your mind and is often more three dimensional than the screen of your mind. What is this screen? Although some believe this is simply a stronger picture played on the screen of your mind, I believe these visions are being seen through your "spiritual eyes."

Visions can be literal or figurative and are often much stronger and will last longer than a mental image. They tend to be closer to the quality of picture you would see with your natural eyes than what you get with a mental image. Sometimes, you can see an object in a vision and also see *through* the object to see what is behind the object you are seeing. This ability to see through an object is something you generally will not see in a mental image of your mind. Often times, visions and an inner witness are received simultaneously. For example, you have a vision of a person and there is a sense of "knowing" that this event happened in the past, or will happen in the future. The Lord may impart other information through an inward witness to give you the background information on what you are seeing in the vision.

The difference between a vision and a trance is the suspension of the physical senses. In some books, a vision in which the person has cognizance of their physical senses is referred to as an *open vision*. In a *trance*, the person's mind is largely shut down and although the body is receiving sensory input from the five senses, the mind is not processing the data and therefore gives the effect that there is no physical sense, thereby giving greater awareness to the vision being seen while in the trance. If this description doesn't make any sense, don't worry. You probably will not be having too many trances.

There are some exercises I will describe later in this chapter which will help you tune your ability to hear the voice of your spirit man through pictorial images. You may not always be able to dial up a vision when you are looking for direction from the Lord, but I will show you how you can clear your screen and then trust what you are seeing. This will help you in your decision making ability and improve your success.

Dreams

Dreams are similar to mental images. Everyone has had dreams and are familiar with them. Similar to mental images, not all dreams are from God. Dreams can originate in your mind, or they can come from your spirit man. They can be influenced by both the Holy Spirit and other spirits. An additional challenge of dreams is they can include elements which are from both God and your soul, making it challenging to figure out which part of the dream is from God and which is from your soul.[7] If that is not challenging enough, dreams are generally intended to be interpreted symbolically or figuratively and not literally.

Many books have been written on dream interpretation and that subject is outside the scope of this book. I will give a few pieces of advice I have learned about interpreting dreams. The first piece of advice is although these books on dream interpretation are helpful, the Holy Spirit is your best guide to interpreting your dream. Pray over the dream and ask Him to tell you what the dream meant. Keep a journal to write down not only your dream but also the interpretation He provides you over time. Second only to the Holy Spirit, you are the best person to interpret your dreams. If you see a boat in your dream, you will find an interpretation of a boat in many dream interpretation books, but more importantly, what does the boat represent to you? In the absence of revelation from Holy Spirit, this is how you should interpret the boat.

Dreams that come from God tend to be stronger and memorable than natural dreams. They might even be repeated. Although I mentioned dreams can include elements that come from God and our soul, in a true spiritual dream from God, every element of the dream is important. That is a revelation the Lord gave me as I asked Him for help interpreting one of my dreams. Every time He asked me a question about the dream, He replied, "That was important." In fact, He told me quite explicitly that in a spiritual dream, every element in the dream is an important detail.

Some people keep a journal and even a voice recorder near their bed to capture their dreams. It is important to write down the dream as soon as you awake, especially since you might fall back to sleep and have another dream and have trouble reconciling the two dreams.

Open and Closed Doors

We have all had doors of opportunities open up for us in life. Looking backwards, we can often see clearly the Lord's hand was in the open door of opportunity. Conversely, we have all experienced the disappointments which came when doors of opportunities we were seeking were closed to us. Later on, we may have sensed the Lord was keeping us from going down a path that would have been destructive if we had pursued it, or simply because the Lord had a better plan for us than the one we were pursuing. We refer to these communications channels as open and closed doors.

The concept of open and closed doors comes from the key of the house of David that has been given to Jesus to open doors no man can shut, and to shut doors no man can open (Isaiah 22:22, Rev 3:7). Open and closed doors seems to be an elementary way God "speaks" to his children, especially when they are young and have yet to learn how to discern His voice. However, open and closed doors can also be counterfeited by the enemy, and I have seen as many clients make wrong decisions through open and closed doors as I have seen use them to make correct decisions about their life and business. This is especially true in the area of open doors of business opportunities.

I have seen many Christian business people walk through an open door of opportunity just because it looked attractive. Frequently, these open doors involved some type of "get rich quick" scheme that was supposed to help them get more clients, more business, greater prestige, more money, or more success in a faster period of time than the path they were currently on. The results of following these get rich schemes are always depressing.

Although open and closed doors are a way God speaks to us, they should never be used by themselves to make an important decision about your life or your business. Always seek confirmation from the Lord for His will in this situation. Pray about the opportunity until you believe you have heard clearly from the Lord on the matter. The best way to use open and closed doors is to pray the Lord controls them. If an open door lies ahead of you, pray if this opportunity is not the Lord, He will close the door to you. At the same time, if a door is closed, pray the Lord will open it to you, at the right time. By faith and patience, I have seen the Lord open doors to opportunities impossible in the natural and seen Him close doors that looked awfully good, but in the end would have resulted in less than His best. Sometimes those doors opened up years later after persistent prayer. But when the Lord finally opens these doors, no man can shut them.

Prophecy

Prophecy is the Holy Spirit speaking to you through another person for the purpose of edification, exhortation, and comfort (2 Peter 1:21, 1Cor 14:3). As believers we are called to covet the spiritual gifts but especially the gift of prophecy (1 Cor 14:1). The subject of the prophetic ministry and your involvement in it is beyond the scope of this book. However, I would like to cover some important concepts you will need to keep in mind when *receiving* prophetic ministry from someone else, especially as it pertains to your ability to make decisions in your personal life and business.

All prophetic words include three basic components: the revelation, the interpretation, and the application of the prophetic word.[8] Revelation is simply the message the person "heard" from the Holy Spirit. No matter how gifted or anointed the prophetic person is, we all see in part, know in part, and prophecy in in part (1 Cor 13:9-12). None of us are infallible at hearing the Holy Spirit correctly.

Even if the prophetic person gets the revelation of the prophetic word correctly, there is another opportunity for error in the interpretation of message. When given an interpretation, ask the receiver of the prophetic word to describe exactly what they felt, heard, or saw. Most likely, they already made an interpretation of the revelation and you want to be able to separate out the revealed message from the Holy Spirit and their interpretation of the message. Then ask them for their interpretation of the message. If their interpretation of the message is different than your interpretation, ask the receiver of the message to explain their interpretation of the message. Don't be afraid to ask them, "Why did you interpret it that way?"

The reason you are asking these questions is not to challenge their prophetic gifting, but to ascertain whether they told you everything about the revelation they received. This is frequently the case when a message comes through multiple communications channels. Many times when someone has a vision, dream, or an inward voice, they also have an inner witness to the revelation. They might see something and know that the revelation refers to something in the past or the future. How did they know? That information was probably not in the dream or vision. They probably didn't hear a voice saying "This pertains to something in the future." So, how did they know? They may have received an inner witness along with that dream or vision. However, when they gave you the revelation, they left the inner witness part out of the revelation and now you hear their interpretation which includes the knowledge that this refers to something in your future. And you can't figure out how they reached that conclusion.

What do you do when your interpretation is different than theirs? Go with your own interpretation, but file their interpretation away. It is possible they might be right, but interpretation of prophecy is often where prophetic people start drifting into error. If God is going to send you a message through someone else, He knows how to word the message in a way it will make sense to you, even if it doesn't make sense to the prophetic person receiving the message.

The application of the prophetic word is another area where errors can be made. Once you receive the prophetic message, what do you do with it? That is a good question. Seek a Word of Wisdom from the Lord on what to do with this prophetic word to apply it correctly to your situation. Hopefully, the person who received this prophetic message from the Lord has already sought a Word of Wisdom before giving you the prophetic message and can give you both the message and the instruction on how to use it. But if not, seek the Word of Wisdom yourself from the Lord on how to apply this prophetic message to your current situation.

As a Christian business owner, I suggest you surround yourself with people with strong prophetic gifting. This is especially true for your intercessory prayer team. Although there is little you can do about how well they receive the prophetic message, you are still the one responsible to ensure the prophetic word is received, interpreted, and applied correctly.

Interpretation of Tongues

As discussed in the Prayer Chapter, the concept of praying in tongues is one which is fairly divisive in the Body of Christ. I am not going to debate the topic theologically, but instead show you how to use the gift of tongues and the interpretation of tongues to receive wisdom and understanding for your personal life and business through some practical exercises. Needless to say, this will require you have already been baptized in the Holy Spirit and have received your heavenly prayer language (tongues). If not, then I highly suggest you seek out ministries that specialize in helping people receive the baptism of the Holy Spirit and releasing their heavenly prayer language.

"For he who speaks in a tongue does not speak to men but to God, for no one understands him; however, in the spirit he speaks mysteries. Therefore let him who speaks in a tongue pray that he may interpret" (1 Cor 14:2, 13 NKJV).

The Bible tells us in these two scriptures that no man understands the gift of tongues because it is a spiritual language. It is a spiritual language between you and God that no man or demonic spirit can understand. The Bible also tells us we can pray for the interpretation of the tongue. Whatever mysteries of wisdom and hidden knowledge were communicated between your spirit man and God, can be revealed by the Holy Spirit to your spirit man. If that communications channel sounds familiar, it should. It is the Holy Spirit – your spirit man – your soul connection we have already discussed.

"A plan in the heart of a man is like deep water, but a man of understanding draws it out" (Prov 20:5).

Later in this chapter I am going to give you a couple of practical exercises you can do, either alone or with a group of intercessors, that will show you how you can receive wisdom and understanding from God through the gift of interpretation of tongues. You will be the man or woman of understanding who draws out wisdom from the deep waters inside of you. These exercises work so well, they will convince you of the power of praying in tongues.

Practical Exercises to Help You Discern The Voice of God

The Lord wants you to hear his voice clearly. He has no problem with creating games and exercises to help you discern His voice over the noise of this world. Here are some examples of ones I have used myself.

1. **Ask the Lord to Speak to You About Something Simple -** Practice asking the Lord to speak to you about something fairly mundane and something which you are not emotional about. As a management consultant, I spent many days in client's buildings. These buildings tend to be large with multiple elevators. The standard elevator group has six elevators; three on one side of the corridor and three on the other side. I would ask the Lord to show me which elevator door would open first. I had to learn to disregard my eyes or ears as they would see lights and hear sounds in the elevator shaft that would lead me to the wrong decision. Most of the time, the Lord would speak to me through an inner witness to tell me which elevator would open first. I got to the point where I would "know" correctly almost every single time. On a more practical side, I learned to trust my inner witness for answers to real-time questions, which gave me greater confidence when the questions I was asking were important and had significant consequences.

2. **Ask the Lord to Give You A Revelation About A Specific Question** – It is very easy to contrive games and exercises which have binary or discrete answers (e.g., yes/no, bid/no bid, which elevator). A more challenging scenario is when you need revelation on a certain situation. Perhaps you are having issues with an employee and don't know why. Perhaps you know your business model is not working but you are not sure what the correct business model would look like. In these types of scenarios, I suggest you get alone with the Lord in your prayer

closet. Play some "soaking music" in the background and get in an atmosphere of worship. Spend about 15 or 20 minutes simply worshipping the Lord. He is Wisdom personified and you cannot help but receive wisdom when you are in His presence. After spending time in worship, close your eyes and try to picture a blank, white screen. Now try to picture the Lord while you are thinking about your problem. If you cannot picture Him, that's ok. Keep your eyes and heart on Him as you prayerfully ask Him for revelation on your problem. Pay close attention to what comes onto the blank screen during the next 15 minutes as often the Lord will show you a mental image or vision. He might also speak to you through an inner witness. If your eyes and your heart are on Him, you can trust what you are seeing, hearing, or feeling. You may only get a partial revelation of the answer. That is ok. You can repeat this exercise until you feel you have received the answer to your question.

3. **Learn How To Discern Between Your Mind and Your Spirit Man -** Many people with strong analytical abilities have trouble discerning between the voice of their mind and the voice of their soul. Without an "off switch," their reasoning faculties make it difficult for them to hear their spirit man since the voice of their mind is always speaking loudly. They are constantly *processing* information making it difficult to *receive* new information. These people have trouble picturing a blank, white screen because their mind is already working on something. It is very difficult for these people to *not* think about something. Here is a technique to discern between the voice of your mind and the voice of your spirit man. Using either the mundane question or blank white screen exercises above, take the time to discern exactly what your mind is working on. Write it down to prove you clearly understand what your mind is processing. As long as your mind in engaged in something totally unrelated to the question you are seeking answers to, this technique will work. If your mind is engaged in something, this preoccupation will show up on the white screen of your mind and in the

impressions you are receiving in your spirit man. Therefore, anything unrelated to what your mind is already processing that shows up on the white screen or in your impressions, should be what you are receiving from your spirit man. Subtract out the part of the revelation that has to do with what your mind was previously processing, and the rest of the picture or inner witness should be revelation coming from your spirit man.

4. **Fast For Greater Spiritual Sensitivity** - To really increase the volume of the voice of your spirit man and to turn down the voice of your soul and body, go on a 10-day juice fast. Why 10 days? After five days of fasting your appetite will leave you. Sure, you may have sympathetic pains every time you see an advertisement for a hamburger, but your hunger will have gone away. Your body will have removed a large amount of waste and toxins and you will start to feel the increase of your spiritual sensitivity and the decrease of your soul and body. You will start sleep soundly and have increased dreams and visions. By the 10th day of the fast, you will definitely see the benefits of fasting.

5. **Learn How To Recognize the Voice of Your Spirit Man** - Where does your spirit man reside and what does he sound like? Here is an exercise to increase your sensitivity to hearing your spirit man and knowing what he sounds like when he speaks to you. Get alone in a very quiet place and pray in tongues for about 20 minutes. Stay in an attitude of worship and keep your eyes and heart on the Lord while praying in tongues. At the end of the time period, stop praying in tongues and then listen very carefully. What do you hear? Although you stopped praying in tongues, you are probably still hearing the tongues. This inner voice you are hearing is your spirit man still praying in tongues. What does he sound like? Where in your body does the sound seem to be coming from? Now you know where your spirit man resides and what he sounds like!

6. **Learn How to Use Interpretation of Tongues to Draw From Your Spirit Man** – Here is an exercise to help your draw out revelation from your spirit man while praying in tongues. Get with a group of intercessors or Spirit-filled believers and pray in tongues for 20 to 30 minutes. You can pray over a certain subject, but this exercise will be more dramatic if you do not have a previous agenda while you begin praying in tongues. Before you start praying in tongues, ask the Lord to give your group the grace to pray in unity of the Spirit. After praying in tongues, ask the Lord to give your group a revelation on what you have been praying. Allow the group another 20 or 30 minutes to seek the Lord for a word. Have the people present their impressions and visions to the group and have someone write them down. They may come in single words, groups of words, or even sentences. After you have given the group sufficient time to seek the Lord for the interpretation of the tongues, start looking at the collective revelation that was written down. It should start coming together like a jigsaw puzzle. You will find that most of the revelation seems to be referring to the same topic, even though none of you had an agenda when you started praying in tongues. After you have done this exercise in a group setting a few times, try it alone. It will still work, but you will probably get much less revelation than you would get in a group setting. This exercise shows another good reason to make sure you are praying with a group of business intercessors on a regular basis.

Principles in Practice

Harold owned a services company well known in the commercial industry but was looking to expand in the Government contracting arena. He engaged me to help his company identify and pursue some Government contracts. At first, his team presented me with 10 different solicitations for which they felt they were qualified and were interested in obtaining the contracts. My experiential knowledge of the Government contracting industry led me to dismiss many of these opportunities. My understanding of my client's capabilities and their lack of experience in the Government arena and knowledge of the capabilities of their competitors, led me to dismiss the remainder of these 10 opportunities. While reviewing these opportunities, I was seeking wisdom from God as to which opportunity was the right one for them. After reviewing the 10 opportunities, I didn't "feel" good about any of them. There was nothing in my spirit man saying "This is the one."

I then asked Harold's team if these 10 opportunities were the only ones they had looked at. They told me they had looked at approximately 30 other opportunities but had dismissed those for various reasons. I asked them if I could review those 30 solicitations. While reviewing these 30 opportunities, I found three opportunities which I felt good about. One solicitation in particular seemed to stand out above the rest. The font on the paper seemed to be in bold font similar to a *rhēma* word. I felt I had received wisdom from God as to which opportunity to bid on.

I then sat down with Harold's team and asked them why they had decided to pass on these three opportunities which I felt good about. One opportunity would have required them to team with another bidder; one was a very attractive large contract that would attract many bidders; and the one which I had a *rhēma* impression on, I could tell they really didn't understand. They had several legitimate concerns about my choice. I explained to them I understood their concerns about the solicitation, but then explained that all of the reasons they felt were reasons to avoid the solicitation, my understanding and experiential knowledge told me it would be a good opportunity for them. This procurement would have few bidders. It was large enough to make some serious profit, but small enough that only a small number of companies would bid.

Wisdom told me that this was the solicitation the Lord was telling us to pursue. My understanding told me the concerns the client had could easily be overcome. My experiential knowledge told me some of the concerns they saw as red flags, were actually green lights to me.

After much discussion and prayer, we decided to pursue this opportunity.

Before submitting their bid on this solicitation, they asked me to read over their proposal. While reading it, the Lord gave me a mental image about something they had left out of their proposal. Additionally, I knew in my spirit their bid price was too high. I had an inner witness for an exact bid price that was about 15% less than their current bid price. I knew that even at the reduced price they would still be making a profit over 35%. Additionally, this contract would provide them a foot in the door with a new client, a Government Agency for which they had never done business before. They submitted their proposal as suggested and won the award without any further contract price negotiation. This is an example of how wisdom, understanding, and knowledge work together to win sales in the business world.

Chris and Simone owned a growing company and were in need of larger facilities. They were in the middle of a multiyear lease in their current building. They were considering approaching their landlord to see if he would be willing to sell them the building when another opportunity arose to buy a distressed property that appeared to be an incredible deal. After performing due diligence and after much prayer with their intercessors, they believed the Lord was giving them this opportunity to acquire this vacant building. In their eagerness to move forward as quickly as possible, they forgot the admonition from their intercessors to talk to their current landlord and have an attorney look at their existing lease, before submitting their offer on the vacant building.

Chris and Simone were able to negotiate and obtain financing to purchase the distressed property at an incredible price. God seemed to be all over this deal. They started the extensive renovations on their newly acquired building and when they were three months away from moving into their new facilities, they sent a letter to their current landlord stating they would be leaving the premises at the end of the year. However, if God was all over this deal, He forgot to tell their existing landlord, who quickly reminded them they had remaining years left on their lease, and he would be expecting immediate payment of the balance of the lease.

One of the intercessors suggested Chris and Simone go to their current landlord with their "hat in their hand" and ask for release from the terms of the lease. They should inform their landlord about the great opportunity they came across and ask him to release them from the remainder of the lease. If that approach didn't work, they suggested asking him how they could work something out to get out of the lease. Chris and Simone even considered offering the landlord help in finding a new renter. However, the meeting with the landlord never happened and very quickly the lawyers got involved. At this point, all communications between Chris and Simone and their landlord were terminated as per their attorneys.

The intercessors heard a very specific amount of money which should be offered to the landlord to settle this lease. However, the attorneys for both parties had figures very far apart. Over a period of several months and significant attorney fees, both parties came to a settlement within $2,500 of the figure the Lord had given the intercessors. Was the new building a God idea, wisdom from God? It probably was. But they probably missed the understanding of how God wanted them to get out of their existing lease. Chris and Simone may have moved too quickly and ended up with anxious months and expenses which were not part of the Lord's plan.

God will give you wisdom and witty ideas to bless you financially and help you to succeed. However, God's plans always have a timing associated with them. If you move ahead too quickly or lag behind, you may struggle to implement God's plan. The wisdom of God will make you smarter than your competitors. Understanding, will give you the details of how and when to execute the wisdom of God.

Theresa owned a small software development company. She owned all the IT equipment in their facilities including the PBX, servers, and routers. Although the equipment was hers, she hired Evan as a subcontractor to setup, configure, and maintain her IT equipment.

Evan provided his technology services to her on a Time and Material basis.

At one point, Theresa questioned a monthly invoice she received from Evan. She couldn't understand how it could be so high during a month when no new equipment was being installed and no configuration changes were being made to the equipment. Evan and Theresa argued over the invoice for about one month without being able to come to a resolution. Then, one Saturday, Theresa received numerous calls saying her company's servers seemed to be down. The emails weren't going through and the developers could not logon to the servers. After some investigation they discovered the reason they could not logon to their servers was because the servers were gone. It turns out, Evan had removed them from the premises!

Not wanting to report this to the police and wanting to get her developers writing software as quickly as possible, Theresa worked out a deal with Evan over the phone where she would pay a large portion of his invoice if he would quickly return the servers. She immediately cut a check and sent it to him via overnight mail and then waited for the servers to return. Although Theresa would call Evan each day to check on the status of the servers, he always seemed to have a reason why they couldn't be delivered that day, but would be returned the following day. After three days of playing this game, Theresa turned to me for advice.

While Theresa was telling me the story, I had both an inner witness and a mental image of Evan selling the servers to pay his bills. I told Theresa what the Lord had shown me and initially she was somewhat offended I would even suggest such a thing. However, the next day she called me to say she had talked to Evan and while he was stalling, she confronted him with the revelation I had given her. Evan confessed he had indeed sold the servers and couldn't return them. Theresa and Evan finally settled their differences without going to court. The wisdom of God will keep you from doing business with the wrong people, even the wrong Christian business people. The wisdom of God will also help you know events going on in your company, which will help you protect your financial investments.

Questions for Reflection

1. What decision stands out the most to you, in which the decision you made was based upon having heard from God? Wouldn't you like all of your decisions to stand out the same way?

2. On a scale of 1 to 10, how clearly have you learned to discern between the voice of your spirit man, your soul, and your body? Ask the Lord to show you what exercises you can do to increase your sensitivity to your spirit man while turning down the volume to your soul and body.

3. Think about the times you were most confident you knew the Lord was speaking to you about something. Through which communications channel (e.g., inner witness, inner voice, dream, or vision) did you receive this revelation? Which communications channel do you have the most experience and confidence when hearing the Lord? Which ones do you have the least experience and confidence?

Chapter 13

Spiritual Warfare

"From the days of John the Baptist until now the kingdom of heaven is forcibly entered, and violent men seize it for themselves" (Matt 11:12).

Bad things happen to good people. Have you ever thought there was someone up there who didn't like you or was out to get you? Well, it turns out you were right. When you became born-again, you were born into a war between the Kingdom of Heaven and the kingdom of darkness. Like it or not, you are called to be a warrior in this epic battle. The enemy of your soul did not lay down his weapons the day you went "all in" with the Lord. In fact, he may have intensified his efforts.

The topic of spiritual warfare is one that is highly divisive in the Body of Christ and fairly complex. The purpose of this section is not to provide you with a tutorial on spiritual warfare, but to help you understand how demonic forces and curses operate and the effect they *will* have in your life and business, and how you can minimize their ability to affect you by closing the entry doors that allow them legal access to your life and business. Knowing the strategies, tactics, and weapons of your enemy, and the strategies and weapons you have to counter the attacks will put you in a position to not only defend yourself, but permit you to take the offensive and bring the Kingdom of Heaven into your life and business.

What is spiritual warfare? Spiritual warfare is an invisible battle in the spirit realm involving a power confrontation between the Kingdom of Heaven and the kingdom of darkness.[1] Although this battle is seen in the spiritual realm, its effects are both seen and felt in the natural realm. The weapons of our warfare are spiritual and their consequences are displayed in the spirit realm, which then causes them to be manifested in the natural realm.

Kingdom Business Success

Where do these "bad things" or spiritual attacks originate from? Most spiritual attacks can be categorized as relating to either a curse or demonic oppression. Curses in the Old Testament were generally tied to judgments, oaths, and covenants. If you broke the oath of a covenant, you would be under a curse. Under the Mosaic Law, God provides an extensive list of specific curses which would come upon and overtake those who failed to keep His commandments (Deut 28:15-68). God says these curses shall come upon and overtake us. He does not say He will send these curses upon us. The inference is that these curses were already in the world due to the fall in the Garden. Whatever protection God was providing for his children against those curses would be removed. God doesn't send curses against us. The curses are already here in our fallen world.

Most of the spiritual attacks that occur due to curses do not happen through the spoken curses of man. The Bible says "a curse without cause will not alight" (Prov 26:2). Although there are people in the world practicing witchcraft and pronouncing curses on you and your business, for the most part, this is generally not the source of the spiritual attacks you are encountering.

The second major source of attacks we encounter comes from demonic oppression.[2] In order to simplify this complex topic, under the category of demonic oppression, I will include temptations, deception, vexation, bondage, and affliction. These attacks can affect believers and non-believers. These include attacks from within (against your spirit, soul, and body), and external attacks (attacks against your environment, city and nation, and your social and economic systems).

Although there are many curses that exist in our world, most of the spiritual attacks Christians will face will come from the category of demonic oppression. Why? Because, when we walk in obedience and abide in Him we are *largely* protected from the curses in the world, but demonic oppression is much harder to avoid if you are living in the world. It is even harder to avoid if you have unknowingly provided a legal right for the enemy to attack you.

In order for the enemy to have success in attacking you, he generally must gain some type of legal access to you through "open doors." When attacked, you must identify these open doors and then shut them. Most of these open doors in your life will come from one of the following channels: unforgiveness, personal sin, the sins of others, generational sins/curses, sins of those in covenant relationship with, and the fact that the Kingdom of Heaven is not yet fully manifested.

Unforgiveness is probably the most common source of open doors for demonic oppression. Unless we learn to forgive people the same way God forgives us, then we have not forgiven the person. "Make friends quickly with your opponent at law while you are with him on the way, so that your opponent may not hand you over to the judge, and the judge to the officer, and you be thrown into prison. Truly I say to you, you will not come out of there until you have paid up the last cent" (Matt 5:23-26). In this parable, the Lord is saying when there is an issue of debt due to offenses, we are to come to terms quickly with the one we are contending with. If you feel you are in prison and the devil is tormenting you, quickly come to terms (forgiveness) with the one who owes you, or the one you owe. If you don't, the Lord promises you will stay in the prison of torment until every penny is paid of those debts. You cannot afford to have any debts or to have someone be in debt to you. Cancel those debts today through true forgiveness. This forgiveness will shut the door which has allowed the enemy legal right to torment you.

Unrepentant and unrepented **personal sin** is probably the second most common source of open doors. Sometimes this is caused by ignorance of our sins. Many Christians become involved in occult practices, rituals, and objects at an early age. No one repents for something until they first understand what they have done is wrong. Ignorance to the Word of God is not bliss. Perhaps even worse than ignorance of our sins, is to reach the point of callousness where we start to accept sin in our lives. The Body of Christ has become calloused to sin and has started accepting behavior God does not consider acceptable. Rather than allowing the Holy Spirit to complete the work of perfection in us, we have found a plateau in the mountain and decided to camp there for a while. This callousness causes unrepentant sin in our lives which opens up a wide door for demonic attacks.

Can the victim of **the sin of others** be a sinner? Yes, quite frequently in fact. This type of sin is sometimes called the trauma sin or victimization sin. The victim did not commit the sin, but the way the victim processed the trauma results in them subsequently sinning. These victimization sins are quite common in the Body of Christ. The ministry of dealing with these soul/spirit wounds is often called inner healing or deliverance ministry. This is best administered with trained ministers who have a prophetic gifting. But unless these sins are dealt with, they will allow an open door for the enemy to torment you. It doesn't seem fair that the victim of a trauma should be punished for how they processed the trauma, but make sure you close the door to any openings by asking the Lord to help you put the traumas of your past aside, so you can walk in the abundance of the new life He has in store for you.

Generational curses associated with generational sins are often caused by unrepented sin by one or more of the ancestors. These associated curses can appear as proclivities towards the same type of sin (e.g., addictions, sexual immorality, anger) or they can appear as failure and death in one's life, family, and finances as the enemy appears to have an open door to kill, steal, and destroy things pertaining to your life. When dealing with generational sins and the resulting curses, similar to dealing with the sins associated with soul/spirit wounds, it is best to seek the help of a trained inner healing/deliverance minister. You want to be sure you are led by the Holy Spirit in identifying these sins. Once the sin is identified, confess and repent of the sin on behalf of yourself and your ancestors. Name the ancestors who were involved with this sin if you know their name, or if the Holy Spirit shows you the person. Once repented of, these open doors will generally close.

Another type of "other people's sins" that can open a door into our lives for demonic oppression are **sins of those we are in covenant relationship with**. Similar to the open doors described above, these are open doors which come into our lives and business through people we are in covenant relationship with. This covenant relationship allows the enemy a legal right to oppress your business through this open door. This means you need to be wise about who you enter into agreements with in the business world. You will need to discern the will of the Lord for the relationship. If the Lord wants you to enter into an agreement with a non-believer, there will be a grace to successfully complete the assignment. However, you should not be presumptuous about these business covenants and agreements and believe you will be automatically protected from any demonic oppression.

Keep in mind, the type of covenant agreements I am referring to in the business world would include business ownership, joint ventures, real estate, financing, wealth transfer, and major contractual purchases with people you are yoked with. I am *not* talking about buying materials from a supplier or selling your products to someone who is not a believer. The latter category does not create an obligation on your part for future commitments you may need to recuse yourself from. The latter category of relationship should not create any open doors.

The last type of open door that I will mention is the open door that exists because the **Kingdom of Heaven has not yet fully manifested** here on earth and the devil still has some authority and power in this world. For scriptural support, I use the storm on the lake Jesus quieted (Luke 8:22-25), Paul's thorn in the flesh (2 Cor 12:7-10), and the death of Stephen, one of the original deacons (Acts 6:6-7:60). There was no open door from sin in the lives of these three men, and yet Satan was able to oppress and eventually kill all of them.

Most of the open doors described so far are considered sin-based oppression and are caused by the sins of a believer or their ancestor. They could be sins of commission or omission. However, the enemy can also bring demonic oppression through temptations to sin, deception to believing something contrary to the Word of God, or outright demonic affliction. Temptations and deception are part of the spiritual war known as the "battle of the mind." The last category is simply demonic influence based upon the limited power and authority the devil and his demonic spirits currently have in this world.

In summary, defensive spiritual warfare can best be performed by repentance and forgiveness. Repentance would include repenting for your sins, and identification repentance for the sins of your ancestors, family, employees, and your government or nation. Forgiveness requires the remittance of the offense; to wipe the slate clean the same way the Lord forgives us. Offensive spiritual warfare generally requires binding (forbidding) and loosing (permitting) declarative prayers. The Lord has given us the power to legislate His government here on earth through the power of binding and loosing (Matt 16:19, 18:18).

The final admonition I would like to give regarding spiritual warfare is to not give credit to the enemy for every bad thing which happens. I believe giving him credit for things he did not cause is a form of worship. We are called to worship God and Him alone. In the midst of your storms, always keep your eyes and heart on Him and not your problems. Stop looking at the enemy and start looking at the Lord. It doesn't matter if your problems are caused by demonic oppression or not. The answers to your problems are *only* found in Him.

Principles in Practice

Gene and Karin had a struggling company troubled by employee issues. They even had one employee who had filed a grievance with OSHA over some minor work environment deficiencies. They struggled to find good employees who would stay with them. Their employees seemed to be a bunch of individuals rather than a team working cohesively together. Although they spent a considerable amount of time screening and interviewing new employees using multiple interviews and personality and skill assessments, they couldn't seem to put together a winning team of employees.

While prayer-walking over their property with their intercessors one day, they started to identify some of the spiritual issues. One of the intercessors sensed there was a familiar spirit watching from the rafters of the building. This familiar spirit seemed to be causing a spirit of division and distrust amongst the employees. Additionally, while praying over one of the desks, the Lord revealed that a former employee who had sat there in the past had been stealing from the company by giving company resources away. There was also a strong sense this person had been watching pornography from the company computer on this desk.

Armed with this discernment of where the enemy had found open doors in the company, Gene and Karin started praying with their intercessors over the offices, desks, building, and even the land where the building was situated. They used identification repentance to ask forgiveness for the sins of their current and former employees and for any sins on their part for not treating their employees with love and honor. They broke off all ties with familiar spirits associated with division, distrust, secrecy, confusion, and pornography. They invited the Holy Spirit to blow a fresh, cleansing wind into the building and blow out anything unclean or defiled. They prayed over their employees and released love, unity, favor, and blessings over each of them.

Almost immediately, they started to see changes in their company especially in the personnel issues. Some of the problem employees quit. Other employees started to step up their commitment to the company. They soon were able to hire new employees who were able to embrace the vision of the company and allow them to go to higher levels of success. The spiritual warfare was working. Light was displacing darkness in their company.

Sam and Halley had seen cyclical success in their business for years. Although they would have streaks of success in their sales and profits, they would also have streaks of setbacks and failures. When things were going well, they attributed their success to their righteousness and the faithfulness of God. When things were not going well, they attributed their demise to demonic oppression. Sam and Halley had been through some inner healing/deliverance ministry, but what that ministry seemed to do was fuel the idea that the reason for their lack of success was largely attributable to the enemy.

Sam and Halley hired intercessors to pray for their company. Although some victories were achieved, especially in areas regarding their family's health, their cycles of success and failure seemed to continue. Although Sam and Halley were convinced their problems originated outside of themselves, their intercessors believed their issues were largely self-inflicted. From Sam and Halley's perspective, the issues were being caused by demonic spirits which were nipping at their heels and eating their harvest. They believed their unsaved family members who were walking in New Age religion were speaking word curses and using witchcraft against them. Sam and Halley were convinced that whatever was causing their cycles of failure was coming from someone else or something else.

Although the intercessors engaged in spiritual warfare against these presumed demonic attacks, they came to the revelation that the issues which were causing these open doors were not coming from without, but were largely coming from within. The intercessors provided guidance that Sam and Halley needed to keep their eyes on the Lord and not on the devil or his demons. They advised them to seek the Lord with all of their heart, soul, and mind and not make the pursuit of sales and money their primary focus. Sales and money were supposed to be seeking them and not vice versa. Sam and Halley needed to spend more time worshiping the Lord and coming into His presence with praise and thanksgiving. Even if there was less to be thankful for in their current financial situation, they had much to be thankful for due to their previous seasons of success. They needed to focus on what the Lord was doing and what He had done and be thankful for it, and not complain about what they didn't have.

Sam and Halley needed to ask the Lord to give them the grace to love their customers, prospects, and employees the way the Lord loved them. The owners needed to look to see how they could bless these people and add value to their lives through their products and services. The more Sam and Halley poured into these people, the more of a harvest they would see from these customers, prospects, and employees.

Our greatest protection from the enemy comes from abiding in Him and He in us. By walking in love, obedience, and humility with God and man, we receive the protection only He can provide us.

Questions for Reflection

1. When a sequence of setbacks starts to occur in your life or business, do you normally assume these misfortunes are caused by you, God, or demonic activity? Do you normally assume you know the source of the misfortune, or do you seek the Lord to identify the source of these misfortunes?

2. Can you think of one instance of failure in your life or business you believe was attributable to a spiritual attack of the enemy? Thinking back over the situation, can you identify one or more open doors which allowed the enemy legal access to attack you at that time?

3. Do you have intercessors who are knowledgeable and experienced with spiritual warfare who can engage the enemy on your behalf, for yourself and your company? If not, who is the person in your company who has the most knowledge and experience with spiritual warfare? Do they have the time and experience to engage in spiritual battle?

Chapter 14

Financial Abundance

"Poverty is not the lack of money, it's the lack of God." - Judy Sullivan

How do you measure success? Jesus said He came so that you would have His *zōē* life and have it more abundantly (John 10:10). Are you living that abundant life? If so, how are you measuring this abundant life? If you don't know how to measure the type of abundance Jesus promised to give you, how do you know how much of it you have or are missing? How will you know you have achieved the success you are looking for?

I know this is not a rhetorical question because this is the primary reason people come to our ministry. They are looking for the abundant life, even if they are unsure of what that means. As part of our assignment, **we help CEOs partner with God for success to fulfill their God-given assignment on the earth, and prosper and grow in their personal life and business**. These CEOs may come to us because they are looking for more money and financial success, but we help them understand that in the Kingdom, the abundant life is multifaceted and can only be found by abiding in Him. However, we also acknowledge that at the end of the day, their financial situation must improve significantly if they are going to feel they are living the abundant life Jesus promised.

In this chapter, we are going to take a look at Kingdom principles for obtaining financial abundance. Everyone is looking for more money and wealth, and we will discuss principles that will bring abundance to your financial situation. But first, I would like to discuss a Kingdom perspective on money and wealth. Otherwise, you might end up with more money and wealth from reading this book, but not be able to answer the question above as to whether or not you are living the abundant life, or knowing how you would measure your success.

Kingdom Business Success

A Kingdom Perspective on Money

I have found Christian viewpoints and emotions on the topic of money run an extreme ambit from believing God wants everyone to be extremely wealthy to a monastic viewpoint that we should all be free of filthy lucre. Similar to many other theological debates, each side has identified scriptures to support their viewpoint.

But what did our King really say about the abundant life He came to give us? What did Jesus say about money and how it applies to our lives and to the advancement of His Kingdom here on earth? Was Jesus only talking about our spiritual life in the context of the abundant life promised in John 10:10, or was He including our souls, bodies, and material needs? I believe the answer to this question lies primarily on which paradigm you are using and your understanding of your assignment here on earth. Let's look at this question from a Kingdom of Heaven paradigm.

> "This is eternal life, that they may know You, the
> only true God, and Jesus Christ whom You have sent"
> (John 17:3).

In this scripture, Jesus is defining the *zōē* life He was talking about in John 10:10. In this scripture, Jesus is saying that outside of His abiding presence there is no such thing as an abundant life. You can have lots of money, but still live in poverty. You can have lots of money, but not be successful in life. As my business partner Judy Sullivan says, "Poverty is not the absence of money, it's the absence of God."

In John 10:10, the word translated *abundantly* is the Greek word *perissos* which means an overflowing amount or an extreme amount.[1] It is never used to characterize an amount that is just enough to get by. This is the type of financial abundance we are called to possess. An overflowing, extreme amount that will serve whatever needs we have in our Kingdom assignment, and then some. Although some of us may be called to be as wealthy as Bill Gates, Donald Trump, or Warren Buffet, all of us are called to have more than enough money to fulfill the call of God on our lives. There is no shortage or lack in the Kingdom of Heaven.

When we abide in Him, we see things from His perspective and not ours. Money and wealth have a Kingdom assignment and not one of personal greed. As we become more like Him, we realize abundance does not consist in our possessions, but in how much of Him we have in our lives (Luke 12:15). With Him in us, we can tap into the resources of Heaven and have whatever we need in His perfect timing. This I believe, is the Kingdom perspective on money and wealth.

How Do You Know When You Are Successful?

Let's go back to the question of "How do you measure success?" Regardless of your theology on money, you will need some type of metric to determine your level of success. The metric you choose will be determined largely by how you define success and what you believe your Kingdom assignment is now. This question of metrics should have been well defined and implemented by now, but you will find almost everyone is measuring money and *not* measuring their level of success in fulfilling their Kingdom purpose or assignment.

If you read the annual reports of most companies, they are measuring their success through financial statements. Financial statements are great at showing the financial health of a company. They are great at showing whether a company is making a profit or loss. But what they don't show is whether or not the company is successful in achieving its purpose in life. They might be selling plenty of products and services and generating a considerable profit, but is that the same as being successful?

Imagine if you knew the Kingdom purpose of your company. Imagine if you established measurable goals for measuring your success in fulfilling your Kingdom assignment. Imagine if you saw each person you served through your company both employees and customers, as recipients of the grace and peace of Christ you were providing them through the products and services your company offered. Granted, you can only do this if you really believe and see yourself fulfilling a Kingdom assignment through your business. This metric would allow you to measure your success in fulfilling your Kingdom assignment before you looked at your financial statements, which could then be used to measure the overall fiscal health of your company.

Imagine if your company made a concerted effort to provide greater value to your customers each year. This would create a larger market share over your competitors and eventually put them out of business and make you the dominant player in your industry. The most successful companies in the world have done just that. Whatever mission your company is attempting to fulfill, seek the Lord for how to continuously increase the value you are bringing to the market. It is a proven formula for success.

Measuring your achievements against your mission statement will help you determine how successful your company is becoming, but what about you personally? How do you measure the increase in the abundant life in your personal life? Here are a few suggestions for taking an annual inventory of the increase of abundance in your personal life:

Abiding in Him – people in love spend as much time together as possible. How is your worship time with the Lord? Is it increasing in quantity and quality?

Love for God and man – God is love and the more you abide in Him, the greater your love for Him should become. You should see everything and everyone in the world becoming insignificant in comparison for your love for Him. By the same token, your love for everyone else should also become greater.

Obedience in the small things – Are you becoming more sensitive to disobedience and realizing all disobedience is rebellion, self-will, and dishonors God? If you are becoming more obedient in the small things, the larger things will take care of themselves.

Being led by Holy Spirit – Are you being led more each day by the Holy Spirit or by your self-will? Who do you check with when making decisions; your mind, will, and emotions, or the Holy Spirit?

Dying to self – Are you dying to your flesh more and more? Death is always a painful process. You will hear the sizzle and smell the aroma of your flesh being burnt on the altar of sacrifice. It may feel terrible, but it is a pleasing aroma to the Lord.

Joy of the Lord – Is the joy of the Lord inside of you increasing? You might have had a bad year financially, but the joy of the Lord is not dependent on external circumstances.

Fruit of the Holy Spirit – Are you increasing in the other fruits of the Holy Spirit including peace, patience, kindness, goodness, faithfulness, gentleness, and self-control? Can others see the increase in you?

Yes, I believe financial abundance is one of the areas that should be increasing as we abide in Him and live out the abundant life He promised. But without abundance in Christ-like qualities, without pursuing and fulfilling your God-given Kingdom assignment, you can end up with an abundance of money in this world and be broke in the Kingdom.

Kingdom Principles for Financial Abundance

So, you have reached the point where you realize the abundant life can only be found by abiding in Him and He in you. You are being led daily by the Holy Spirit and dying to yourself every day. However, you have also reached the point where in order to fulfill your Kingdom assignment, you need an abundance of money in your personal life and in your business. What can you do to obtain this wealth using Kingdom principles? Here are some principles guaranteed to work. Why do I say guaranteed? Because not only are these Kingdom principles delineated in the Word of God, but many of them are principles of success that have been used extensively by non-believers to accumulate incredible wealth. The subject of how non-believers succeed using Kingdom principles will be discussed in Chapter 15.

All Good Things Are Received by Faith

The way you receive anything in the Kingdom is through faith. This includes your salvation and finances. Remember, it is your Father's good pleasure to give you the Kingdom (Luke 12:32). You simply need to ask for it. Begging is not the same as asking and believing. Most people don't have a problem believing God for their salvation which they cannot see, but struggle to believe God for things that can be seen. We need to have just as much faith in things we can see such as our finances, as in those things we cannot see such as our salvation.

The world wants to see results first and then believe. In the Kingdom, the order is to pray, believe, and then see (Mark 11:23-24). It takes no faith to believe in something that can be seen, and without faith it is impossible to please God (Heb 11:6). Doubt is the opposing force to faith. Doubt is the force that makes us double-minded and prevents us from receiving anything from the Lord (James 1:6-7). Doubt is the sin that so easily entangles us and prevents us from receiving the promises of God through a life of faith (Heb 12:1).

I have heard all kinds of "cookbook recipes" for receiving financial miracles from God. These included giving double and triple tithes, sowing with an expectation of a hundred-fold return, praying in tongues every day, giving prayer requests in conjunction with offerings, and meditating on God's Word. Many of these are noble actions that have benefit, but the way we receive anything from God is through the grace that comes by faith in Christ Jesus. If we could earn these financial blessings by works, then they would come with an attached earnings statement.

The Just Shall Live By Faith

I have known many Christians whose financial goal was to reach the point where they had enough money in the bank that they would not have to live by faith for their financial needs. To those of us who have walked with the Lord for a while, that idea may sound somewhat naïve, knowing we are called to live by faith (Heb 10:38). However, all of us at one time or another look for financial solutions which are contrary to the will of God for our lives. We want living by faith to be our "Plan B," while we continue to look for our "Plan A."

Until our relationship with the Lord is truly the most important thing in our life and our character matures to a Christ-like person, an abundance of money is an impediment to the mountain of spiritual maturity we are called to climb. When given a choice, man will always opt for the short cut rather than the arduous climb necessary to mold us properly. I believe the Lord wants us to have an abundance of wealth, but in direct proportion to the rate we mature (3 John 1:2).

Sometimes, the Lord has to dry up the streams of provision in our life in order to get us to abandon our dependence on our bank account and learn to be totally dependent on Him. We may even ask ourselves, *"What's wrong? Why isn't it working?"* and not realize it *is* working. It is working God's way. He is forcing us to learn to live by our faith. However, as wonderful as it sounds to know the Lord will meet our every need when we live by faith, it sounds much better to use this as a "Plan B." This is why the Lord has to encourage us and even force us at times to learn to walk by faith. This doesn't mean you can't have a big bank account someday, but not to the detriment that it prevents you from learning to live by faith.

Ask in Accordance With His Will

There are many Christians who feel they cannot pray with confidence unless they know for sure that what they are praying for is the will of God. These same Christians also believe it is impossible to know the will of God and therefore get stuck in a rut. However, to a large extent we *do* know the will of God because the will of God is revealed in Christ Jesus (Heb 1:3). Whatever Jesus said or did is the will of God. We don't have to ask whether it is the will of God to heal the sick, raise the dead, cast out demons, heal the broken hearted or provide for the poor. Jesus did these things and therefore they *are* the will of God for our lives.

Additionally, the Bible is full of examples where God gave his children what they asked for even though it was against His will to do so. Unless it is something the Word of God clearly says is not the will of God, I believe we should seek the direction of the Holy Spirit how to pray for it, and start praying and believing for it. However, here is where balance is needed in regard to the "ask in accordance to His will principle." Many times, we can pray for things which are not necessarily wrong in principle, but simply not in agreement with the Lord's way of solving a problem, or in agreement with His timing.

You may be praying for a particular new home, but the Lord wants to give you one even better. You may be praying for finances to pay some debt, but the Lord wants to give you favor to have the debt forgiven. You may be trying to keep a struggling business alive, but the Lord wants that business to die so He can give you a better one. Learn to seek His will for your situation. You will have much greater success in answered prayer when you pray in accordance to His will. Instead of asking God to join you in what you are working on and bless it, find out what God is working on in your life. His plan is already blessed! Then join Him in what He is already doing in your life. You will be amazed at how much less prayer is required to get God to bless what He is working on, and has already blessed.

Ask, Seek, Find

Although we receive all things by grace through faith in Christ Jesus, there are some things that asking alone will not accomplish. Some things you will need to seek out and some things will only come after knocking on doors.

> "Keep on asking, and you will receive what you ask for. Keep on seeking, and you will find. Keep on knocking, and the door will be opened to you. For everyone who asks, receives. Everyone who seeks,

finds. And to everyone who knocks, the door will be opened" (Matt 7:7-8 NLT).

If God gives you a "God idea" to put into a business plan, don't expect the first investor who reads your business plan to see the hand of God written all over it. Sometimes, God wants you to seek and knock on doors so you will be able to appreciate the incredible favor He is giving you. When a door opens for you that would never open in the natural, then you know the favor of God is operating in your life. But in order to get there, you may have to seek and knock on a few doors to obtain the things God already wants you to have.

Seeking and knocking are not actions you perform to get a reluctant God to help you. They are things you do as part of what God wants to do in your life. Expect some things to come to you just by asking for them. Others will be obtained only by seeking them. Others will not come until you have knocked on many doors. Keep asking, keep seeking, and keep knocking to obtain the abundant life Jesus promised you. Persistence is a characteristic of the wealthy.

Wisdom, Understanding, and Knowledge

Grace money. That's what I call it. Unexpected money that comes to you from out of nowhere. Don't you just love it? Who doesn't? I doubt there is a person in the world who doesn't have a prayer list that includes a large amount of grace money coming in for some purpose. Perhaps you want a new car, a home, or simply to pay down some debt. We all want God to supernaturally provide the finances to meet our needs. Frequently, He does give us grace money through various ways, especially when there is an urgent need for cash. However, this grace money is not without its limitations and drawbacks, and like the allowance our parents gave us when we were young, it was never intended to be the primary way we obtain money and wealth in our lives.

As discussed in previous chapters, the way the Lord generally provides wealth to you is not through grace money but through investing in people and increasing their value. The more people you serve, and the greater the value they perceive they have received from your products and services, the greater the return to you. Wisdom, understanding, and knowledge are the keys to understanding what you should be doing, who you should be doing it to, and how you should be doing it. They will show you how to give them the greatest value for your service, while providing you with the greatest return on your investment in those people.

Whatever the financial issue, God wants you to seek Him to obtain the wisdom to understand your fundamental problem and His solution for solving it. You may think you have a cash flow problem, but what you really have is a wisdom problem. This means you have a shortage of God problem. Get into His presence and seek wisdom, understanding, and knowledge and deal with the root of the problem, and the cash flow issues will be resolved.

What Do You Have of Value?

What talents did the Lord leave with you? It is interesting that we describe the special abilities people have as their talents. The origin of the word *talent* in Latin and Greek was a weight of money. A talent of silver or gold was about 75 pounds of the precious metal.[2] I do not know how talents of money evolved into becoming talents of special abilities in our language, but perhaps somewhere along the way, someone realized the special talents and abilities the Lord has given us could be exchanged or transferred into money and wealth. It seems the talents the Lord gave to each of us were intended to be used to provide valuable service to others and thereby provide a financial return to us.

Whatever talents the Lord gave you, He wants you to put them to work until He returns. These talents include the special abilities, intellect, people-skills, and even financial assets you have. If you want to become wealthy, you need to take stock in your true value. What unique combination of talents and assets do you have and how can they be used to advance the Kingdom of God? You need to take inventory of your talents because this is what you are called to put to work, and this is generally *the primary way* the Lord will bless you financially.

Often times, others who know you well can help you identify talents and gifts you were not aware of or felt were insignificant. These hidden talents and abilities might launch you into a new business that will make you wealthy. It is sad, but neither our educational system nor our corporate organizations take the time to help people identify their talents, abilities, strengths, and passions. They seem to focus on knowledge and experience and not your God-given intrinsic value. Take the time to know what you have. God gave you those talents and abilities for a reason. The law of stewardship applies here. Be faithful with what He has given you and He will give you more. To those who claim they have none, even what they have will be taken from them.

In Chapter 6, we talked about the importance of passion being a key to determining your Kingdom assignment. If you can figure out what you are passionate about, and add to it an understanding of your strengths, talents, abilities, and experiences you have that make you valuable, you should be well on your way to identifying what you have that will make you money. More importantly, it will show you what you possess to uniquely serve and invest in other people. The greater the value they receive from the service you invest in them, the greater the harvest or return on investment that will come back to you, and make you wealthy. "A man's gift makes room for him and brings him before great men" (Prov 18:16).

Don't Eat Everything In The Fruit

In the Bible, fruit is symbolic of a blessing or a harvest. The money you are looking for is the fruit or harvest of the service you provide to people. Everyone is looking for a big harvest. This is understandable. However, not everything in the fruit is meant to be consumed by you.

Along with its fruit, the apple includes a stem, seeds, and a core. The seeds are necessary to create additional apples, the core is good for feed for animals, and the stem is good for fertilizer. Not everything in the apple is meant to be eaten by you. The same can be said about your financial fruit, your money. It is not meant to be consumed entirely by you. Even under the Mosaic Law, not everything the Israelites received was meant to be consumed by them. As we discussed in the Stewardship Chapter, there were multiple tithes and offerings they were required to give at various times. Additionally, there were laws about harvesting their land that prevented them from gleaning everything from their land. They were required to leave some of the harvest for the poor, the widows, and the aliens. They were required to open their hand and give generously to the poor (Lev 19:9-10, Deut 15:10-11).

Under the Kingdom of Heaven paradigm, everything we receive belongs to the King. We are simply the stewards of His financial harvest. The Lord wants us to be good stewards of His finances and bring increase to His Kingdom, but not at the cost of forsaking the poor and needy.

The business people we work with who have been the most blessed financially and personally, are also the most generous people. These people never assume their financial harvest is meant just for them. They instinctively know they are called to share their harvest with others. This includes worthy causes in the community along with providing for the needy and the poor. These people would never consider eating everything in the fruit. They know that everything in the fruit has a purpose in the Kingdom.

Don't Tempt God

As stewards of the King's finances, it would only make sense that we never spend a dime without asking the Lord what He wants us to do with His money. If we never spent a dime without seeking His permission, we would save ourselves from a lot of financial worry and embarrassment. Instead, many of us spend the money as if it was ours to spend and end up tempting or testing God (Matt 4:7, Luke 4:12, 10:25, 1 Cor 10:9).

How do Christians tempt God? By following their self-will and doing what they want to do, and then defending their actions with scripture just as the devil did in the desert. This is especially true when it comes to spending money. I have seen many Christian business owners who bought new cars, homes, and even other businesses when they lacked the finances and specific direction from the Lord to do so. They tend to support their actions with phrases such as "God doesn't want us to have a poverty mentality," or "We are walking in faith that God will provide the finances we need." This is not faith, but presumption. They are tempting God to provide for them in a way and a time of their choice. This is not how the Kingdom of Heaven works. We are called to pray His will is done here on earth; not our will.

As a business intercessor, I am engaged in praying for specific financial needs of our clients every day. Praying and believing God will provide the financial resources our clients need is something I breathe every day. But, I always admonish our clients to abstain from spending the money until it comes in. We must leave it up to Him as to when and how He determines to provide for us. His ways are not our ways and His timing is not our timing. We must learn to live in accordance with His will and not ours.

I know there are times when the Lord will ask us to step out on faith and be proactive when there are no finances within sight. I have heard stories where God has told people to submit an offer on a piece of property when they lacked the finances to consummate the deal, or go to a bank and apply for a loan when they lacked collateral, or to stand in line at an airport when they lacked the finances for a ticket. However, in all of these successful stories, each person heard the Lord speak to them to perform these acts of faith. Another qualifier of these faith stories is that none of the people wanted to perform those acts of faith for fear it might not work out. They did it out of obedience to what they were told to do, more than their faith in what they were doing (Luke 5:4-5).

When people come up with their own plan for financial deliverance, I have seldom seen that plan work. Presumption is not the same as

Kingdom Business Success

faith. God has a plan for your financial success. Spend time in His presence to get the plan and follow it. This is walking by faith. Don't spend money you do not have. Don't tempt God by spending His money without seeking His direction. It doesn't matter how many scriptures you can come up with to support your argument for self-will. "For all who are being led by the Spirit of God, these are sons of God" (Rom 8:14).

Owe No Man Nothing But Your Love

Debt is a terrible task master and a burden the Lord does not want you to carry. The abundant life Jesus promised is one with burdens which are light and not heavy. The Bible says "The rich rules over the poor, and the borrower *becomes* the lender's slave" (Prov 22:7).

What do you do if you owe someone money but cannot afford to pay them? Remember the Second Commandment and treat others the same way you want them to treat you (Matt 7:12). Go to them and explain your situation. Keep them informed of your situation and when you believe you will be able to make the payment. If you can't pay it at all, explain that to them and ask for forgiveness. Don't run from them, run to them. Learn from your mistakes and remember to avoid future debt. "Owe nothing to anyone - except for your obligation to love one another" (Rom 13:8a NLT).

As stewards of His financial resources, we need to ensure we are led by the Holy Spirit in everything we do. Do not borrow money without hearing from Him first. Do not invest in anything without having heard from Him first. Be extremely cautious and wary about accumulating debt. I have learned the hard way that one God idea is better than one hundred good ideas when it comes to generating wealth.

Win-Win Mentality

In the Kingdom, we are called to love the people we are doing business with and to treat them as we would want to be treated ourselves. In order for this to happen, we need to ensure we have our business partners and our customer's best interests at heart when we are doing business with them. We need to see the deal from their perspective and ensure they are getting what they want from the deal. We need to ensure they are truly satisfied with the deal and not just going along with it because they can't find anything else at the moment. Anything less than their satisfaction will result in a disgruntled business partner or customer down the road. The world calls this type of business negotiation a "win-win" transaction.

There was a time when I took great pride in haggling with someone to get a better deal for myself. Now, I like to ensure the people I deal with are getting at least what they want and preferably more. I have given contractors more than the amount they bid in their proposal. They often seem confused as if they didn't think I heard them correctly the first time. I heard them correctly. But now, I want everyone to enjoy the experience of doing business with me. I always try to provide more value than what they are expecting. I always try to treat the people I do business with the same way I want to be treated myself. This is the way favor is received and financial abundance is generated in the Kingdom of Heaven.

Principles in Practice

Wyatt and Felicia had tried their hand in several different businesses. Although they had some success in these various business enterprises, they could not say they were entirely successful at any of them. When asked what they thought their Kingdom assignment was, they could only shake their head and say they had not figured it out yet.

Like the dog chasing his tail, Wyatt and Felicia were so busy trying to earn an income they forgot to take the time to figure out what they should be doing. They were chasing money and not pursuing their Kingdom assignment. When a door of opportunity opened up for them to do something different or do their current business differently, they had no standard to use to help them determine if this new opportunity would move them closer to their destination. When you don't know where you are heading, it is hard to know if the road you are on is the correct one. They kept spending money on various marketing programs intended to help them become more successful at what they were doing, but never saw the return on investment for their time and money.

Perhaps the saddest commentary about people who chase money instead of their Kingdom assignment, is that people who are struggling in a business but know it is a business they have been called to, have the benefit of knowing they are doing what the Lord has called them to do. They just need to figure out the correct business model to use to start making money from it. The person who struggles in a business which is not their calling has nothing to console themselves with during the dry times which all businesses go through at one time or another.

It pays to take the time to get before the Lord and seek your Kingdom assignment. If it takes you ten years to discover what it is, it will save you much heartache over the future years of your business endeavors. Seek His Kingdom and His assignment for your life. Don't chase money. Chase the Lord and His Kingdom. Let money chase you!

Jordan and Tori were business owners who understood that not everything in the fruit was meant to be eaten by them. They never believed that everything in their paycheck was meant to be consumed by them. During a time period when their business was barely keeping its head above water and most owners would have plowed their profits back in the company to grow the business, Jordan and Tori were taking profits out of their business to invest in Kingdom purposes and believed the Lord would build their company while they built His Kingdom.

Although Jordan and Tori had several children, they adopted one more that the Lord had put on their heart. In addition, they became the legal guardian for an elderly neighbor of theirs. Jordan and Tori were actively involved in their community and took their civic responsibilities very seriously. They invested their time and money into organizations and groups that were trying to make serious changes in the way small businesses were supported. They invested heavily in non-profit organizations that were attempting to bring biblical values back into our government and society. They also invested in many ministries from the profits which came from their business.

While Jordan and Tori were sowing heavily outside of their business and personal lives, the Lord kept blessing their business and personal income. They would receive uncommon favor with their customers and prospects. Doors, not normally open to a small business would open to them. The Lord caused them to be recognized and honored in both the government and business environments. Jordan and Tori were good stewards of the finances the Lord gave them and learned that not everything He provided was meant to be consumed by them.

Kimberly was the owner of a startup services business. In her first several years of operations, she ran her company from the basement of her home. Most of her employees were onsite at her client's place of business, so she didn't need much space for herself and her four support personnel. By keeping her overhead and G&A expenses to a minimum, Kimberly was able to generate a good profit from her small business in the first few years of operations.

As the company grew, Kimberly wanted to break out of her basement office and move into leased office facilities. Since the large majority of her work was still being performed at the client's site, the urgency to move to leased offices was more about presenting the right image to a prospect than a practical necessity. Her current clients didn't seem to care that she operated her company from her home. Since things were going well in the company, she decided to lease new co-op style offices not too far from her home. Although the new lease came with a high price, Kimberly believed she was walking in faith and God was going to provide the additional business to cover the significant new expense which she would have with the leased offices.

God's timing for the new business was not the same as hers, and pretty soon Kimberly could not afford to pay the lease on her new offices. To compound the problem, the lease prevented her from subleasing any of the space to another company. Kimberly was stuck in a long-term lease she could not afford.

It was understandable that Kimberly would want and eventually need new office space. Many times we make business decisions based upon image and not necessity. We reason that the decision makes sense and after all, God wants us to have an abundant life. Anything less than God's best could be perceived as a "poverty spirit" by some. Unfortunately, God's plans and God's timing are seldom ours. If Kimberly had prayed for the new office space and waited for the Lord to show her the right office, she might have obtained office space which was affordable, albeit perhaps not as nice as what she wanted at the moment.

Sometimes, we have to go through several offices or automobiles before we get the one we always wanted. God promised to give us the desires of our heart, but He doesn't promise when or how He would do that. When we attempt to force God's hand by making drastic decisions that will force God to provide for us our way and in our time, we are not walking by faith, we are tempting God. Don't tempt God!

Heath and Suzanna were business owners who understood how to walk by faith for finances and to ask, seek, and knock for provision for their Kingdom assignment. They believed whatever the Lord put on their heart, that if they would step out in faith to pursue it, He would give them the strategy for how, when, and the resources necessary to fulfill their assignment.

Heath and Suzanna had multiple businesses and non-profit ministries they started simply by following the leading of the Holy Spirit and their heart's desires. They always prayed for direction and timing and expected the Lord's confirmation would come as they stepped out in faith. Whenever there was a financial need, they would simply ask the Lord for it and then believe and wait for it. They never ran ahead of the Lord or tempted Him to provide in a way or timing outside of His will. If the finances seemed to be held up, they simply prayed to hear the Lord's will in the matter to discern if they were going in the right direction. When they only had partial finances or a partial revelation as to the next steps, they would only do what they could do at the time without going into debt or trying to force the Lord's hand to do things their way.

Heath and Suzanna were good stewards of the business and ministry the Lord gave them, and never looked at them as being "theirs." They were simply stewards of what He had given to them. Because of their good stewardship, He kept giving them more. Not only did He give them more resources and success in their existing businesses and ministry, but He gave them new opportunities to pursue. Heath and Suzanna had learned that the Lord delights to give us our hearts desires, especially when they are the sanctified desires He already put on our hearts. When the Lord orders the meal, He always pays the bill. But He reserves the right to choose how and when He pays for it.

Questions for Reflection

1. What is your Kingdom assignment? How do you measure your progress in pursuing and fulfilling that assignment? What changes can you make to start measuring your success in fulfilling your assignment from a mission or Kingdom perspective rather than a financial one?

2. When you ask God for financial resources, do you believe He will provide, or do you feel your prayers are pretty much "hit or miss?" Ask the Holy Spirit to show you the fundamental reasons you are having doubts in the area of receiving finances. Remember the order of pray, believe, and receive.

3. How much of your paycheck belongs to you and how much belongs to God? Are you basing this division of ownership upon the Mosaic Law or the Kingdom of Heaven paradigm? How do you determine how your paycheck is spent, invested, or

consumed? Ask the Holy Spirit to show you what He wants you to do with your paycheck.

SECTION 4: EPILOGUE

Chapter 15

Why Some Are Wealthy

"Jesus said to him, 'If I want him to remain until I come, what is that to you? You follow Me!'" (John 21:22).

I thought of naming this chapter *Why Do the Wicked Prosper?* But as you'll see, this chapter is not about the wicked but about the wealthy. This chapter is intended to answer the question why non-believers and those not abiding in the Lord succeed in business and life, and often achieve greater success than you or I or other devout Christians. Some of these successful people profess to be Christians without any fruit or evidence of that transformation in their life, while others are clearly following other gods including themselves.

We know we shouldn't do it, but we tend to compare our experiences in life with those around us. Perhaps it's part of a "works" mentality, but we all feel rewards and blessings in life should be based upon how good we have been or how well we have played the game of life. We believe there should be some sort of "fairness police" ensuring each person gets what they deserve out of life. We believe a *good* God would also be a *fair* God and would not allow any unfairness in the world. Certainly not in the area of financial success.

Why are some of the most successful business people in the world non-believers? In this chapter, I am going to attempt to answer the question why some outside the Kingdom succeed. To ignore this question, would ignore the elephant in the room. I don't profess to have all the answers to this question, but I am going to explain some of the reasons the Lord has shown me over the last thirty years why others succeed, when you and I do not. I will also explain the biblical response He gives to people who ask the question "What about them, Lord?" and how that answer may impact your quest to bring the Kingdom of Heaven into your business.

As you read these reasons for their success, note how many of the reasons align themselves with Kingdom principles we have discussed in this book. Let's examine *why* these people are wealthy.

1.   There Is a Call of God On Their Life

Some of these people may not be following the Lord today, but there is a call of God on their life. They have a call to follow Him and a call to wealth. Without getting into predestination, some of these people are supposed to be following the Lord but have yet to make that choice. All of us at one time or another were without God and only the Lord knows when or if these people will give their lives to Him and follow Him. We look at them in their current state and judge them for who they are and what they are doing, while God looks at them through the eyes of eternity.

The gifts and the calling of God upon man are irrevocable (Rom 11:29). Sometimes, these people do not follow the destiny the Lord planned for them and never get around to being "all in." However, they still get to keep the gift of financial success which was part of their calling. This may not seem fair in our eyes, but that is His way.

2.   They Have A Cyrus Anointing

We often believe the only people God would use to accomplish His will are men and woman of God who are virtuous and sanctified. But this is not true. God uses believers and non-believers to accomplish His will here on earth. Even people who don't know God can find themselves used by Him to accomplish His will. Cyrus, king of Persia was one of those people. Although he was neither a Christian nor a Jew, the Lord used him to deliver the Israelites out of Babylon and ordered them to return to their own country and rebuild their temple. He also returned the sacred vessels from the temple and paid for the rebuilding of the temple with money from his treasury (Ezra 6:3-5).

If you look at some of the most successful business people of the last century, you will see many of them were not devout Christians. But I believe many of those successful non-believers were used by God as modern day Cyruses. Warren Buffet, Bill Gates, Henry Ford, and Thomas Edison weren't looking to create something that would be beneficial for themselves or a small group of people. They were trying to enrich the lives of the masses. They would have been successful and become millionaires if they only served themselves and a small group of people. Their legacy, honor, and incredible wealth came from enriching the lives and adding value to the lives of the masses.

I believe the key to their success is they were not self-seeking with their power and wealth, but were looking to add value and blessing to the lives of the masses. They provided for and served others more than themselves. Therein lies a key to success. Find new ways to enrich the life and add value to every person you meet. If you do, you won't have to chase money, money will chase you.

3. They Have Passion For Their Assignment

The Lord loves people who have passion and zest for life. He would prefer to have someone whose passion is in the wrong direction than someone who is lukewarm about life. The person whose passion is misguided can be turned around, but what do you do with someone who has been salted but still lacks flavor (Matt 5:13)?

It takes passion to be successful because your passion will compel you to keep moving forward when everyone else moves backwards. Great accomplishments are generally preceded by great disappointments and failures. Passion will make someone look past the failures and keep believing it will work. People without passion will quit when the money dries up. They are only passionate about the idea when they are being paid. But people with passion will find a way to make money while they continue to work on their passion.

It is easy to be a tuna and swim with the current, but it takes passion to be a salmon and swim upstream.

> "I know your works, that you are neither cold nor hot. I could wish you were cold or hot. So then, because you are lukewarm, and neither cold nor hot, I will vomit you out of My mouth" (Rev 3:15-16 NKJV).

4. They Have Purpose

Similar to passion, successful people have purpose for everything they do. They understand the "why" behind what they are trying to accomplish. Passion for a goal will put some people in the Guinness World's Record for their accomplishments, but seriously, what is the purpose behind how many dominoes can be successfully toppled? You can have passion for something which has limited value to anyone. You can have passion with myopic vision. Successful people have both passion and purpose that benefits others and not just themselves.

There is a saying *provision* always follows *vision*. This makes sense since provision is actually pro-vision, or the favor of the vision. People are attracted to visionaries who have a vision with a purpose they can relate to. If the purpose of the vision is important to the people, the people will rally behind the vision and support the vision with provision. People who are successful in business always have a significant reason or purpose behind the ventures they pursue. They have a purpose that goes beyond just making money and becoming wealthy. They have a purpose which attracts others to support their vision, and that is why they are successful.

5. They Are Disciplined With Time and Money

If you study the lives of successful billionaires, you will discover they accomplish more in one day than the average business person does in a week. How do they do that? Good secretaries, I guess. But seriously, all successful people learn an important premise about time that most people never learn in an entire lifetime.

> "Time is our most valuable asset, yet we tend to waste it, kill it, and spend it rather than invest it. Time is more valuable than money. You can get more money, but you cannot get more time."[1]

When it comes to spending money, successful people spend less than they earn, avoid buying status symbols of success, risk money only if the rewards outweigh the risks, and avoid debt by not spending tomorrow's money today.[2] They value wealth (no pun intended) and understand how to leverage it rather than spend it. Stewardship is an important principle in the Kingdom of Heaven. God rewards people who are good stewards of His resources regardless of their religion. Study the biographies of the billionaires of this century and you will discover most of them didn't follow the Lord. But all of them were great stewards of time and money.

6. They Are Wise Business People

Although successful business people are very passionate about their businesses, they are also very prudent about their business ventures. They do not engage in anything without exercising shrewd judgement on carefully designed plans. They do not start or purchase a business without a well-developed and researched business plan. Their projections are always realistic and based upon reliable data. They know that in order to accomplish the objectives of their business plan and be successful, they will need wisdom, understanding, and knowledge. They are looking for the right thing, the right timing, and the right way.

Successful business people study their business market segment and competition. They know the direction the market is going and steer a course to intercept the market's future. Like a good football coach, they have a calculated game plan and know success will be based upon how well they follow their game plan. Successful business people are planners. Success doesn't just happen to them, they carefully plan for success and move progressively toward it.

Successful business people study their competitors to the point where they often know more about what their competitors are doing than many of the mangers employed by their competitors. They are objective about their own strengths and weaknesses and those of their competitors. They exploit their competitors' weaknesses while performing risk prevention on their own weaknesses.

7. They Are Not Afraid of Failing

Successful business people know that in order to be successful, you have to leave home port and sail into uncharted waters. You must be willing to do something different than what others are doing. You must be willing "to boldly go where no man has gone before." Success requires taking risks and not being afraid to fail. Successful business people know most business ventures are destined for initial setbacks, so they are very calculated on which risks they are willing to pursue. They are adventurers, but they never jump out of an airplane without a parachute.

Successful business people overcome their fear of failure by overcoming inertia. They take small steps toward their goals. They don't look at setbacks as failures, but see them as opportunities to become wiser and more experienced in what they are pursuing. They see opportunities to succeed, rather than seeing them as opportunities to fail. Successful business people are very patient and astute concerning opportunities. They will wait years for the right moment in the market and economy to strike. During the waiting time, they will continue their intelligence gathering and preparations for involvement. Preparation time for them is never wasted time.

Successful business people are not afraid of what others think about them or how they are perceived in the community. They are too busy looking forward to be looking behind or around them. They have so much passion and purpose for what they are attempting to accomplish, they just assume everyone else is on their side and not against them. They tend to be fearless in regard to fear of man and are unaffected by fear of rejection.

8. They Are Relationship Oriented

Successful people understand no one accomplishes anything great in life on their own or for themselves. Therefore, they tend to be relationship oriented. They build and nurture relationships and treat them as valuable assets. In fact, they realize the quality and depth of their social capital is arguably the greatest asset on their balance sheet. They are very strategic about the process of building those relationships and nurturing them. They honor their relationships and are very win-win in their strategy for helping each other succeed.

Successful business people are community-oriented and not loners. They do not possess an orphan spirit and do not operate in a vacuum. They might not have a large group of people they interact with, but the ones they do interact with are highly valued and nurtured. They are connected to their community. Although the media might not be very favorable to some of them, their close business relationships and customers tend to love them for the results they achieve and the passion and purpose they exhibit.

9. They Value Wealth

Successful business people value wealth. They probably value being wealthy as well, but they also put a high value on wealth. They realize wealth is not something to be taken for granted and they do everything they can to generate and retain wealth. They do not have an "easy come, easy go" mentality when it comes to wealth. The Bible says, An inheritance gained hastily in the beginning will not be blessed in the end" (Prov 20:21 NKJV).

Wealthy business people preserve wealth and don't consume it the same way others do.

It's true that some of these wealthy business people have made wealth their god and an object of worship, but they also have a better appreciation of wealth than the average person. If you ask the average person what they would do if they received a gift of $1 million, they will probably start telling you about the house, the car, and the boat they will purchase. If you ask a person who values wealth what they would do with the same $1 million, they will probably tell you their plans to invest the money and live off the interest or increase of the investment. Therein lies the difference between someone who values wealth and someone who doesn't.

Successful business people are focused on building wealth and wealth is attracted to them. They see themselves as being successful and speak words of life and success into what they are working on. They attract other successful business people who have a similar mindset. Although some of these successful business people might be overly focused on building wealth, God appreciates the good stewardship mentality they have concerning how they create and maintain wealth.

10. They Are Meant To Serve As A Contrast

Every story needs a protagonist and an antagonist; a hero and a villain. You can't have one without the other since they serve to provide contrast and definition to each other. The kingdom of darkness is the antagonist to the Kingdom of Heaven. The spirit of mammon is the antagonist to the abundant life, the *zōē* life that is available in the Kingdom of Heaven. If someone is going to achieve wealth using Kingdom principles, then we need to have someone achieve wealth using principles of the spirit of mammon in order to provide contrast and definition to the abundant life of the Kingdom of Heaven.

There have been many successful business people over the years who have accumulated significant wealth outside of an abiding relationship with the Lord. Some of them, although without an intimate relationship with the Lord, used Kingdom principles to achieve that wealth. Others used principles of the spirit of mammon. Either way, they serve as a contrast to those of us called to accumulate wealth in this world for Him. Until we do it His way, being led by His Holy Spirit and using Kingdom principles, then there is nothing to serve as a contrast.

The players in the battle of the Kingdom of Heaven versus the kingdom of darkness have been introduced and are well in place. You are one of them. The time is short and we are getting near the end of the age. The world is just waiting for us to rise up as the protagonists of this epic battle. We are called to be the heroes in this story, but like all true heroes we cannot cheat. We need to ensure we win playing by His rules, the principles of the Kingdom of Heaven.

One of my favorite scriptures illustrating how people have changed little over the years is found at the end of the Gospel of John. Jesus had just had a conversation with Peter discussing Peter's future and the nature of his death (John 21:18-22). There must have been a million great questions to ask the Lord in this situation. But since the spotlight was on Peter, Peter attempted to deflect the conversation away from himself. His only question appears to be "What about him?" in regard to what type of death the apostle John would face. Jesus brings the conversation back to Peter and says "If I want him to remain until I come, what is that to you? You follow me!" (John 21:22).

In the end, it really doesn't matter how or why others have succeeded in accumulating massive amounts of wealth. We should learn from them, but we are not called to be like them. We are called to follow Jesus and be like Him. We are called to abide in Him and He in us. We are to be led by the Holy Spirit in everything we think, say, and do. We are called to a higher life and with it, a higher way of living. Let us embrace the abundant life and do life and business with Him, and do it His way using Kingdom principles of success. In the Kingdom, it *does* matter how you play the game. In the next chapter, we will look at an action plan for how to bring the Kingdom of Heaven into *your* business.

Chapter 16

Bring The Kingdom of Heaven Into Your Business

"Do not fear, little flock, for it is your Father's good pleasure to give you the kingdom." (Luke 12:32 NKJV).

"*What's wrong? Why isn't it working?*" If you have made it this far in the story, you have probably come to the conclusion that there is no single answer to what you have been doing wrong in your business that is preventing you from enjoying the abundant life Jesus promised. It is probably a combination of several things. Therefore, there is no single solution to your problem either. It will take adjustments in several areas.

Perhaps you have come to the realization you have been operating under an incorrect paradigm of the Kingdom of Heaven and are still living under the Mosaic Law. You offer up your own sacrifices without realizing the only sacrifice He wants from you is you - all of you. That means everything you are and all you have. He wants you to be "all in." Beyond that, He is not looking for any sacrifices from you and any attempts to impress Him with your sacrifices have probably been disappointing.

Perhaps you have been attempting to serve the Lord the best you know how and have come to realize He is not impressed with what you can do for Him. He wants you to serve *with* Him and not *for* Him. He is looking for you to do life and business with Him and not for Him. Your best efforts to serve Him will never compare to what He can accomplish in your life working through you.

Perhaps you've taken the time to clarify how you have been defining success and come to realize you have been defining success by the definition and measure the world uses, by how much money and wealth you have accumulated. You have come to realize the Lord has something better in mind for you and you have decided to seek and pursue your Kingdom assignment. You want purpose instead of self-fulfillment. You want what the Lord has in mind for you, sight unseen, knowing it must be better than the path you have been pursuing.

If there is a key to Kingdom success, it is to abide in Him and He in us. The key is to be led by His Holy Spirit from moment to moment and do those things He tells us to do. No matter how difficult or simple His request, we just need to be obedient in everything. He promises to lead us to the place where we have His *zōē* life operating in abundance in each area of our lives. This is why He died for us. As long as we are submitted to His will, moving in the right direction, and becoming more and more like Him, we should expect to see the Kingdom of Heaven operating in our lives and businesses. We don't have to wait until we have been perfected. He is merciful and not legalistic. His mercy triumphs over legalism.

For those who only need small tweaks in their paradigm or walk with the Lord, this book should help you to stay on track with your path towards success. If however, you believe you have significant changes to make to bring the Kingdom of Heaven into your life and business, I have composed an action plan to help you. This plan will help someone who does not intimately know the Lord, develop a personal relationship with Him and start down the path necessary to bring the Kingdom of Heaven into your business.

Bring the Kingdom of Heaven Into Your Business Action Plan

1. Develop a Personal Relationship With The Lord

You must be born-again to enter the Kingdom of Heaven (John 3:5). You must become a disciple of Christ and learn to walk like He walked. You must be "all in." Life in the Kingdom is always preceded by death. You cannot be resurrected with Christ until you have first died with Him. This means death to your flesh and self-will. Along with becoming your Savior, He must become the Lord of your life. Dead men do not control their own lives.

Along with becoming your Lord and Savior, He must also become your lover, your best friend, your confidant, your provider, your protector, your joy, your reason for being, and your everything. He is a jealous God and like a jealous spouse, He wants your greatest desire to be for Him. If you've never completely given your life to the Lord, I have included a prayer in Chapter 17 that will allow you to dedicate yourself to Him and go "all in."

2. Be Led By The Holy Spirit In Everything You Do

When we become born-again, the Holy Spirit comes and abides in our spirit man. However, there is also a baptism of the Holy Spirit the disciples were told to wait for, the promise of the Spirit. This baptism of the Holy Spirit can come at the same time as conversion but frequently happens as a separate, life-changing event. Jesus baptizes us in the Holy Spirit so we can abide in Him and He in us. The Holy Spirit is our advocate, our teacher, our comforter, our intercessor, our best friend, and our guide to walk in Truth and receive the Wisdom of God for every situation we need. He is the third person of the Godhead and we can grieve Him through our thoughts, words, and actions. Develop a personal relationship with Him the same way you are pursuing a personal relationship with the Father and Jesus. To the extent you are led by Him in everything you do, you become a mature son or daughter of God and will see the abundant life in everything you do.

I have included a prayer to receive the baptism of the Holy Spirit in Chapter 17, but I have found this infilling is often received more readily and more demonstratively when received under the ministry of someone who is called to minister this baptism. When the Holy Spirit fills someone, there are various manifestations that can occur to the recipient, such as speaking in tongues, but generally there will be a feeling of love and peace that will come upon them that is not coming from their mind. It might feel as if someone is pouring love and peace into you intravenously. Don't get hung up about the different manifestations people might have, rather allow the Holy Spirit to bring the fruit of the Spirit into your life in a greater measure each day.

3. Consider Inner Healing/Deliverance Ministry

Although there is no mention of inner healing or deliverance ministries in the Bible, I have found the average Christian has strongholds in their life they struggle to eliminate. This spiritual baggage they are carrying with them holds them back and prevents them from living the abundant life. If you are struggling with an orphan spirit, rejection, fear, resentment, bitterness, hatred, anger, or unforgiveness, I highly recommend you seek out some inner healing/deliverance ministry to deal with these issues. You must get rid of this spiritual baggage.

These strongholds will create open doors in your life that will allow the enemy to persecute you. You will feel like you are being held in a prison and tormented over and over again. Just when you start to feel some relief, the persecution and setbacks will return. Understand, you are in a self-made prison and only you hold the key to let yourself out. Pray about seeking professional ministry support to help you break free of this oppression. I have personally gone through three different inner healing/deliverance ministries for these type of issues and know of their benefits. Remember, the key to defensive spiritual warfare is through repentance and forgiveness. If you are struggling in this area, get some professional ministry help. I have recommended several ministries in the Notes Chapter.[1]

4. Do Life and Business With Him and Not For Him

When you became born-again, you became the tabernacle of God and He goes wherever you go. Like a spouse, God wants to be a part of your life and do everything with you. He wants to go where you go, pray with you, work with you, exercise with you, make sales calls with you, write proposals with you, and vacation with you. If you are going to be married to the Lord, you can't leave Him at home or at the door when you go to work. No matter what you are doing, no matter how trivial the task, ask Him to do it with you. You will find that you don't need to beg Him to join you. He's been waiting for you to ask Him all along.

Once you start practicing doing life and business with God and not for Him, you will discover what you are really seeking is not God doing business with you, but you doing business with God. You must see yourself as being joined to Him as two oxen pulling a cart. You must surrender the lead ox role to Him and let Him steer your course. Now, you are not asking Him to be part of what you are doing, you are asking to become part of what He is doing. This is where you will see the Lord doing incredible things through you. This is where you will really start seeing the Kingdom advancing in your life.

5. Reorder Your Day to Put Him First Place

In order to develop an abiding presence with the Lord you will need to reorder your day to put Him first place in your heart and life. Remember, idolatry is putting someone or something in a place in your heart where only He belongs. Stop saying you don't have time to spend with Him. Stop saying you don't have time each day to read your Bible, pray, or give Him praise, worship, and thanksgiving. Whatever else you have in your day, including your spouse, children, and business, *must* take a distant second to your relationship with Him. This is not optional. Any other plan amounts to idolatry. This will generally require you reorder your day and priorities to put Him first place.

You must reorder your day to have a set time when you and the Lord come together like husband and spouse in a good marriage. Some people call this devotional time, but it really is "us time." This is quality time for you and Him to come together and build your intimate relationship. This is the time when you will pour out your heart to Him and He in turn will pour out His heart to you. It is in this quiet time you will learn to recognize the still small voice of the Lord and the different ways He speaks to you that we discussed in Chapter 12.

Let the Holy Spirit lead you and guide you during your devotional time. I encourage every business person to spend at least 30 minutes per day in devotional time. In addition, you should spend at least 15 minutes each day, preferably with your spouse, praying for your needs, the needs of your family, and your business. I also suggest you include another 15 minutes per day reading and studying your Bible.

6. Ask For The Grace To Love Like Him

Since most of us come into the Kingdom clueless about *agapē* love, we tend to love the same way the world loves, which is a fairly worthless commodity. Ask the Lord to give you a revelation of His love that goes beyond mental ascent. You must reach the point of being able to feel His love. You will never be able to love others beyond the point where you yourself feel loved. If you are struggling with this, then I strongly suggest you seek out some professional inner healing/deliverance ministry to help you achieve the breakthrough you need. As you spend more and more time soaking in His presence during your times of devotion, you should find yourself becoming changed and becoming more like Him as you behold Him on a daily basis.

The Bible says we love God because He first loved us (1 John 4:19). His *agapē* love is poured out within our hearts through the Holy Spirit when we became born-again, which explains why we can't *agapē* love until we become born-again (Rom 5:5). As we become transformed and become like Him, our capacity to love like Him is also increased. This type of love is a grace we need to pursue earnestly in order to become like Him and abide in Him. On a daily basis, keep asking for the grace to love Him and others the same way He loves you.

7. Remove All Idols From Your Life

The definition of idolatry is putting someone or something in a place in our heart where only God belongs. We are commanded to love God with all of our heart, soul, mind, and strength. This is a tall order, but is doable with His grace. Everyone comes into the Kingdom with their idols in tow, simply because we cannot know or understand *agapē* love until we are born-again. But at the entrance to the Kingdom, we are required to expunge all our idols.

When you think about all of the relationships you have had in your life, including your spouse and children, can you honestly say there is no one you have loved more than God? Can you honestly say you've *never* pursued any business deal, real estate, car, jewelry, boat, food, or fun more than you have passionately pursued God? If your answer is "yes" to these questions, then you are a rare person indeed. For the rest of us, God tends to be like coffee. He is an acquired taste. Like coffee, once you acquire a taste for Him, you will find you cannot live without Him. You will seek Him early and passionately each day.

Ask the Lord to show you the idols in your life. Ask him to show you the people, places, business deals, symbols of wealth, television, food, and activities you love more than Him. Ask Him to show you if there is anything sitting in a place in your heart where He alone is meant to reside. He is not asking you to give up your spouse, your children, or even your business. But He is a jealous spouse and He will not permit you to love anyone or anything more than Him.

8. Ask For Grace To Love Others With Christ's Love

Everyone who walks with the Lord will have to pass the test of betrayal. If you are in the business world, you are probably quite familiar with this test. This is the test where people you trusted betray you by their words and actions. Sometimes the betrayal comes in the form of what they did and sometimes it comes in the form of what they didn't do for you. Betrayal is the feeling of a cold knife stuck in your back when you weren't looking.

Regardless of the betrayal, we are required to love and forgive our betrayers. It is easy to say you have forgiven someone who has betrayed you. It is much harder to forgive them and remit their sins the same way we want Christ to remit our sins. This requires a special grace to love others the same way Christ loves us. This is the type of love where the person who was betrayed is willing to pay the price for the sins and mistakes of the betrayer and keep no record of wrong. This is the type of love where the person betrayed would lay down their right to receive recompense so the betrayer could live the abundant life. This is an extremely high calling, but it is also the type of love Jesus requires us to have for others.

9. Honor Everyone The Way You Want To Be Honored

Honor can best be described as an outward manifestation of our *agapē* love toward one another. Honor is a valuation. When you honor people, you are showing the world that you value them. Honor is also the process of making people look better than they are and let's admit it, we all need that grace in abundance! Value people's strengths and overlook their weaknesses and mistakes the same way you want the Lord to honor you. To dishonor the creation and those He created is to dishonor the Creator. Become a person of honor.

Eliminate the idea that people need to earn your respect or honor. This is the mindset of the flesh. The word of God commands us to "Honor all people, love the brotherhood, fear God, honor the king" (1 Peter 2:17). Honor your employees, even the incompetent ones and the ones who steal from you. Honor your children, even when they disobey you. Honor your competitors, even when they dishonor you or steal business from you. When you learn to honor everyone regardless of what they say or do to you, the Lord will promote you and honor you in front of them.

10. Repent of All Known Disobedience

When it comes to obedience you cannot be a little bit pregnant. All disobedience is sin. God considers rebellion as sinful as witchcraft and stubbornness as sinful as idol worship (1 Sam 15:23 NLT). Make a decision to start walking in obedience in every area of your life. Many Christians look at the Ten Commandments and feel they are walking in obedience since they are not overtly breaking any of them. However, to the point we know what we should be doing and are disobedient to it, for us it becomes sin (James 4:17).

Most Christians are the lord of their own life and direct their own footsteps. They operate in self-will and pray that God will bless their decisions and actions. Practice asking the Holy Spirit to lead you moment by moment each day and let Him direct and guide your footsteps into the life He has already blessed for you. When you learn to be obedient to the Holy Spirit in small things, the bigger things will become easier to obey. Remember, it is impossible to walk in disobedience and faith at the same time.

11. Dedicate Your Business To Him

If you have never dedicated your business and given it to the Lord for His purposes, then this would be a good time. The Lord gives man free will and if you choose to run your own company, He will let you do that. He will even let you run it into the ground. But if you are tired of carrying the burden of your business on your own shoulders, then it is time to give it to Him and let Him run it. It is generally more profitable to be a steward of His company than to run your own.

Don't be surprised if He brings changes to this new company. He might purge some employees, products, and customers; but He will also bring in new relationships, employees, products, and ideas to get your business to higher levels of success. He will bring His *zōē* life to areas of your business that were once dead.

241

I have included a prayer of dedication in Chapter 17 you can use to dedicate or rededicate your business to Him. If they are agreeable, you should also invite your spouse and business partners to this solemn event. I suggest performing this dedication at your offices and taking communion after the dedication ceremony.

12. Seek Your Kingdom Assignment

If you do not already know it, seek to understand your Kingdom assignment. What are you called to do in the Kingdom? What purpose does your assignment have? You must know who you are, what you are called to do, where you are called to do it, and who you are called to do it to. Don't be surprised if it takes years to discover. While seeking your assignment, keep working at your current assignment but never settle for anything less than God's best for your life. Once you know your assignment, ask the Lord to show you how to get from where you are to where you are called to serve. The transition itself may take years to accomplish, but the Lord will lead you to your assignment.

What are you passionate about? What are you so passionate about that the idea of dying before you see it accomplished brings you to tears? Your passion is the key to discovering your Kingdom assignment. Ask the Lord to give you a very strong passion for your assignment and to diminish the passion for anything not associated with His will for your life.

13. Know the Purpose For Everything You Do

It is important you not only know your Kingdom assignment but understand the significance or purpose behind the assignment. A Kingdom assignment will have reason or purpose that goes far beyond making you successful and wealthy. A Kingdom assignment will have a vision that attracts others to your assignment. Those people may be your customers, but they could also be part of the provision you need for your assignment. Provision always follows vision.

A Kingdom assignment will have purpose or vision that will benefit many people and not just a few. Your ability to sell your vision is dependent on you showing the value people will get from what you are attempting to accomplish. People are never motivated by *your* vision. It is *their* vision that will motivate them. Show them how your vision will help them accomplish *their* vision and they will jump onboard with your vision.

14. Seek To Be The Best At What You Do

Whatever you put your hand to, do it with all your might as unto the Lord (Col 3:23). Run the race to win. Seek to become the best at your assignment. If you are called to be a widget maker, seek to become the best widget maker on the mountain. Seek *mastery* instead of *mediocrity* in your Kingdom assignment. Become the expert in your field. Study your competitors to the point where you know their strengths and weaknesses better than they do. Study the current market dynamics and the future market trends. Become the person in your field the world thinks of when they are looking for an expert. Ask God to give you the wisdom, understanding, and knowledge to become the very best at what you are called to do. Similar to Joseph being called before Pharaoh, when you become the expert in your field, God is able to promote you and bring you before leaders of industries and governments for the purpose of bringing His Kingdom solution into their situation.

You might believe you are not called to be at the top of your mountain. You might be right. But you may be called to support the person at the top of the mountain. The best support person is someone who is qualified to do the job themselves. You might be called to be that support person. One day, the person called to be at the top of your mountain may not show up for work, and the Lord might promote you into that position. You don't have to be God's first choice to end up being His best choice.

15. Don't Chase Money – Let Money Chase You

This flies contrary to the success secrets of the self-help gurus and business coaches who encourage you to keep your financial goals in the forefront of your thoughts. As Christians, we are called to continually seek His Kingdom and His righteousness and everything else will be provided to us (Matt 6:33). The most successful business people in the world aren't focused on their personal financial needs. They are focused on their assignment and the purpose behind it. They are passionate about what they are trying to accomplish and their passion consumes them.

Money follows value. As you provide solutions to bigger and bigger pain points, people will pay you more money for the value you bring to their lives. They will seek you out. Money will be chasing you. Focus on chasing the Lord and walking in the same righteousness He walked in. Seek to bring His Kingdom into your situation and pursue your Kingdom assignment with fervent passion. Money and wealth will follow closely behind the value you bring to people's lives.

16. Put Aside All Falsehood

Since Jesus is the Truth, you cannot abide in Him if you are telling lies, exaggerating the truth, or deceiving people. As a business person, I know this is easier said than done in the 21st Century. But if we let our tongues be led by the Holy Spirit, we can purge ourselves of all falsehood and set ourselves apart as children of the Light.

One of the best ways to avoid being cornered to the point where you are tempted to speak falsehoods is to make a concerted effort to speak slowly and speak less. The Bible says "Where there are many words, transgression is unavoidable, but he who restrains his lips is wise" (Prov 10:19). When asked a question, think before you speak. Think about what you are about to say and ask yourself if it is entirely truthful. Ask yourself if someone could possibly misinterpret what you are saying and be deceived. If so, be careful to frame your words in such a way to prevent misunderstanding.

17. Embrace the Position of Steward and Not Owner

When you entered the Kingdom and went "all in," you gave up your ownership rights. You are now a steward of everything He entrusts to your care. You must learn to look at everything you have as belonging to the Lord, and you must be willing to give away or manage it according to His desires. This is a concept most Christian business people understand conceptually, but quickly lose sight of during the work day. Remember, someday you will be asked to give an account for your stewardship of everything He entrusted to you.

Like Linus van Pelt's security blanket, most business people are attached to their business, their Kingdom assignments, and their families. It is easy to say you have given something to the Lord until He asks you to give what you perceive to be yours to someone else. This is when the flesh will want to hold that security blanket close to your head and remind you it is "Mine, mine, mine." Whatever He has given you, be ready at all times to walk away from. I have learned that whatever you are willing to give up, you generally get to keep. Whenever you believe you can't live without something, He is on a mission to prove you wrong.

18. The Worker is Worthy of His Wages

The question you need to answer is "What are your wages?" He has promised that if you will delight yourself in Him that He will give you the desires of your heart (Psalm 37:4). What are your desires? What type of home would it take to make you happy? What kind of car would you need to drive? How much of a salary would you need to afford the lifestyle you desire? Be careful of what you ask for because you are probably going to get it. Remember, your Father has already given you the two most precious gifts He possesses: the blood of His only Son, and His precious Holy Spirit. How much more will He give you, including the wealth you need to live an abundant life here on earth.

Don't expect Him to give you everything you desire overnight. His ways are perfect and His timing is perfect. Despise not the day of small beginnings. You may be currently renting and have your eye on a $1 million home. Don't be surprised if along the way you own a couple of smaller homes before arriving at your dream home. Be thankful for everything and in everything you go through. Give Him thanks for His Lordship and provision. Even if you are evicted along the way, give Him thanks for that experience. When you finally enter your dream home, it will make the experience seem so much sweeter. Never allow the wealth you are asking for to come before your desire for Him, and your Kingdom assignment. When determining your wages, think eternity and not just the next decade.

19. Steward As If You Will Be Held Accountable

Two areas of stewardship that separate successful business people from the unsuccessful are time and money. The more valuable of these two commodities is time. You can make more money, but you cannot make more time. Treat these two commodities with the honor they deserve and don't waste them. Read *80/20 Sales and Marketing*[2] and apply the Pareto principle to your time management. Remember, 1% of your activities will produce 50% of your results in any given area. Spend the bulk of your time doing those 1% activities and learn to delegate or hire someone else to do the bulk of the other 99% of your activities. This is a time management secret of the wealthy.

Do not spend money you don't have. Pray and believe the Lord will provide you with everything you need to prosper and accomplish your Kingdom assignment, but don't spend it until it arrives. To do otherwise is to tempt God. Don't purchase or give anything away, even a charitable offering, without first checking with the Lord. Remember, it is not your money to use or give away. Embezzlement is a felony offense, even in the Kingdom of Heaven.

20. Don't Be Afraid to Fail

If you are going to do anything great in life, you are going to have to get out of the boat and attempt to walk on water. You will have to conquer the demonic spirits of fear of failure and fear of man. The key to overcoming these fears is to have settled in your heart that you are pursuing your Kingdom assignment. You are doing what God has told you to do. If you are passionate about what you are doing and know the purpose behind what you are attempting to accomplish, your ears will become deaf to the voice of the naysayers.

Don't look at failure as the end, but the beginning of something new. If God allows you to fail at something, it is probably because He has something better in mind for you. If He blessed everything you are doing, would you leave what you are currently working on and go work on what He wants you to work on? Probably not. Look at failure as a chance to reset your focus and priorities in life. God may be letting you fail because He has something better in store for you.

Learn to take calculated risks and not foolish ones. The best project management advice I ever heard was "think big, start small." Keep in mind very few people get their business model correct the first time. Keep seeking wisdom, understanding, and knowledge concerning the correct business model. Break your goals up into bite size pieces. If one of those bite size ventures fails, you haven't lost everything. Learn from your setbacks and make adjustments prior to each new attempt. Even when you have success with one business model, keep seeking wisdom whether there is a better model that will bring better results.

21. Seek Wisdom, Understanding, and Knowledge

Where you are today is a reflection of the decisions you made yesterday. Where you will be tomorrow will be based upon the decisions you make today. If you don't like where you are in life today, change your decision making process. Seek the Lord daily and wait at His doorpost to receive wisdom, understanding, and knowledge for the decisions you need to make (Prov 8:34). He wants to give you the strategies and skills you need that will empower you to succeed in your assignment. But He also wants you to earnestly seek out these nuggets of gold He has concealed along the way (Prov 25:2).

Use your prayer team to help you obtain this wisdom and understanding. Good ideas are nice, but one God-idea can be the difference between becoming successful or becoming a billionaire. Make a decision to become skilled at hearing the Lord's voice. Develop this ability like you would any skill. Seek out people who are more gifted than you in this area and learn from them. Some things are easier caught than taught.

Whenever I counsel a struggling business, I always ask to see their business plan. When they tell me they don't have one, or one that has been updated since inception, I always remind them that their struggling business is actually tracking the path of their business plan. Business people often say they can't afford $25,000 or even $50,000 for a business plan, but can they afford to lose hundreds of thousands of dollars per year without a plan? Plan your business success, and then work your plan. If you don't have a plan for success, don't be surprised if you are not succeeding.

22. Build A Prayer/Spiritual Warfare Team Around You

Like Jesus, become a person of prayer. Read *The Autobiography of George Muller*[3], *Praying Hyde*[4], and *Rees Howells Intercessor*[5]. The stories of these three men will inspire you to believe God wants to help you in your Kingdom assignment, and that prayer is the key to obtain provision from God. Remember, "From the days of John the Baptist until now the kingdom of heaven is forcibly entered, and violent men seize it for themselves" (Matt 11:12). Fight the good fight of faith. Prayer is the weapon of your warfare to bring the Kingdom of Heaven into your situation.

Build a prayer team of intercessors around you. Look for people who are called to this assignment and not people who are simply looking for a job. Who else are they praying for and what type of results have they seen? Are they experienced in spiritual warfare? Work closely with your intercessors and make sure they are praying each day for you, your family, your employees, your business associates, and your customers and prospects. The greatest breakthrough you will have is when they pray onsite with you. If you are having trouble finding business intercessors or want training for a team of your intercessors, contact Sozo Services (www.sozoservices.com).

23. Bless And Don't Curse

Make sure you are blessing everyone and not cursing them. Remember, your words are spirit and they will contain either life or death in them. Speak only words of life into people and situations. Ask the Holy Spirit to prick your conscience whenever you speak words contrary to His words.

Similarly, as a man thinks in his heart, so is he (Prov 23:7). Your thoughts contain spiritual force. Make sure you are seeing everything from God's perspective. This includes His perspective on you, your life, your marriage, and your Kingdom assignment. Ensure your thoughts are agreeing with His and not with thoughts the enemy is trying to implant. See yourself succeeding. See yourself walking in the same favor He walked in. Make sure your thoughts and words are in agreement with His and you are only thinking and speaking *zōē* life. Bless and don't curse. Release His *zōē* life everywhere you go and to everyone you meet.

24. Develop A Win-Win Mentality

Remember the Second Commandment in all your business transactions and relationships. Do unto other as you would have others do unto you. Treat each person the way you want to be treated. Make every attempt to walk around to the other side of the table and see the business transaction from the other person's perspective. Do not assume they are happy with the transaction simply because they accepted the deal. This selfish mentality creates disgruntled employees, unhappy customers, and untrusting business associates. Remember, you are responsible to ensure they win on this transaction. Later, if they feel they received a bad deal, they will blame you. If you don't believe me, ask them who they blame.

The key to win-win negotiating is to take the time to see the transaction from their perspective. Be proactive in asking questions about their level of satisfaction and understand why they are satisfied. Don't make any assumptions. Ask them if this is the deal that they were looking for. Ask them if they will be happy with the transaction as proposed. Ask them if they will feel like they have "won." When they tell you they will be happy with the transaction, ask them why this transaction meets their needs? Don't be afraid to ask, "Are you sure?" Always attempt to provide more value in the transaction than what they were expecting.

Most business people would not dare ask these questions for fear the business transaction would fall apart before being signed. That shouldn't be your biggest concern. Your concern should be in leaving a trail of people who will never want to work for you or do business with you again. If you master win-win negotiating, your company will become the place all employees want to work. You will be the person everyone wants to do business with. You will be bringing the Kingdom of Heaven into their lives.

25. Always Look to Bring Greater Value to Your Customers

The greater the value your products and services provide to your customers, the more valuable you will be to them and the more they will be willing to pay. Never become content with what you are providing them. Always look to provide more while managing your profit margin. Remember, you are sowing value into your customer's lives. The greater the value they receive from the product or service you are investing in them, the greater the harvest or return on investment that will come back to you.

Value comes in many forms and sometimes exists in the customer experience. Nordstrom's is a good example. They neither sell the best clothes nor have the lowest prices, but there are scores of loyal Nordie shoppers. Why? It's the shopping experience they provide. How many shoe stores will sell you a pair of shoes of different sizes at the same price as a normal pair of shoes? For people with different size feet, their shopping experience is extremely valuable.

If you are providing the same product or service to your customer you provided two years ago, and have not increased the value they are receiving from you, you are at risk of losing your customer to a competitor. This is especially true for new competitors who were not on the scene two years ago, who have done their competitive analysis on your business and figured out your strengths and weaknesses. Companies that continually strive to bring increased value to their customers will eventually put their competitors out of business and become the dominant player in their industry.

26. Don't Eat Everything In The Fruit

Remember, everything belongs to the Lord and you are only the steward of what He gives you. This includes your paycheck and the profits of your company. Don't spend a dime without praying over the money and discussing it with the Lord. Not everything He gives you is meant to be consumed by you. Part of what He gives you is meant to be given to the poor and the needy. Part is meant to be given to your community and your local church.

How much should you give away? How much are you allowed to keep for yourself? Avoid cookbook formulas and ask the Master. He has a personalized plan for your life. Many people like cookbook formulas because they do not require taking time to seek the Lord's will. But He desires that you come to Him daily seeking His will and direction for your life and finances. Ask Him what He wants you to do with His money and His bills. He will answer you if you take the time to listen. Even if you don't get it perfect, He will honor your attempt to be a good steward of His finances. Whatever you do, don't eat the entire fruit. It is not all meant for you.

27. Owe No Man Nothing But Your Love

Avoid all debt whenever possible, especially consumer debt. Use lines of credit and credit cards as tools to moderate the cash flow needed to keep your company running. Be wary if you are borrowing money because the revenue is not supporting your operations. This is a red flag that you have deeper problems. That revenue problem cannot be solved by borrowing more money. Never purchase anything for your personal life or business you cannot afford.

If you owe someone money and cannot afford to pay them, remember the Second Commandment and go to them and explain your situation. Keep them informed and let them know when you believe you will be able to make the payment. If it doesn't look like you will ever be able to pay it, explain that to them and ask for forgiveness. At the same time, make sure you are forgiving those who cannot pay you (James 2:13). Remember, mercy is given to those who show mercy (Matt 5:7).

28. Remain Teachable

This could also be the first step in your action plan. As a disciple of Christ you need to remain teachable. You are in the process of becoming like One who is by definition, perfect Himself. This will be a lifelong process. If you ever feel that you have arrived at a level of maturity where you can coast, you are positioned to fall. The high calling in Christ Jesus is always upwards. You will know you are on the right track if you feel like you are dying to yourself more and more every day. Remember, He gives grace to the humble, but He knows the proud from a distance.

Closing

I pray this book will motivate you to seek the Lord with all of your heart, soul, mind, and strength. I pray you reach the point where you know your Kingdom assignment and start to live the plan for your life He has already blessed, and stop asking Him to bless *your* plans. I pray you start doing life and business with the Lord and remember that when you are abiding in Him, everything you do is sacred. There is no more separation of sacred versus secular in your life. You are holy because He is Holy. Whatever you put your hand to is holy.

Strive to be the best at whatever you put your hand to and plan to take the mountain you are called to subdue. Even if you are not the one called to be the leader of your mountain, that person will need someone like you supporting them. Remember, it is your Father's good pleasure to give you the Kingdom (Luke 12:32). He is on your side. He wants you to win. You don't have to beg him to help you. He is begging you to get with His plan for your life and business.

I pray that the *zōē* life, the abundant life of the Lord Jesus comes into every area of your life and business, and you succeed in everything you put your hand to. Go forward and bring the tabernacle of the Lord with you everywhere you go. Be blessed and prosperous, in Jesus' mighty name.

Chapter 17

Prayers For Your Life and Business

Three best prayers are simple, child-like, heartfelt prayers. When
your heart connects to the Lord you will know your prayers are
being heard and answered. If you have never dedicated your life or
business to the Lord, here are a few prayers to help you bring the
Kingdom of Heaven into your personal life and business and provide
spiritual protection against the wiles of the enemy.

Prayer to Dedicate Your Life to the Lord

Father, I thank you for the blood of the Lord Jesus Christ. I believe
He died and rose from the dead for me and washed away my sins.
Jesus, I give my life to you today and ask you come into my heart and
be my Lord, my Savior, and my all-consuming desire. Lord, I give you
all I am and all I have. I surrender my will for Your will in my life. I
repent of all sin and disobedience in my life and ask that you give me
the grace to pick up my cross and follow after you wholeheartedly from
this day forward. Help me Lord to abide in you and you in me all the
days of my life. This I pray in Jesus' mighty name.

Prayer for the Baptism of the Holy Spirit

Father, I thank you for the promise of Your Spirit. You said you
would give your precious Holy Spirit to those who asked for Him. Lord
Jesus, I ask that you baptize me right now in Your Holy Spirit. Holy
Spirit, I ask that you come right now and fill me to overflowing with
your living waters of *zōē* life. Come and magnify Jesus in my heart and
teach me and remind me of everything He said and did. Be my
counselor, my Truth, my wisdom, my protection, my deliverer, and my
best friend. Lead me and guide me every moment of the day so I will
always walk in His Truth and righteousness. Holy Spirit, right now by
faith I receive your indwelling presence. Give me my new prayer

language and teach me to worship the Father in Spirit and in Truth. This I pray in Jesus' mighty name.

Although some people receive the baptism of the Holy Spirit while alone and praying a prayer similar to the one above, most people receive this precious gift easier while being ministered to by someone who has a gifting for this ministry, or while in a corporate environment where the Holy Spirit is in charge and being manifested. As they say, some things are easier caught than taught.

Prayer to Dedicate Your Business to the Lord

Lord Jesus, we set apart this day to dedicate this business into Your service; to announce to the seen and unseen realms that (business name) belongs to You and exists for Your purposes. We place all of our works of service on the altar of consecration and ask You Lord to bring life, purpose, and direction to the affairs of this business. May Your Holy Spirit and His favour and blessing rest here. May every officer, employee, contractor, vendor, and customer recognize Your hand in our business affairs. We dedicate ourselves to You Lord as well, to be set apart for Your service as stewards of Your inheritance and the advancement of Your Kingdom in this business. We bless (business name) in the name of our Lord Jesus Christ.

From this day forward we seek to bring You honor and glory in all we put our hands to as stewards of Your business. As Your faithful stewards, we are the recipients of all the blessings, favor, grace, and honor due to You to advance this cause. This is our appointed time to advance Your Kingdom purpose here on earth. We declare that all provision that has been stored up for us and everything that rightfully belongs to us is being released into our hands today. We command the north, south, east, and west to give up every resource necessary for our business to prosper in this calling.

We bless our staff, employees, families, clients, vendors, and associates to be safe under the Lord's covering. We stand on the Word of the Living God that says no weapon formed against us shall prosper.

We repent and break agreement with the spirits of fear, doubt, unbelief, and failure and stand on the Word of God that says the same Spirit that raised Christ from the dead dwells in us. We put on Kingdom authority, clothe ourselves with the full armor of God, take up the weapons of our warfare, and defend what is rightfully ours.

We put a halt to all plots and plans of the enemy to take us off course, meddle with our heritage or cause harm to our business, family, employees, associates, and clients. We build a hedge of protection and draw a blood line around this business. We deny the enemy access to all who work for (business name) and we command that demonic interruptions in our affairs cease now. We rest in the safety and protection of our Lord and Savior, Jesus Christ. The Blood of Jesus covers us, we are now hidden from the enemy's lies, schemes and tactics.

We decree and declare that we are free from every demonic influence, curse, debt, sickness, and bondage that has come upon us through the kingdom of darkness. We put a halt to every witchcraft prayer, spell, curse, and every harsh, critical and ill-spoken word against this business, employees, associates, family, and customers. We decree and declare that they shall not stand, they shall not take root, and they shall not come to pass.

From this day forward we operate according to God's timetable. God's agenda is our agenda. Our ears and eyes are in tune to Heaven's frequency and what God is doing in this hour, we are doing, what He is saying in this hour, we are saying. Our set time will not be frustrated. We will not suffer shame. The mountain of our assignment will not be surrendered. Divine boundaries and borders are hereby established and the laws of the Kingdom of Heaven now govern all our business activities. Blessings, favor, and every good thing abounds in our life and in this business from this day forth. We seal this today in Jesus' mighty name.

Kingdom Business Success

The owners and corporate officers should be present for this dedication or rededication. It is suggested that you seal this dedication ceremony with communion.

Prayer for Spiritual Protection[1]

Father, I thank you for your covering of protection over my life, my family, my finances, and our business today. I ask for angelic protection against the powers of darkness. I decree and declare that the weapons of our warfare are not carnal, but mighty through God. I enforce God's original plans and purposes over every plan and purpose of the kingdom of darkness. I walk in the power and anointing of the risen Jesus Christ and I am lead by His precious Holy Spirit in everything I think, say, and do.

I bind every spirit of witchcraft, confusion, deception, sickness, disease, poverty, lack, and death that would attempt to come against me, my family, or our business. I overrule and nullify all ill-spoken words, ill wishes, enchantments, divinations, spells, hexes, curses, witchcraft prayers, and every idle word spoken contrary to God's plans of *zōē* life for my life, family, and finances. I reverse the curse associated with these demonically inspired utterances and decree and declare that they shall not stand, they shall not come to pass, they shall not take root, and their destructive effects are returned to their demonic originators.

I nullify, dismantle, and forcefully oppose any satanic impressions, illusions, projections, suggestions, suspicions, and deceptions setup as a decoy or ambush to my soul. I cast down strongholds and vain imaginations and every thought that lifts itself against the knowledge of the Lord Jesus Christ. He who the Son sets free, is free indeed and I decree and declare that I, my family, and this business are free from all satanic oppression and influence from this moment forward. I thank you Father that you have given me the victory in Christ Jesus. Amen.

Prayer for Releasing Forgiveness and Blessing

Father, I lift up (include your family, employees, and customer names). As an ambassador of the Lord Jesus Christ, I release forgiveness today on your behalf and remit their sins through the blood of the Lord Jesus Christ. I release the grace and peace of the Lord Jesus Christ to come into their lives today to make them whole: spirit, soul, and body. I decree and declare that they are highly favored and blessed today by God and man, in Jesus' mighty name.

NOTES

Chapter 1 – Abiding in Him

1. Dr. Lance Wallnau, *The Seven Mountain Strategy* (San Bernardino, CA: International School of Ministry (ISOM), 2009).
2. W.E. Vine, Merrill Unger, and William White, Jr., *Vines's Complete Expository Dictionary of Old and New Testament Words* (Nashville, TN: Thomas Nelson, Inc., 1996), 367. Strong's #2222.

Chapter 2 – Love

1. Vine et al., *Vines's Complete Expository Dictionary of Old and New Testament Words*, 381. Strong's #25.
2. Ibid., 382. Strong's #5368.

Chapter 3 – Obedience

1. Francis Frangipane, *Holiness, Truth And The Presence of God* (Cedar Rapids, IA: Arrow Publications, 1986), 75.
2. A.A. Allen, *The Price of God's Miracle Working Power* (Printed by Create Space Independent Publishing Platform, 2012), 61.

Chapter 4 – Honor

1. Vine et al., *Vines's Complete Expository Dictionary of Old and New Testament Words*, 114. Strong's #3519.
2. Ibid., 310. Strong's #5092.

Chapter 5 – The Kingdom of Heaven

1. Vine et al., *Vines's Complete Expository Dictionary of Old and New Testament Words*, 313. Strong's #3624.

Chapter 6 – Your Kingdom Assignment

1. Liz Freedman, "The Developmental Disconnect in Choosing a Major: Why Institutions Should Prohibit Choice until Second Year," *Penn State Division of Undergraduate Studies*, June 28, 2013, https://dus.psu.edu/mentor/2013/06/disconnect-choosing-major/.
2. Peter Weber, "Why most Americans hate their jobs (or are just 'checked out')," *The Week*, June 25, 2013, http://theweek.com/articles/462832/why-most-americans-hate-jobs-are-just-checked.
3. Wikipedia, "DOS," *Wikipedia the Free Encylopedia*, October 7, 2015, https://en.wikipedia.org/wiki/DOS.
4. Wikipedia, "Donald Trump," *Wikipedia the Free Encyclopedia*, October 9, 2015, https://en.wikipedia.org/wiki/Donald_Trump#cite_note-26.
5. Wikipedia, "Richard and Maurice McDonald," *Wikipedia the Free Encyclopedia*, September 13, 2015, https://en.wikipedia.org/wiki/Richard_and_Maurice_McDonald.

Chapter 7 – Stewardship

1. James Strong, *The New Strong's Expanded Exhaustive Concordance of The Bible: Red Letter Edition* (Nashville, TN: Thomas Nelson, Inc., 2001), 176, Strong's #3623.
2. Ibid., 172. Strong's #3551.

Chapter 8 – Truth

1. Vine et al., *Vines's Complete Expository Dictionary of Old and New Testament Words*, 645. Strong's #225.
2. Ibid., 366. Strong's #5579
3. Ibid., 151. Strong's #538.

Chapter 9 – Fearless

1. Vine et al., *Vines's Complete Expository Dictionary of Old and New Testament Words*, 89. Strong's #3309.
2. Ibid., 79. Strong's #3372.

Chapter 10 – Discipline

1. Brian Tracy, "Successful People Are Self Disciplined," *Brian Tracy International*, August 25, 2015, http://www.briantracy.com/blog/time-management/successful-people-are-self-discipline-high-value-personal-management/.
2. Vine et al., *Vines's Complete Expository Dictionary of Old and New Testament Words*, 242. Strong's #4561.
3. Franklin Hall, "Atomic Power with God Through Fasting and Prayer," *Sozo Services*, August 25, 2015, http://www.sozoservices.com/PDFgallery.htm.

Chapter 11 – Prayer

1. Vine et al., *Vines's Complete Expository Dictionary of Old and New Testament Words*, 185. Strong's #6419.
2. Ibid., 480. Strong's #4336.
3. R.A. Torrey, *The Power of Prayer* (New York, NY: Fleming H. Revell Company, 1924), 201-202.
4. E.M. Bounds, *Purpose in Prayer* (New York, NY: Fleming H. Revell Company, 1920), 79.
5. Kenneth E. Hagin, "Why Pray?", *Cfaith*, August 25, 2015, http://www.cfaith.com/index.php/blog/24-articles/prayer/18165-why-pray
6. Oswald Chambers, *My Utmost for His Highest* (Grand Rapids, MI: Discovery House Publishers, 1992).

Chapter 12 – Wisdom, Understanding, and Knowledge

1. Dr. Horace Morson, *Where Did I Go Wrong* (Bloomington, IN: Xlibris Corporation, 2011), 5.
2. Vine et al., *Vines's Complete Expository Dictionary of Old and New Testament Words*, 290. Strong's #2451.
3. Ibid., 273. Strong's #8394.
4. Ibid., 131. Strong's #1847.
5. Tyndale House Publishers, "The One Year Bible Online," *The One Year Bible Online*, August 25, 2015, http://oneyearbibleonline.com/.
6. Vine et al., *Vines's Complete Expository Dictionary of Old and New Testament Words*, 683. Strong's #4487.

7. Larry Randolph, *Spirit Talk: Hearing the Voice of God* (Fort Mill, SC: Morningstar Publications, 2006), 58.
8. Steve Thompson, *You May All Prophesy: Practical Guidelines for Prophetic Ministry* (Fort Mill, SC: Morningstar Publications, 2003), 13.

Chapter 13 – Spiritual Warfare

1. Rebecca Greenwood, *Authority to Tread: An Intercessors Guide to Strategic-Level Spiritual Warfare* (Grand Rapids, MI: Chosen Books, 2005), 21.
2. Thomas B. White, *The Believer's Guide To Spiritual Warfare* (Ann Arbor, MI: Servant Publications, 1990), 21.

Chapter 14 – Financial Abundance

1. Vine et al., *Vines's Complete Expository Dictionary of Old and New Testament Words*, 6. Strong's #4053.
2. James Strong, *The New Strong's Expanded Exhaustive Concordance of the Bible: Red Letter Edition* (Nashville, TN: Thomas Nelson Publishers, Inc., 2001), 246. Strong's #5007.

Chapter 15 – Why Some Are Wealthy

1. Jim Rohn, *The Treasury of Quotes: America's Foremost Business Philosopher* (Dallas, TX: Success Books, 2006).
2. Thomas J. Stanley and William D. Danko, *The Millionaire Next Door: The Surprising Secrets of America's Wealthy* (New York, NY: Pocket Books, 1996).

Chapter 16 – Bring The Kingdom of Heaven Into Your Business

1. Inner healing/deliverance ministries that I'm familiar with and would recommend would include: Restoring the Foundations, Sozo Healing Ministry (iBethel), Father's Heart, Ancient Paths, and Communion With God.
2. Perry Marshall, *80/20 Sales and Marketing: The Definitive Guide to Working Less and Making More* (Irvine, CA: Entrepreneur Press, 2013).

3. George Muller, *The Autobiography of George Muller* (Springdale, PA: Whitaker House, 1984).

4. E.G. Carre (edited by), *Praying Hyde: The Life Story of John Hyde, Apostle of Prayer* (Orlando, FL: Bridge-Logos, 1982).

5. Norman Grubb, *Rees Howells Intercessor* (Fort Washington, PA: CLC*Publication, 1952).

Chapter 17 – Prayers for Your Life and Business

1. Cindy Trimm, *The Rules of Engagement* (Lake Mary, FL: Charisma House, 2008), 23-37. Substantial material borrowed from Ms. Trimm's Prayers of Activation for Spiritual Warfare.

ABOUT THE AUTHOR

Jeff Ahern is co-founder of Sozo Services, Inc., an executive coaching, spiritual advisory firm helping business leaders succeed and achieve their personal and corporate goals by using Biblical, Spirit-led solutions. Jeff works closely with Christian CEOs and business leaders and serves in a role that can best be described as a combination of business intercessor, prophetic voice, and business confidant. Jeff helps business owners and CEOs understand that where they will be tomorrow will be based upon decisions they make today, and then helps them obtain wisdom and understanding from the Lord in order to make better decisions. Jeff's passion is to help business leaders succeed in all areas of their life and business and fulfill their God-given assignment as marketplace ministry leaders.

A born-again, Spirit-filled Christian, Jeff has been walking with the Lord since 1985 and has been involved in providing management consulting and professional services to Fortune 500 and Government clients for over twenty years. He has a B.S. in Electronics Engineering and has served in the computer security, telecommunications, software development, and financial industries. As a former U.S. Naval Officer, he served on two destroyers. He is also a former member of the MITRE Corporation's Security Technical Center having provided computer security services to the Government, military, and Intelligence communities. Jeff has served as a Trustee and Board member for several non-profit and for-profit organizations and resides in Northern Virginia. He can be reached at www.sozoservices.com.

OTHER RESOURCES FROM SOZO SERVICES

Available in paperback and eBook at Amazon.com

Made in the USA
Middletown, DE
07 September 2016